The Politics of Combined and Uneven Development

The Politics of Combined and Uneven Development

The Theory of Permanent Revolution

Michael Löwy

Haymarket Books
Chicago, Illinois

First published by Verso in 1981
© 1981 Michael Löwy

This edition published by Haymarket Books in 2010, and has been abridged for
length. Part two of the 1981 edition has been omitted.

Haymarket Books
P.O. Box 180165
Chicago, IL 60618
773-583-7884
info@haymarketbooks.org
www.haymarketbooks.org

Trade distribution:
In the U.S., Consortium Book Sales and Distribution, www.cbsd.com
In Canada, Publishers Group Canada, www.pgcbooks.ca
In the UK, Turnaround Publisher Services, www.turnaround-uk.com
In Australia, Palgrave Macmillan, www.palgravemacmillan.com.au
All other countries, Publishers Group Worldwide, www.pgw.com

ISBN: 978-1-60846-068-7

Cover design by Josh On.

Special discounts are available for bulk purchases by organizations and institutions.
Please contact Haymarket Books for more information at 773-583-7884 or
info@haymarketbooks.org.

This book was published with the generous support of the Lannan Foundation and
the Wallace Global Fund.

Library of Congress CIP Data is available.

10 9 8 7 6 5 4 3 2

Printed in the United States.

Contents

1 Conceptions of Revolution in Marx and Engels   1
2 Permanent Revolution in Russia   30
3 The Emergence of the General Theory   70
4 Conclusions   101
5 Permanent Revolution in the Twenty-First Century
    Interview with Michael Löwy by Phil Gasper, 2010   145

Index   155

1
Conceptions of Revolution in Marx and Engels

The theory of permanent revolution, first formulated by Leon Trotsky in 1905-6, defines a theoretical field whose principal, dialectically linked problems are: (a) the possibility of proletarian revolution in 'backward' (underdeveloped, semi-feudal, pre-capitalist or pre-industrial) countries; (b) the uninterrupted transition from the democratic to socialist revolution, as so-called bourgeois-democratic tasks (national independence and unity, the emancipation of the peasantry, democratic enfranchisement, and so on) are undertaken by workers' power in ineluctable combination with specifically socialist tasks; (c) the international extension of the revolutionary process and the construction of socialism on a world scale. The formulation of this theory, and the new problematic it entailed, unquestionably signalled a bold and original break from the evolutionist Marxism of the Second International. At the same time, however, it initiated a controversy that persists to this day: does Trotsky's theory of permanent revolution represent a creative development of classical socialist theory, or is it, in fact, a heretical rupture with the fundamental principles of historical materialism as conceived by Marx?

It is a cliché of anti-Marxists of every stripe, repeated *ad infinitum*, that 'according to Marxism, the proletarian revolution should have been the final outcome of industrialization, and not *vice versa*, and it should have come first in the highly industrialized countries, and only much later in Russia'.[1] Unfortunately, this platitude has acquired dogmatic validity to the extent that it has also been accepted and embellished by a surprising number of Marxists from the end of the nineteenth century down to the present day. For example, no less an authority than Kautsky—the 'Pope' of German Marxism—proclaimed in 1909: 'Marx and Engels acknowledged . . . that a revolution could not be made at will, but only as far as it was

[1]Karl Popper, *The Open Society and Its Enemies*, vol. 2, London 1962, p. 111.

the necessary product of determinate conditions, and to the extent that these conditions were lacking, revolution was thus impossible. It is only where the system of capitalist production has achieved a high level of development that economic conditions permit public power to transform the means of production into social property.'[2] Moreover, it was in the name of this thesis that Kautsky criticized the October Revolution, stressing that the working class of so backward a country as Russia was not capable of introducing socialism, and that it should, therefore, refrain from installing a dictatorship of the proletariat.

This near-unanimity between many Marxists and their most hostile critics concerning the unilinear link between economic development and socialist revolution has reinforced a certain interpretation of Marxism that claims that historical materialism has proved itself analytically bankrupt. Indeed, if Marx simply believed what was imputed to him by Kautsky, then the actual unfolding of twentieth-century history confounds all Marx's predictions. In particular, the direct reduction of revolutionary possibility to economic potential on a *national scale* makes the sequence of revolutions and revolutionary movements since 1917—centred as they have so often been in the 'weak links' rather than the economic fortresses of world capitalism—almost inexplicable in theoretical terms. For some commentators, this apparent dissonance between theory and reality has only ratified their belief in the fundamental invalidity of Marxism as a whole; for others, especially right-wing social democrats, it has demonstrated the 'anti-Marxist adventurism' of the Bolsheviks' and later attempts to leap over iron laws of history. Even revolutionary socialists in Western Europe originally had great difficulty reconciling the success of the Bolsheviks with an 'orthodox' understanding of Marxism. Thus the young Gramsci was brash enough to hail October as the 'revolution against *Capital*'.[3] This *double entendre* expressed the terrific tension that the eruption of the Russian Revolution created within the mental apparatus and world outlook of a generation of socialist militants conditioned to expect that the 'last fight' would begin in Berlin, London or Chicago rather than Petrograd, Shanghai or Havana.

[2]*Le chemin du pouvoir*, Paris 1969, p. 3. See also Massimo Salvadori, *Karl Kautsky and the Socialist Revolution 1880-1938*, London 1979, p. 224.

[3]'In Russia, Marx's *Capital* was more the book of the bourgeoisie than of the proletariat. It stood as the critical demonstration of how events should follow a predetermined course: how in Russia a bourgeoisie had to develop, and a capitalist era had to open, with the setting-up of Western-type civilization, before the proletariat could even think in terms of its own revolt, its own class demands, its own revolution. But events have overcome ideologies.' ('The Revolution Against "Capital"', in *Selections from Political Writings, 1910-1920*, Quintin Hoare, ed., London 1977, p. 34).

Thus, before examining Trotsky's seminal break with this mechanical model of the socialist transition, it is necessary to interrogate the works of Marx and Engels. Did the Kautskian orthodoxy of the Second International faithfully reproduce, as its grey-bearded leaders always insisted, the letter and the spirit of Marx's theory of socialist revolution; or did it flatten and distort its complex folds and nuances? It is my opinion that a rigorous analysis of the writings of Marx and Engels, in fact, reveals a problematic far more complex and subtle, pregnant with ideas and hypotheses that offer a groundwork for the conception of permanent revolution as eventually theorized by Trotsky. It is, of course, undeniable that certain texts of the 'founding fathers' are marked by an explicitly *stagist* perspective—the supposition of an unvarying succession of historical (economic and/or socio-political) stages. Rather than skirt this contradiction, I will try to situate it in its proper context relative to unresolved theoretical and strategic problems in the thought of Marx and Engels. In the absence of previous systematic inquiry into the question of permanent revolution as conceived by Marx and Engels, I attempt in this chapter to disentangle the different threads of theory—'stagist' and 'permanentist'—that comprise their reflections on the revolutions of the nineteenth century. At the same time I will endeavor to answer the paradoxical question raised by Gramsci in 1917: was the Russian revolution the living negation of *Capital* and classical Marxism?

How did Marx and Engels envisage revolutions in backward, semi-feudal and absolutist countries? Did they believe in an inevitable repetition of the model of past bourgeois revolutions or did they look forward to the uninterrupted development of the revolutionary process towards the consolidation of proletarian power? These questions find a far from univocal and coherent answer in their writings. Indeed, one discovers contradictory elements that express the contradictory social reality and transitional nature of their period. To begin with, the very concept of 'bourgeois revolution' was itself never formalized or rigorously defined in their political thought. Occasionally, the concept was anchored by certain common features putatively shared by two great bourgeois revolutions of the past—1648 and 1789. As Marx explained in the pages of the *Neue Rheinische Zeitung* in 1848: 'In these revolutions the bourgeoisie gained the victory; but the *victory of the bourgeoisie* was at that time *the victory of a new social order*, the victory of bourgeois property over feudal property, of nationality over provincialism, of competition over guild, of the partition of estates over primogeniture . . . of enlightenment over superstition . . . of industry over heroic laziness, of civil law over privileges of medieval origin.'[4] More typically, however, it was the Great French Revolution alone that provided Marx and Engels with the 'classical' prototype of bourgeois revolution; for, unlike its English predecessor, 'it constituted a complete breach with the traditions of the past; it cleared out the very last vestiges of feudalism'.[5]

The concept of a 'revolutionary bourgeoisie' is, then, intimately linked to the model of 1789, and the French bourgeoisie of this epoch becomes the measure of the revolutionary or non-revolutionary character of the European bourgeoisies of the nineteenth century—especially the German. In his journalism during the revolution of 1848, Marx repeatedly contrasted the revolutionary fortitude of the bourgeoisie of 1789 with the pusillanimity of the German middle classes. Whereas the French bourgeoisie had upheld its anti-feudal alliance with the peasantry, the German bourgeoisie in 1848-50 cravenly betrayed the peasants in order to mollify the aristocracy and king.[6] In contrast to the German middle classes, the French bourgeoisie of 1789-94 had really acted (in Marx's view) as the incarnation of the general interests of modernity in confrontation with the old feudal order.[7] It is beyond the purview of the present study to weigh the historical accuracy of Marx and Engels's estimate of the French bourgeoisie; suffice to say that on other occasions they openly acknowledged that the prime mover of the revolutionary process was not actually the bourgeoisie but the sans-culottes.[8] Later on, in the Second International, it was precisely the socio-political category of 'bourgeois-democratic revolution' that became the basis of a generalized, stagist interpretation of Marxism; in particular it provided the strategic horizon of political debates within Russian Social Democracy. Yet there is plenty of evidence that Marx and Engels themselves were uncomfortable with the concept. As early as the *Communist Manifesto*, Marx had conceived 'democracy' as a specific task of socialist rather than bourgeois revolution ('. . . the first step in the revolution by the working class is to raise the proletariat to the position of ruling class, to

[4] *The Revolutions of 1848*, Harmondsworth 1973, pp. 192-3.

[5] Engels, Special Introduction to the English Edition of *Socialism: Utopian and Scientific* (1892) in Marx and Engels, *Selected Works*, London 1970, p. 387. In his *Political Power and Social Classes* London 1975, pp. 173-180), Poulantzas questions whether the Revolution of 1789 really provided the exemplary pattern for other 'bourgeois revolutions'. Although a discussion of this question lies outside the boundaries of his study, it should be noted that Poulantzas wrongly attributes the responsibility for a paradigmatic interpretation of 1789 to Gramsci, when in fact it was Marx and Engels themselves who introduced it.

[6] See 'The Bill for the Abolition of Feudal Burdens', in *The Revolutions of 1848*, pp. 137-43.

[7] See 'The Bourgeoisie and the Counter-Revolution' (December, 1848) in ibid, pp. 193-4.

[8] See Marx, 'Moralizing Criticism and Critical Morality' (1847) in *Collected Works*, vol. 6, London 1976, p. 319.

win the battle of democracy'[9]). In later years both Marx and Engels were to question further whether the bourgeoisie actually required a 'revolution' to accomplish its 'historic tasks'—the abolition of feudal institutions and barriers, the free development of industry, national independence and unification and so on. For example, in his 1895 introduction to Marx's *Class Struggles in France*, Engels suggests the following hypothesis concerning the historical roles of Napoleon III and Bismarck: after 1851, 'the period of revolutions from below was concluded for the time being; there followed a period of revolutions from above. . . . The general result, however, was that in Europe the independence and internal unity of the great nations, with the exception of Poland, had become a fact. . . . The grave-diggers of the Revolution of 1848 had become the executors of its will'.[10] Although the idea was never codified by Marx and Engels, their writings seem to suggest that the prospect of future bourgeois revolutions would become less certain as the bourgeoisie became able to attain its aims through non-revolutionary means—revolutions 'from above'—without popular mobilization or political rupture.

If the concept of bourgeois revolution is ambiguous in Marx and Engels, the question of the character of the revolutionary process in countries with feudal-absolutist structures is even more contradictory in their writings. In a series of texts, especially those of Engels, one can find the clear outlines of a stagist doctrine that defines bourgeois revolution and/or industrial capitalism as the necessary historical condition(s) of autonomous revolutionary intervention by the proletariat. This thesis is sometimes justified on economic grounds, sometimes socio-politically; the approaches in the two cases are different and need to be examined separately.

In the most extreme version, the economic foundation of stagism is given as the level of the development of the productive forces. Capitalism can only be abolished at the point where it has exhausted its ability to nurture technological creativity and expand production. As Engels observed in 1895, this was manifestly not the case in 1848: 'History has . . . made it clear that the state of economic development on the Continent at that time was not, by a long way, ripe for the elimination of capitalist production; it has proved this by the economic revolution which, since 1848, has seized the whole of the Continent . . .—all on a capitalist basis, which, in the year 1848, therefore had great capacity for expansion.'[11] Compare this

---

[9]*Manifesto of the Communist Party* in *The Revolutions of 1848*, p. 86.
[10]In *Selected Works*, p. 647-8.
[11]Ibid. p. 646.

with Marx's celebrated remark in the 1859 Preface: 'No social order is ever destroyed before all the productive forces for which it is sufficient have been developed . . .'.[12] Certainly if Marx and Engels had confined themselves to this rigidly economistic and deterministic problematic, and its equation of revolution with the breakdown of a moribund capitalism, then not a single nineteenth-century society—not even late Victorian England—could have been adjudged ripe for socialism. Indeed, if the exhaustion of potential for economic development in some abstract sense is the overarching structural precondition of socialism, what country could meet this criterion even today?

But in the very same texts one can also find a more subtle version of economic stagism which focuses attention less on the maximum development of the productive forces, and more on the transformation of the *relations* of production. Here the decisive material condition of the socialist revolution becomes the formation and centralization of the factory proletariat as industrialism dissolves pre-capitalist layers of peasants, artisans and small producers in general. It thus follows that revolution is only possible where capitalism has simplified and polarized the social structure into openly opposed armies of proletarians and bourgeois.[13] This is why Marx and Engels in certain writings present England as the country most 'ripe' for socialism, or, indeed, sometimes as the *only* country where proletarian revolution has become the order of the day.[14]

In contrast with these straightforwardly economistic justifications of an inevitable bourgeois-revolutionary stage, Marx and Engels also argued from a socio-political perspective that adumbrated an explicitly permanentist conception of revolution. In this transitional problematic the bourgeois revolution appears as a precondition to the extent that, by abolishing the monarchy and the power of the feudal nobility, the political terrain is simplified into the direct contraposition of bourgeoisie and proletariat. 'The workers . . . know that their own struggle against the bourgeoisie can only dawn with the day when the bourgeoisie is victorious. . . . They can and must accept the *bourgeois revolution* as a precon-

---

[12]Preface to A *Contribution towards the Critique of Political Economy*, Moscow 1970, p. 21.

[13]Cf. Marx, 'Montesquieu LVI' (21 January 1849), *Collected Works*, Vol. 6, p. 266; Engels, 'The Movements of 1847' (20 January, 1848), ibid., pp. 520-529; *Introduction to Class Struggles in France*, pp. 646-47.

[14]'England, being the metropolis of capital, the power which has hitherto ruled the world market, is for the present the most important country for the workers' revolution, and moreover, the *only* country in which material conditions for this revolution have developed up to a certain degree of maturity.' (Marx to S. Meyer and A. Vogt, 9 April 1870, in Marx and Engels, *On Britain*, Moscow 1957, p. 507).

dition for the *workers' revolution*. However, they cannot for a moment regard it as their *ultimate* goal.'[15] The change here from previous formulations is considerable: the focus has shifted from a fixed succession of generation-long economic stages to a telescoped sequence of political phases. The stagist dimension remains, but it has been reduced to the somewhat abstract categorical assertion that bourgeois revolution remains the *sine qua non* of revolutionary proletarian politics.

For Marx, the stagist theory of revolution did not exclude the possibility of a 'premature' accession to power, although in his view such an experience could not be more than an ephemeral episode. Indeed, if the proletariat were, by some unexpected and contingent turn of events, to come to power in van of the bourgeois revolution, it would find itself doomed to become a political instrument or temporary surrogate of the socially ascendant bourgeoisie. Marx claimed (not very convincingly in my opinion) to find an historical precedent for such an event in the Jacobin dictatorship of Year Four.[16] Brought to power by the sans-culottes, the Committee of Public Safety found itself nonetheless constrained to serve the logic of bourgeois, not plebeian, emancipation. During the debate within the Central Committee of the Communist League in 1850, Marx further elaborated this idea, now stressing the overwhelming social weight of the petty-bourgeois layers and their ideology in France. In a country so little transformed by modern industry, a victorious working class would be obliged to share power with the numerically preponderant peasantry and lower middle classes. The proletariat would be forced to defer its own class demands while legislating the programme of its allies.[17] Engels gives a different twist to this thesis in a letter to Weydemeyer in 1853. Where Marx had emphasized the captivity of a revolutionary government to the stage of social development, Engels now fretted over the dangers of adventurism as he confided his fear that if 'our party' were forced to take power in Germany '*before* its own time', it might be tempted 'to make communist experiments and leaps' that were 'premature' and would lead to total defeat.[18] These cautionary allusions left a profound imprint upon the politics of the Second International in the form of a conception of proletarian power that, in countries like Russia, was confined to alliance with the peasantry and the execution of bourgeois-democratic tasks.

---

[15]'Moralizing Criticism . . .', pp.331-3.
[16]Ibid.
[17]'Minutes of the Central Committee Meeting of 15 September 1850,' in *Revolutions of 1848*, p. 343.
[18]See *Ausgewählte Briefe*, Berlin 1953, pp. 93-4.

All these various formulations, however, provide only one scenario of revolution to be found in the writings of Marx and Engels. In a contradictory manner—sometimes literally side by side with stagist conceptions—there appears the *idea* of permanent revolution: that is to say, the concept of an uninterrupted revolutionary process enabling the proletariat to overturn capitalism and maintain state power, even in the peripheral, backward and semi-feudal countries of Europe. I say 'idea' and not 'theory', because it is not possible to speak of a coherent and systematic theory of permanent revolution in Marx and Engels. Rather, there is a series of fragmentary conceptions, prophetic intuitions and inchoate perspectives, which intermittently appear and reappear but are never ordered in a rigorous doctrine or global strategy. Their importance is above all methodological: they show that Marx and Engels had admitted the *objective possibility* of a rupture in the succession of historical tasks; that these tasks have a complex, dialectical articulation; and that historical materialism—at least as practised in the writings of its founders—cannot be reduced to a metaphysical and economistic evolutionism.

The term 'permanent revolution' is first employed by Marx in his 1844 text, *The Jewish Question*. It occurs in a passage criticizing Jacobinism as a terroristic attempt to impose the supremacy of the political sphere over bourgeois society (although this was, of course, its actual foundation): 'But it only manages to do this in *violent* contradiction to the conditions of its own existence, by declaring the revolution *permanent*, and for that reason the political drama necessarily ends up with the restoration of religion, private property and all the elements of civil society (*bürgerlichen Gesellschaft*), just as war ends with peace.'[19] Of course this utilization of the mere *term* in 1844 had little relationship to the idea of permanent revolution as the uninterrupted process leading the proletariat to power in backward countries. The Jacobins were far from being the precursors of the revolutionary proletariat, and Marx in this period tended to employ the term in an imprecise manner. Consider, for example, its appearance in a well-known passage from *The Holy Family* (1845) concerning Napoleon: 'He perfected the Terror by substituting *permanent war* for *permanent revolution*.'[20] It was only in 1850 that Marx first used the term to designate

[19]In *Early Writings*, Harmondsworth 1975, p. 222.
[20]In *Collected Works*, vol. 4, p. 123. What is the origin of the phrase 'permanent revolution'? Many authors have attributed it to Blanqui, but I have not been able to find any instance of it in his writings, and, besides, Marx began to use the term at a time when he was unacquainted with any work by Blanqui. It may be, however, that the phrase comes directly from Jacobin usage. During moments of revolutionary crisis the Jacobin Club would declare itself assembled 'en permanence'—in permanent session. This expression appears in a German study of

the concept in a familiar sense. Still, one may wonder whether the term was truly adequate in its reference to the problematic involved; does not the connotation of perpetual and ceaseless motion introduce an element of misunderstanding and confusion? Perhaps an expression like 'uninterrupted and combined revolution' would have been more precise. Nonetheless, revolutionary tradition for nearly a century has invested Marx's formula with a rich signification that transcends its literal sense—scarcely a unique example of lexical overdetermination in socialist discourse (just think of the loaded, multiple meanings compressed within signifiers like 'socialism', 'communism', and so on). Trotsky openly recognized this problem when he referred to 'this rather high-flown expression'.[21]

The crucial question is, what actual ideas are denoted by the term 'permanent revolution' in the various texts of Marx and Engels that concerned themselves with the problem of revolution in continental Europe? In fact, the richest and most rigorous development of the concept can be found in their texts on *Germany*. Although the German Empire would be the industrial giant of Europe by the century's end, it should not be forgotten that the 'Germany' of 1844-56 was still semi-feudal, pre-industrial and politically fragmented. Its most powerful core state—the Prussia of Kaiser Wilhelm II—was one of the purest examples in Europe of unreformed absolutism. It is interesting to observe, therefore, that the first work in which Marx explicitly recognized the revolutionary agency of the proletariat is simultaneously the first work in which he sketched a 'permanentist' prospectus for the class struggle in Germany: the Introduction to 'The Critique of Hegel's Theory of Right', published in the *Franco-German Yearbook* for 1844. Marx's personal experience of direct collaboration with the German liberal bourgeoisie, as the crusading young editor of the *Rheinische Zeitung* (1842-43), gave him a negative view of that class's revolutionary capacity. In particular, the servile capitulation of the paper's shareholders to Prussian censorship so disgusted him that he resigned (in

---

[21]Preface to the First Edition (1922), *1905*, New York 1971, p. vi. When Nicolas Krasso ('Trotsky's Marxism', *New Left Review* 44 [July-August, 1967], pp. 67-68) tries at all cost to expose Trotsky's supposed confusion ('He called this process "permanent revolution"—an inept designation that indicated the lack of scientific precision even in his profoundest insights'), he very simply forgets that Trotsky had only appropriated the term from Marx.

---

the Revolution that was certainly known to Marx, who took notes on it in Kreuznach in 1843: W. Wachsmuth, *Geschichte Frankreichs im Revolutionsalter*, Hamburg 1842, vol. 2, p. 341—'Von den Jakobinern ging die Nachricht ein, dass sie in Permanenz erklärt hatten.' On this, see J. Bruhat, 'Marx et la révolution française', *Annales d'Histoire de la Révolution Française*, 184, April-June 1966, p. 138.

March 1843) rather than concede to 'moderation' of the editorial line. A little while later, in a letter to Ruge, he expressed his scorn for the bourgeois philistinism that accepted a sheepish subservience rather than struggle to become 'free men—that means republicans'.[22] In the 1844 Introduction this conclusion is sharpened and amplified: for Marx, the German bourgeoisie does not posess 'the consistency, acuteness, courage and ruthlessness which would stamp it as the negative representative of society'. It lacks 'that revolutionary boldness which flings into the face of its adversary the defiant words: *I am nothing and I should be everything*'.[23] He thus ironically chastises the German bourgeoisie with the defiant words of Sieyès's *Qu'est-ce que le Tiers Etat?*, that incomparable manifesto of the revolutionary French bourgeoisie of 1789.

Why was the German bourgeoisie of the 1840s so weak-kneed and timid in comparison with the French middle classes of a half-century earlier? The remarkable sociological explanation outlined by Marx in the Introduction contained the seeds of some of the decisive elements of the modern theory of permanent revolution. In particular, Marx analysed with great acuity the *simultaneously backward and advanced character* of German society: 'Every sphere of civil society . . . experiences defeat before it celebrates victory, and asserts its narrow-mindedness before it has had a chance to assert its generosity. As a result, even the opportunity of playing a great role has always passed by before it was every really available, and every class, as soon as it takes up the struggle against the class above it, is involved in a struggle with the class beneath it. Thus princes struggle against kings, bureaucrats against aristocrats, and the bourgeoisie against all of these, while the proletariat is already beginning to struggle against the bourgeoisie. The middle class scarcely dares to conceive the idea of emancipation from its own point of view, and already the development of social conditions and the progress of political theory have demonstrated this point of view to be antiquated or at least problematic.'[24] It is, therefore, the working-class menace 'below' that makes the German bourgeoisie conservative and prevents it from becoming a revolutionary force of any consequence. This leads Marx to conclude that only a 'universal class', lacking any hierarchy of privilege or power to defend against a more subordinate class, could possibly liberate Germany from the shackles of the past. This class is, of course, the proletariat. But the emancipation to which the

---

[22]'Letters from the *Franco-German Yearbooks*', *Early Writings*, p. 201. For a more detailed analysis of this period, see my *La théorie de la révolution chez le jeune Marx*, Paris 1970.
[23]*Early Writings*, p. 254.
[24]Ibid., p. 255.

proletariat aspires is not simply a reform of regimes; as a class with 'radical chains', it requires a radical revolution and general human emancipation— that is to say, communism. Consequently, 'it is not *radical* revolution or *universal human* emancipation which is a utopian dream for Germany; it is the partial, *merely* political revolution, the revolution which leaves the pillars of the building standing. . . . In Germany universal emancipation is the *conditio sine qua non* of any partial emancipation.'[25] Of course at the moment when Marx was writing this, the German workers' movement hardly existed, so his audacious thesis was actually more an extrapolation from the French situation (he was just then receiving his first introduction to the Parisian underground of secret revolutionary societies and communist artisans) than an accurate description of German conditions. However, the great revolt of the Silesian weavers a few months later seemed an astounding confirmation of Marx's prevision. In August, Marx used the Silesian events as a backdrop in his continuing polemic with Ruge, arguing that this first uprising of the German working class demonstrated that 'just as the impotence of the German bourgeoisie is the *political* impotence of Germany, so too the capacity of the German proletariat . . . is the *social* capacity of Germany'. Moreover, he added, one could find 'the first rudiments necessary for an understanding of this phenomenon in my Introduction to the *Critique of Hegel's Philosophy of Right*'.[26]

Three years later, the *Communist Manifesto* offered a more ambiguous gloss on the probable course of a German revolution; and partisans of stagism and permanent revolution have both managed to find passages that seem to support their respective positions. In contrast with the 1844 texts, the *Manifesto* hypothesizes the possibility of a revolutionary role for the bourgeoisie—in which case, Marx and Engels argue, it would be necessary for the proletariat to form a common front with it against the old order. It may be that this hypothesis was a reaction to the clash between the bourgeoisie and the monarchy during the meeting of the German Assembly in March 1847. At all events, even if Marx and Engels envisioned circumstances in which a *tactical* alliance with the bourgeoisie might be necessary, the *strategic* conceptions advanced by the *Manifesto* remained on a clearly permantist terrain: 'The Communists turn their attention chiefly to Germany, because that country is on the eve of a bourgeois revolution that

[25]Ibid., pp. 253, 255. (Cf. p. 257: 'Germany can emancipate itself from the *Middle Ages* only if it emancipates itself at the same time from the *partial* victories over the Middle Ages. In Germany *no* form of bondage can be broken without breaking *all* forms of bondage.')

[26]'Critical Notes on the Article "The King of Prussia and Social Reform. By a Prussian"' (1844), in ibid., p. 417.

is bound to be carried out under more advanced conditions of European civilization, and with a much more developed proletariat, than that of England was in the seventeenth, and of France in the eighteenth century, and because the bourgeois revolution in Germany will be but the prelude to an immediately following proletarian revolution.'[27] This famous passage contains several notions that would be decisive in the future elaboration of the theory of permanent revolution: (1) the idea that the level of social and economic development ('civilization') as an index of 'revolutionary maturity' could not simply be measured in a single nation-state, but had to be evaluated within the appropriate international context (European in the nineteenth century); (2) the understanding that the social and political weight of the German proletariat precluded the repetition of a 'classical' bourgeois-democratic revolution of the English or French types; (3) (and although the affirmation of the *necessary priority* of bourgeois revolution did open the door for a stagist reading of the *Manifesto*) the intuition that, rather than *two distinct historical stages*, the bourgeois and proletarian revolutions might in fact constitute only *two moments* of the same *uninterrupted* revolutionary process.

During the course of the Revolution of 1848-49 in Germany, Marx and Engels had the concrete opportunity to test the strategic orientation they had outlined in the *Manifesto*. With the aid of Fernando Claudín's remarkable study of the evolution of their political thought in this period,[28] we can compare the trajectory of positions adopted in the *Neue Rheinische Zeitung* with the perspective they advanced on the eve of the revolutionary storm.

In the first period (spanning most of 1848) Marx and Engels tried to implement the first tactical priority of their strategy: the common struggle with the bourgeoisie against absolutism. They joined the Democratic Association of Cologne and attempted to enlist the participation of several leading middle-class activists in the launching of the *Neue Rheinische Zeitung* (described simply as an 'organ of democracy').[29] Although their bourgeois

---

[27] In *Revolutions of 1848*, p. 98.

[28] *Marx, Engels y la revolución de 1848*, Madrid 1975.

[29] It is instructive to compare the different commentaries of twentieth-century Marxists regarding the legitimacy of this tactic. Lenin, for example, wrote in 1905 that such collaboration with the bourgeoisie appeared 'astonishing and unbelievable from our current point of view' and was only explicable in light of the 'petty-bourgeois atmosphere in the Germany of this period'. Rose Luxemburg, moreover, in 1905 averred that this tactic could only fail and had been grasped at by Marx in a 'totally hopeless and isolated' situation. In contrast, Stalin, writing in 1927 to justify the Chinese Communist Party's suicidal alliance with the Kuomintang, argued that Marx's tactic was entirely 'correct'. (Cf. Marx, Engels, Lenin, Stalin, *Zur Deutschen Geschichte*, Band II, 1. Halbband, Berlin 1954, pp. 213, 576; and Rosa Luxemburg, *Gesammelte Werke*, Band 2, Berlin 1974, p. 212.)

associates deserted the paper after a few weeks, Marx and Engels persisted in searching for a basis of unity; as late as January, 1849 Marx published an article that presented a rather stagist defence of democratic solidarity.[30] Yet in the same period they also wrote articles that questioned the tactic of alliance with the bourgeoisie. Most notably there was an article by Engels, published in September 1848 shortly after the shameless capitulation of the Frankfurt Assembly to the monarchy and the bloody suppression by Prussian troops of attempted resistance by workers and peasants. According to Engels, the struggle that had become the order of the day 'in Vienna as well as Paris, Berlin as well as Frankfurt, London as well as Milan, is the political overthrow of the bourgeoisie'; raised now on every barricade of the continent was 'the symbol of the European proletariat's unity in combat'— the red flag, under whose banner the German workers had fought the reactionary 'parliament of the combined junkers and bourgeoisie'. The bourgeoisie now felt itself directly threatened by every popular uprising, so the masses had to struggle not only against the military-bureaucratic state, but also 'against the armed bourgeoisie itself'.[31]

After December 1848 Marx undertook to further develop this position in the well-known series of articles entitled 'The Bourgeoisie and the Counter-Revolution'. 'A purely *bourgeois revolution* . . . is impossible in Germany. What *is* possible is either feudal and absolutist counter-revolution or the *social-republican revolution*.'[32] But what would be the motive forces of such a revolution? In an article of February 1849, he gave the answer: 'the most radical and democratic classes of society', the workers, peasants and petty bourgeoisie.[33] By April, Marx had resigned from the Democratic Association and was now concentrating all his energies on building the Workers' Association of Cologne. This shift in his political focus was also reflected in the publication of his famous essay, *Wage-Labour and Capital*; whose introduction warned that any revolutionary uprising in Europe would be doomed to defeat until 'the revolutionary working class is victorious. . . .

---

[30]'But we say to the workers and the petty bourgeoisie: it is better to suffer in modern bourgeois society, which by its industry creates the material means for the foundation of a new society that will liberate you all, than to revert to a bygone form of society, which, on the pretext of saving your classes, thrusts the entire nation back into medieval barbarism.' (Marx, 'Montesquieu LVI', p. 266.) This extreme formulation is highly atypical of Marx's general orientation in the *Neue Rheinische Zeitung*, and is obviously dissonant with his overall perspective. Nonetheless, the Russian (and Menshevik) historian Nicolaievski in his biography of Marx has seized upon this anomalous quotation with great zest: 'never before nor later in the *Neue Rheinische Zeitung*, does Marx express himself with "such clarity"'. (B. Nicolaievski and O. Maenchen-Helfen, *Karl Marx*, Paris 1937, p. 157.)

[31]'The Uprising in Frankfurt' (20 September 1848), *Collected Works*, vol. 7, p. 444.

[32]*Revolutions of 1848*, pp. 193-4, 212.

[33]'The *Kölnische Zeitung* on the Elections' (1 February 1849), *Collected Works*, vol. 8, p. 289.

[Every] social reform remains a utopia until the proletarian revolution and the feudalistic counter-revolution measure swords in a world war.'[34] Thus, just before the closure of the *Neue Rheinische Zeitung*, Marx had completely discarded the *Manifesto*'s insistence on a preliminary phase of bourgeois revolution in Germany, and had reoriented the entire problematic towards the international scene. This was the culmination of Marx's increasing distrust of all attempts at tactical reliance on the middle classes; each bourgeois betrayal of the workers and surrender to the monarchy had pushed Marx back toward the permanentist orientation first outlined in 1844.

It is interesting to compare this second cycle of Marx's disillusionment with the revolutionary capacity of the bourgeoisie and his original break with liberalism after the suppression of the *Rheinische Zeitung* in 1843. In both cases, the initial assumption—however qualified by various doubts and reservations—had concerned the capacity of the bourgeoisie to mount serious and consequent opposition to the feudal-absolutist system. In both cases, bitter practical experience forced Marx to set this belief aside. (As we shall see a little later, a somewhat similar analytic evolution was repeated in the case of Spain in the 1850s.) Nothing distinguished Marx and Engels more from some later 'Marxists' than this capacity to correct and to amend erroneous theoretical presuppositions in the light of the class struggle.

Exiled in England, Marx and Engels continued to radicalize their conception of the dynamics of the German revolution. For example, in March-April 1850, Engels published 'The Campaign for the German Imperial Constitution', with the following conclusion: 'Ever since the defeat of June 1848 the question for the civilized part of the European continent has stood thus: either the rule of the revolutionary proletariat or the rule of the classes who ruled before February. A middle road is no longer possible. In Germany, in particular, the bourgeoisie has shown itself incapable of ruling; it could only maintain its rule over the people by surrendering it once more to the aristocracy and the bureaucracy . . . the revolution can no longer be brought to a conclusion in Germany except with the complete rule of the proletariat.'[35] At the same time, Marx and Engels were also writing the document that would outline most clearly, coherently and explicitly their perspective of permanent revolution: 'The Address of the Central Committee to the Communist League'. Their starting-point was a condemnation of the unholy alliance between the 'liberal' bourgeoisie and absolutism. Against this reactionary coalition, they championed the common action of

---

[34]*Wage Labour and Capital, Collected Works*, vol. 9, p. 198.
[35]'The Campaign for the German Imperial Constitution', ibid., vol. 10, p. 237.

the proletariat with the democratic parties of the petty bourgeoisie. But their conception of 'democratic unity' was now inserted within a much more internationalist and permanentist conception of the revolutionary process: 'while the democratic petty bourgeoisie want to bring the revolution to an end as quickly as possible . . . it is our interest and our task to make the revolution permanent until all the more or less propertied classes have been driven from their ruling positions, until the proletariat has conquered state power and until the association of the proletarians has progressed sufficiently far—not only in one country but in all the leading countries of the world—that competition between the proletarians of these countries ceases and at least the decisive forces of production are concentrated in the hands of the workers.'[36] This striking passage contains three of the fundamental themes that Trotsky would later develop in the theory of permanent revolution: (1) the uninterrupted development of the revolution in a semi-feudal country, leading to the conquest of power by the working class; (2) the application by the proletariat in power of explicitly anti-capitalist and socialist measures; (3) the necessarily international character of the revolutionary process and of the new socialist society, without classes or private property.

Given this perspective, what form must the revolutionary movement of the proletariat take? Marx assumed that the next revolutionary wave would carry the democratic party (bourgeois/petty-bourgeois) to power in Germany, but 'alongside the new offical governments they [the workers] must simultaneously establish their own revolutionary workers' governments, either in the form of local executive committees and councils or through workers' clubs or committees, so that the bourgeois-democratic governments not only immediately lose the support of the workers but find themselves from the very beginning supervised and threatened by authorities behind which stand the whole mass of the workers.'[37] Need we emphasize the extraordinary similarity between this action programme and the October Revolution: organization of workers' councils, dual power, permanent revolution? The resemblance becomes even more unmistakable when Marx and Engels go on to stress the need to centralize the workers' councils and provide them with 'red guards'.[38] Finally, the 'Address' ends

---

[36] In *Revolutions of 1848*, pp. 323-4.

[37] Ibid., p. 326.

[38] 'The workers must try to organize themselves independently as a proletarian guard, with elected leaders and with their own elected general staff; they must try to place themselves not under the orders of the state authority but of the revolutionary local councils set up by the workers.' (ibid., p. 326.)

with a ringing appeal to the German workers not to be deceived by hypo-
critical slogans of the democratic petty bourgeoisie, but to organize their
own independent party. 'Their battle-cry must be: The Permanent
Revolution.'[39]

For obvious reasons this text has always been an embarassment and
irritation to dogmatically stagist interpreters of Marx's political thought.
For some it proposes a revolutionary programme literally 'incompatible
with historical materialism', while for others it constitutes only a 'brief
Jacobin-Blanquist aberration' in Marx's thought.[40] The Menshevik historian Nicolaievski, for example, thinks it is 'difficult to accept that this
document really reflects, in all its details, the opinion of Marx', and that it
was actually the product of a 'compromise' between Marx and the extremist
wing of the Communist League.[41] Most of these commentators, however,
have accepted the accusation first made by Bernstein in 1899 that the
'Address' and its theory of permanent revolution reveal the indelible influence of 'Blanquism'.[42] This is totally erroneous, for not only does the
problematic of the 'Address' diverge entirely from Blanquism (how, for
example, could its central insistence on the revolutionary self-organization
of the working class be squared with Blanqui's conception of a con-
spiracy?), but the theme of 'permanent revolution' is most emphatically not
of Blanquist origin. To my knowledge, neither the term nor the concept
ever surface in the writings of Blanqui; moreover, when Marx first used the
term in 1844-45, he was virtually ignorant of Blanqui's works. In reality,
for Bernstein to be able to calumniate Marx's ideas in 1850 as 'Blanquist',
he was first obliged to 'redefine' radically the conventional meaning of the
concept. Thus for Bernstein, 'Blanquism' was no longer simply the theory
of a revolutionary coup d'etat organized by a secret society (a 'superficial
definition'), but rather 'the theory of the unlimited power of revolutionary
violence and of its corollary: expropriation'.[43] Of course, within such an
expansive definition, every revolutionary socialist current would *a priori*
become 'Blanquist'. . . . On the other hand, Bernstein did demonstrate a

[39]Ibid., p. 330.

[40]Cf. J. Plamenatz, *German Marxism and Russian Communism*, London 1963, p. 127; and
George Lichtheim, *Marxism*, New York 1962, p. 125.

[41]*Karl Marx*, p. 173. This thesis is shared by other authors, especially Richard Hunt (*The
Political Ideas of Marx and Engels*, London 1975) for whom the 1850 text is the expression of
Marx's 'tactical concessions'. Robin Blackburn criticizes these artificial interpretations in
'Marxism: Theory of Proletarian Revolution', *New Left Review* 97 (May-June 1976), pp. 12-13.

[42]*Les presupposés du socialisme*, Paris 1974, pp. 58-67.

[43]Ibid., p. 59.

more profound philosophical intuition when he saw that the ultimate source of the 'Blanquist error' in Marx and Engels was nothing other than the *dialectic* itself. For Bernstein, the concept of the transformation of the coming revolutionary explosion in Germany into a 'permanent revolution' was the fruit of the Hegalian dialectic ('all the more dangerous because it is always totally false') which permits the 'brusque passage from economic analysis to violence' as well as 'the transformation of each thing into its opposite'.[44]

Indeed, it was only by virtue of their dialectical approach that Marx and Engels were able to transcend the rigid and intransigent dualism between economic evolution and political violence, between democratic revolution and socialist revolution. It was their understanding of the contradictory unity of these different moments, and of the possibility of qualitative leaps ('brusque passages') in the historical process that this made possible, that allowed them to lay the foundations for the theory of permanent revolution. Against this dialectical method Bernstein could propose only 'a return to empiricism' as 'the sole means of avoiding the most terrible errors'.[45] No one could have thrown into sharper relief the contrasting methodological premises of stagism and permanentism!

It is, of course, entirely true that the 'empirical' events foretold in the 'Address'—the next revolutionary round in Germany, the victory of the democratic party, and so on—failed to come true. But just as history confounded the short-term predictions of the 'Address', it also eventually vindicated the brilliance of its prefiguration of the proletarian revolutions of the twentieth century.[46] The extraordinarily fertile dialectical approach of Marx and Engels touched on a broad spectrum of problems related to the class struggle in more backward capitalist countries. Indeed, their writings in the early 1850s even contain an intuition that revolution would break out more easily at the periphery than at the centre of the capitalist system. 'These violent convulsions must necessarily occur at the extremities of the bourgeois organism rather than at its heart, where the possibilities of

[44]Ibid., p. 67.
[45]Ibid.
[46]Trotsky made a comment on the predictive errors of Marx and Engels in 1850 which, it seems to me, is very incisive: 'Marx regarded the bourgeois revolution of 1848 as the direct prelude to the proletarian revolution. Marx "erred". Yet his error has a factual and not a methodological character. The revolution of 1848 did not turn into a socialist revolution. But that is just why it also did not achieve democracy.' (*The Permanent Revolution*, New York 1969, p. 131.) This distinction between factual error and methodological correctness is paradoxical, but it nonetheless constitutes the key to interpreting Marx's writings on the revolutions of 1848-50.

restoring the balance are greater.'[47] (For Marx in 1850 the 'heart' was obviously Britain, while the 'extremities' were the countries of the Western and Central Europe). Another seminal idea first canvassed in this period was the question of the peasantry. Reflecting on the failure of the revolution in Germany, Marx commented in a letter to Engels (April 1856): 'The whole thing in Germany depends on the possibility of backing the proletarian revolution by some second edition of the Peasants' War.'[48] Lenin was later to interpret this passage in the following terms: 'while the democratic (bourgeois) revolution in Germany was uncompleted, Marx focused every attention, in the tactics of the socialist proletariat, on developing the democratic energy of the peasantry.'[49] Actually, the position of Marx was much more radical, since its problematic was not that of a bourgeois-democratic revolution, but of peasant support for a *proletarian revolution*— an idea that reappears as a central theme in Trotsky's writing after 1905.

It is clear that the permanentist strategy outlined by Marx and Engels between 1848 and 1850 was inspired *in its form* by the rhythms of the French Revolution of 1789, with its succession of increasingly radical forces assuming power amidst a continuing process of political and social upheaval. When, more than a generation after its demise, Engels drafted a balance-sheet of the *Neue Rheinische Zeitung*, he emphasized that he and Marx had, at the time, envisioned the stormy period of February-March 1848 as 'the starting point of a long revolutionary movement . . . in which, as in the great French upheaval, the people would develop themselves still further through their struggles . . .'.[50] Engels believed that Marat was a precursor of this orientation to the extent that he had envisaged a process of revolution '*en permanence*'.[51] But Engels did not sufficiently stress in this passage everything that distinguished the *social content* of the French Revolution (and its process of deepening radicalization) from the perspective of permanent revolution. Beyond the level of formal analogy, entirely different historical stakes were involved, since the revolutions

---

[47]*The Class Struggles in France* in Marx and Engels, *Surveys From Exile*, Harmondsworth 1973, p. 131.

[48]*Ausgewählte Schriften*, II, Moscow 1934, p. 440.

[49]'Karl Marx' in *Selected Works*, vol. 1, Moscow 1967, p. 58.

[50]'Marx und die "Neue Rheinische Zeitung" 1848-49', in *Zur Deutschen Geschichte*, II/1, p. 220. In an 1849 article Engels had compared the Jacobin dictatorship and the Hungarian Insurrection in the following terms: 'The *lévee en masse*, the national manufacture of weapons, the *revolution in permanence*, in short all the chief characteristics of the glorious year 1793 are to be seen again in Hungary as armed, organized and galvanized by Kossuth.' (my italics; 'The Magyar Struggle', in *Revolutions of 1848*, pp. 213-4.)

[51]'Marx und die "Neue Rheinische Zeitung"', p. 221.

of 1848 opened the new epoch of proletarian power. Thus the reference to Marat is obfuscatory inasmuch as he—unlike Babeuf—did not have a truly anti-capitalist programme.

The 1848 Revolution in France was also visualized by Marx and Engels as a process of permanent revolution, despite the fact that it involved a country that had not only known a bourgeois revolution but was also the most industrialized on the Continent. The existence of a monarchical state and the nearly exclusive concentration of political power in the hands of a financial aristocracy dictated certain revolutionary-democratic tasks; while the numerical superiority of the petty bourgeoisie and peasantry was a formidable obstacle to a workers' revolution. Thus the France of 1848 constituted a social formation intermediate between the 'backwardness' of Germany and the 'ripeness' of England in relation to the development of the productive forces and the polarization of the class structure. This complex situation was analysed in a contradictory manner in Marx's *Class Struggles in France*. On one hand, he affirmed that 'it is only the rule of the bourgeoisie which serves to tear up the material roots of feudal society and level the ground, thus creating the only possible conditions for a proletarian revolution'. On the other, with the exception of Paris, the proletariat 'is almost submerged by the predominance of peasant farmers and petty bourgeoisie'. This argument seems to revive an economistic vision that postponed the possibility of proletarian revolution until a much later historical stage, when France had been fully industrialized and the middle layers proletarianized. Yet in the very same paragraph, he added, 'The French workers could not move a step forward, nor cause the slightest disruption in the bourgeois order, until the course of the revolution had aroused the mass of the nation, the peasants and the petty bourgeoisie, located between the proletariat and the bourgeoisie, against this order, against the rule of capital, and until it had forced them to join forces with their protagonists, the proletarians. The workers were able to gain this victory at the price of the terrible defeat of June.'[52] In focusing on the trajectory of the revolutionary process itself, Marx shifted from a rigid stagism towards a perspective of permanent revolution. For example, he considered the victory of the left in the by-elections of March 1850 as the first achievement of this vast popular coalition under proletarian leadership: 'It was a *general coalition against the bourgeoisie and the government, as in February*. But this time the *proletariat was the head of the revolutionary league*.'[53] And at the head of the proletariat was revolutionary socialism—

[52]In *Surveys From Exile*, pp. 46-7.
[53]Ibid., p. 125.

communism—'for which the bourgeoisie itself has invented the name of Blanqui. This socialism is the declaration of the permanence of the revolution, the class dictatorship of the proletariat as a necessary intermediate point on the path towards the abolition of class differences in general, the abolition of all relations of production on which they are based . . . '[54]

Socialist revolution was, therefore, recognized by Marx as possible in France provided that the proletariat won the following of other popular strata, especially the peasantry. In a famous passage of the *Eighteenth Brumaire* this idea is extended to the entirety of 'peasant nations': generalized industrialization and proletarianization are no longer proposed as absolute preconditions for workers' power; rather the problem is recast in political terms—it is the capacity of the proletariat to assume hegemony over the movement of the plebeian masses that arbitrates whether a dynamic of permanent revolution can take hold.[55] Marx also conceived the proletarian revolution in France as permanent revolution because of its necessary international resonance and extension: 'The new French revolution will be forced to leave its natural soil immediately and to *conquer the European* terrain, on which alone the social revolution of the nineteenth century can be carried out.'[56] He outlined a dialectical relationship between revolutions in France and England that anticipated the Bolsheviks' conception of the interdependence of the Russian and German revolutions: the victorious rising of the French working class would be the first step in the emancipation of Europe, provided that the French revolution was not isolated and eventually defeated by the economic power and world supremacy of England. Thus only the capture of power by the English working class could ensure that the 'social revolution would pass from Kingdom of Utopia to the Kingdom of Reality'.[57] In a passage of *The Class Struggles in France*, he criticized the nationalist illusions of the French workers' movement from the standpoint of an internationalist conception of proletarian revolution that emphasized the global character of capitalism and the linkages it perforce established between class struggles in different national contexts. 'Just as the workers believed that they could emancipate themselves alongside the bourgeoisie, so they believed that they could accomplish a proleta-

---

[54]Ibid., p. 123.

[55]'In despair and disappointment at the Napoleonic restoration, the French peasant will abandon his faith in his smallholding, the entire state edifice erected on the smallholding will fall to the ground, and *the proletarian revolution will obtain the chorus without which its solo will prove a requiem* in all peasant countries'. (*The Eighteenth Brumaire of Louis Bonaparte* in *Surveys From Exile*, p. 245.)

[56]*Class Struggles in France* in *Surveys From Exile*, pp. 61-2.

[57]'The Revolutionary Movement' (1 January, 1849), *Collected Works*, vol. 8, p. 215.

rian revolution within the national walls of France alongside the remaining bourgeois nations. But French relations of production are determined by France's foreign trade, by its position on the world market and by the laws of this market; how was France to break these laws without a European revolutionary war, which would have repercussions on the despot of the world market, England?'[58] Although this type of formulation had the unquestionable merit of posing the problem of the international dimension of the revolutionary process, it also underestimated—as would certain of Trotsky's texts—the *unequal* character of this process, and, thus, the actual autonomy of the crisis and mass movements in each country.

Several years after the defeat of the French and German revolutions, echoes of the 1848-50 events were heard in a rather unexpected country: Spain. In June 1854 the 'liberal' generals, O'Donnell and Espartero, supported by the barricades of the people, staged a military uprising that liberated political prisoners and promised reforms. In a series of articles in the *New York Daily Tribune*, Marx carefully analysed these events, stressing the contradictions between the military (who wanted to preserve the monarchy) and the people (who demanded universal suffrage, the confiscation of the property of counter-revolutionaries, and so on). Nonetheless he was not very sanguine about the possibility of a Spanish version of June 1848; on the contrary, it was his opinion that 'the social question, in the modern sense of the term, lacked a real foundation in a country whose resources were still as undeveloped and population as reduced (merely fifteen million) as Spain.'[59] The second part of Marx's argument may seem rather capricious in retrospect; after all, Prussia—where Marx considered the 'social question' definitely on the agenda—had only about seventeen million inhabitants, just a few more than Spain. But the first part of the argument was more cogent: because of its economic and social underdevelopment, the 'social question' in the sense of the struggle of the proletariat was not yet the order of the day in Spain. Yet two years later Marx abandoned this quasi-stagist conception in the face of another round of revolutionary crisis in Spain. In July 1856, O'Donnell in complicity with the throne seized power in a coup d'etat. The still liberal Espartero went into hiding, while the Cortes, after a timid attempt at resistance, *de facto* dissolved itself and advised the (bourgeois) national militia to disperse. Only the working-class districts of Madrid continued to fight until—after several days of desperate

[58]*Surveys From Exile*, p. 45.
[59]Marx and Engels, *Revolution in Spain*, New York 1938, p. 126 (retranslated).

urban guerrilla warfare—they were crushed by the regular army. The Spanish proletariat had been capable of its heroic 'June' after all. Amending his earlier commentary, Marx now concluded that these events showed how 'the proletarians were betrayed and abandoned by the bourgeoisie', and that in Spain in 1856, 'we no longer have simply the Court and the army on one side and the people on the other, but that we now have also the same divisions in the ranks of the people which exist in the rest of Western Europe'.[60] The social logic of the Spanish coup was ultimately the same as that of the Eighteenth Brumaire of Louis Bonaparte: while the industrial and commercial bourgeoisie did oppose military despotism, they were more afraid of the mobilization of the workers, and, therefore, preferred the ignoble embrace of the generals to a democratic alliance with the proletariat.[61] Marx concluded his first article on the 1856 events with a phrase which indicated not only his evident surprise at the Spanish developments, but also the extent to which he was forced to reconsider his presuppositions about the country's relative 'immaturity': 'that his lesson should also be demonstrated in Spain is as impressive as it is surprising'.[62] In a second article (18 August 1856), he continued with an analysis of how the 1856 insurrection had transcended the liberal bourgeois and putschist framework of the Revolution of 1854, predicting that 'the next European revolution will find Spain ripe to cooperate with it. The years 1854 and 1856 have been transitional phases that it had to pass through to achieve this maturity.'[63]

What European revolution was Marx thinking of? In a letter to Engels around this time he expressed his conviction that 'on the Continent revolution is imminent and will immediately take a socialist character'.[64] Although this prognosis was obviously incorrect, it does clarify Marx's particular interpretation of the Spanish situation. First, he clearly believed that Spain was ready to play its part in an imminent European socialist revolution. Second, Spain's 'maturity' was the product neither of economic expansion nor of industrial revolution, but rather a result of a sequence of socio-political developments, including especially the counter-revolutionary role of the bourgeoisie and the experience acquired by the proletarian masses in the process of struggle. The shift of optic from an earlier determinist vision of distinct stages to a new scenario of permanent

---

[60]Ibid., pp. 144, 151 (retranslated).
[61]Ibid., p. 147 (retranslated).
[62]Ibid., p. 148 (retranslated).
[63]Ibid., p. 154 (retranslated).
[64]Letter of 8 October, 1858, *Ausgewählte Briefe*, p. 133.

revolution recalls the earlier revolution in Marx and Engels's strategic conception of the German revolution. Here, however, the revision was more drastic, since Marx's starting point had been the denial of the possibility of any specifically proletarian movement in Spain.

Marx's reflections on permanent revolution in Spain—which have remained generally forgotten and undiscussed—are the last chapter in the ensemble of texts dealing with the revolutionary period around 1848 (from its first premonitions in the 1840s until its last, dying echo in the 1850s). As the debates on revolutionary strategy faded away, the question of permanent revolution also tended to sink below the immediate political horizon. It would only reappear after a hiatus of more than twenty years, but this time in the context of another country, the social formation in which the first historical concretization of uninterrupted and combined revolution would occur: Russia.

In order to understand the methodological basis of Marx's approach to the Russian question, it is necessary to recall his polemic with the populist theorist Mikhailovsky in 1877. Accused of wanting to transpose onto Russia the model of 'primitive accumulation' described in *Capital*, Marx responded: 'For him [Mikhailovsky] it is absolutely necessary to change my sketch of the origin of capitalism in Western Europe into an historio-philosophical theory of a Universal Progress, fatally imposed on all peoples, regardless of the historical circumstances in which they find themselves.'[65] Is there any point underlining the exceptional clarity and importance of this passage for understanding Marx's views on Russian and other 'backward' nations in the world market? The same problem is raised again in a letter to Vera Zasulich written in 1881 when the ideals of populism still gripped most of the revolutionary intelligentsia in Russia. Marx complained about certain Russian 'Marxists' who attributed to him a 'theory of the historical necessity for all countries of the world to pass through the phases of capitalist production'. In reply, the author of *Capital* insisted that his analysis of the necessity of the expropriation of the peasantry as outlined in the chapter on primitive accumulation was 'explicitly restricted *to the countries of Western Europe*'.[66] These remarks clearly dissociate Marx from any evolutionist, unilinear, mechanical or abstract conception of historical motion and socio-economic development. Indeed, the refusal to enshrine the Western European case as a universal model allowed him to recognize

[65]Marx and Engels, *The Russian Menace to Europe*, London 1953, p. 217.
[66]Ibid., pp. 277-8.

the multiform character of concrete social development. It opened the theoretical possibility of a distinct succession of social and historical stages in Asia, and the 'periphery' in general, which differ from those analysed in *Capital* (feudalism, the crisis of feudalism, mercantilism, manufacture, heavy industry). Transcending the antinomy between the metaphysical universalism (*geschichtsphilosophie*) of the self-proclaimed Russian 'Marxists' and the mystical, slavophile particularism of the Narodniks, Marx achieved in his writings on Russia between 1877 and 1882 a remarkable dialectical synthesis between the general and the particular that allowed him to understand the specific contradictions of the Russian economy and society in this epoch.

What would be the character of the Russian revolution that Marx and Engels anxiously anticipated from the 1870s onwards? For Engels (in 1894) the Russian bourgeoisie was unlikely to play a liberal, much less a revolutionary role: 'If meanwhile it [the bourgeoisie] is still tolerating the despotic autocracy . . . this is only because this autocracy offers it greater security than would a change—even in a bourgeois liberal direction—the consequence of which, given the internal situation in Russia, no one can foresee.'[67] What might be the 'unforeseeable' consequences of a revolutionary uprising in Russia? Several times Engels speaks of a 'Russian 1789', which would necessarily be followed by a 1793'.[68] The problem, of course, is that the significance of '1793' is just as ambiguous in Engels as in Marx. Sometimes it appears as the synonym of the revolution '*en permanence*' (as in Engels's 1849 article on Hungary), while other times it denotes simply the realization of the tasks of bourgeois revolution via plebeian means (as in Marx's 1848 articles on the bourgeoisie and counter-revolution). On another occasion (in a message to a meeting of slavic revolutionaries) Marx and Engels employ the different historical analogy of the 'future establishment of a Russian Commune'.[69] Is this simply a rhetorical formula corresponding to the tenth anniversary of the Paris Commune? It seems to me that its meaning is, in fact, more profound; but to understand it, we must first consider Marx and Engels's attitudes towards the thesis (familiar in some populist circles) that Russia might be able to utilize the traditional rural commune as the social basis for a revolutionary short cut through the calamities of capitalist development. In his 1877 letter, Marx spoke of the

[67]Ibid., p. 240.
[68]'Die Arbeiterbewegung in Deutschland, Frankreich, den USA und Russland' (1878), *Werke*, 19, p. 115; see also the letter to Vera Zasulich (23 April 1885) in *Ausgewählte Briefe*, p. 457.
[69]*Werke*, 19, p. 244.

danger that Russia might squander 'the finest occasion that history has ever offered a people not to undergo all the sudden turns of fortune of the capitalist system'; later, in his 1881 reply to Zasulich, he clarified this remark by straightforwardly asserting that the *obschtchina* (the Russian rural commune) 'is the strategic point of social generation in Russia'.[70] Finally, there is a surviving draft of a letter in which Marx tackled this problem most explicitly, with special emphasis on the *political* conditions that would allow the rural communes to provide the cellular structure for a transition to socialism. 'Only a Russian Revolution can save the Russian village community. . . . If such a revolution takes place in time, if it concentrates all its forces to assure the free development of the rural community, this latter will soon become the regenerating element of Russian society, and the factor giving it superiority over the countries enslaved by the capitalist system.'[71]

This letter has had a strange history. Portions of it were first found by Riazanov in 1911, who asked Zasulich, Plekhanov and Axelrod, one after the other, whether they had been the recipient of the final version. All replied in the negative; but in 1923 the full letter was unexpectedly discovered amongst Axelrod's papers. The amnesia of the three Menshevik· leaders is symptomatic, prompting the observation that they had probably repressed the memory of the letter because it so blatantly contradicted their construction of Marxist orthodoxy and its application to Russia.[72] Yet it would be mistaken to think that Marx intended to provide succour to the Narodniks by his comments on the *obschtchina*. Whereas the populists insisted that Russia could only be redeemed by its spiritual and political separation from a decadent and corrupt Europe, Marx saw the potential role of the rural commune in terms of European and international frameworks. Thus in fragments of a letter intended for Zasulich in 1881, Marx emphasized: 'Russia finds itself in a modern historical environment. It is contem-

---

[70]*The Russian Menace to Eruope*, pp. 217, 278-9.

[71]Ibid., p. 226.

[72]On this subject see the editorial note on page 279 of *The Russian Menace to Europe*. Equally significant is the interpretation given to this letter shortly after its publication in 1924 by the eminent Menshevik historian Nicolaievski. Aware of the contradiction between this document and the Menshevik version of 'orthodox' Marxism, he tried to explain the letter as the product of tactical needs: because of his sympathy for the courageous fight of the *Narodnaya Volya* against Tsarism, Marx did not want to expose his differences with the populists or provide ammunition which the proto-Marxists in *Tcherny Peredel* (led by Plekhanov, Axelrod and Zasulich) might use in their polemical battles against *Narodnaya Volya*. (See B. Nicolaievski, 'Marx und das Russiche Problem, *Die Gesellschaft*, I Jahrgang, 4 (July 1924), pp. 364-66). However any comparison of the original draft with final version sent to Axelrod is sufficient to rebut this rationalization.

poraneous with a superior civilization, it is tied to a world market in which capitalist production predominates. By appropriating the positive results of this mode of production, it is in a position to develop and transform the yet archaic form of its village community, instead of destroying it.'[73] How could this 'appropriation' be achieved? Already, in an 1873 article which was probably the first attempt to theorize the role of the *obschtchina* in Marxist terms, Engels had argued that a revolution in the West would be a necessary precondition, since only then could the farm machinery and other advanced inputs become available for the modernization of the communes. 'If there is anything which can save the Russian system of communal property, and provide the conditions for it to be transformed into a really living form, it is the proletarian revolution in Western Europe.'[74] It is hard to establish whether Marx shared this viewpoint, but in the 'preface' to the 1882 Russian edition of the *Manifesto* the dialectical reciprocity of the two revolutions is affirmed by both authors: 'If the Russian revolution sounds the signal for a proletarian revolution in the West so that each complements the other, the prevailing form of communal ownership of land in Russia may form the starting point for a communist course of development.'[75]

After Marx's death Engels began to manifest an increasing scepticism about the future of the *obschtchina* and Russia's chances to escape the capitalist stage.[76] In an 1892 letter to his populist acquaintance Danielson, for example, he stated, 'I am afraid we shall have to treat the *obschtchina* as a dream of the past, and reckon, in future, with a capitalist Russia.'[77] Engels had good reason to be pessimistic about the rural commune, since the rapid development of industrial capitalism in Russia after 1890 was rapidly dispelling the illusory hopes that he and Marx had invested in the possibility of a non-capitalist path. *Yet once again a predictive error contained a more fundamental truth*: namely, that Russia might embark on a 'communist

---

[73]*The Russian Menace*, pp. 222-3.

[74]'Russia and the Social Revolution' (1873) in ibid., p. 213. Another of Engels's arguments for the necessary link between revolution in Russian and the industrial West was that only when capitalism had been defeated in its heartland, that is, 'only when the backward countries see by this example "how the job is done", how modern industrial productive forces can be made to serve the collectivity as socially owned property', could backward countries like Russia hasten their march toward socialism. (See "Russia and the Revolution Reconsidered"' (1894) in ibid., pp. 234-5.)

[75]Ibid., p. 228.

[76]This does not mean, however, that he began to accept all the positions of Plekhanov, especially his violent attacks against the *Narodnaya Volya*. On Engels's reservations concerning Pekhanov, cf. his letter to Vera Zasulich (23 April, 1885) in *Ausgewählte Briefe*, pp. 455-57 and Kautsky's latter to Bernstein (30 June 1885), cited by Kurt Mandelbaum, *Sozialdemokratie und Leninismus*, Berlin 1974, p. 76.

[77]*Ausgewählte Briefe*, p. 531.

course of development' simultaneously or even before industrialized Western Europe. In more general terms, Marx and Engels's reflections on Russia
provided the crucial indications for a theory of how a revolution might
break out in a backward country with a broad pre-capitalist residuum;
how such a revolution might begin the transition toward socialism; and
why the success of this monumental enterprise would depend to a very
great measure upon the extension of the revolution to the West. It is
almost needless to add that the whole course of twentieth-century history
has tended to confirm these previsions and intuitions; or that the reason
their insight into the logic of the historical process was so profound was
that it grew out of the recognition that history moves dialectically—not
unilinearly—through innumerable combinations, fusions, discontinuities,
ruptures and sudden, qualitative leaps. One of the decisive methodological
aspects of their writings on Russia was a rejection of any form of 'infra-
structural fatalism', of any conception (like that held by the Mensheviks)
that Russian history was preordained by its economic structure. Socio-
economic conditions indisputably delimited the field of the possible and
defined viable alternatives, but the ultimate decision of history depended
upon those autonomous political factors: the revolutions in Russia and
Europe.

In conclusion I would propose that writings of Marx and Engel on the
question of revolution in underdeveloped and semi-feudal countries reveal a
double contradiction: first, a contradiction between stagist and permanentist
visions of revolution; second, a contradiction in the heart of the permanentist texts themselves, between short-term empirical error and profound historical intuition. These persistent contradictions in their political
theory, moreover, are the refraction of a contradiction in reality itself—a
contradiction in the nature of the historical epoch in which Marx and
Engels lived. As Trotsky pointed out in his *Results and Prospects* (1906),
during the nineteenth century in countries like Germany 'capitalism had
developed sufficiently to render necessary the abolition of the old feudal
relations, but not sufficiently to bring forward the working class, the
product of the new industrial relations, as a decisive political force. The
antagonism between the proletariat and the bourgeoisie, even within the
national framework of Germany, had gone too far to allow the bourgeoisie
fearlessly to take up the role of national hegemon, but not sufficiently to
allow the working class to take up that role.'[78] In other words, it was too

---

[78]London 1962, p. 189. Also see Alain Brossat's excellent study, *Aux origines de la révolution permanente: la pensée politique du jeune Trotsky*, Maspero, Paris 1974, p. 18.

late for the bourgeois revolution but still too early for the proletarian. The shifting positions of Marx and Engels must be situated in terms of this dilemma, as at one moment they insisted on the incapacity of the bourgeoisie to play a revolutionary role, while at another they emphasized the immaturity of the proletariat. They grappled heroically with this dilemma, but its solution evaded them because it involved a transformation in social reality itself.

Nevertheless, Trotsky's comment needs to be relativized and qualified: while it is certainly true that after 1848 the bourgeoisie no longer played a hegemonic revolutionary role comparable to that of 1789, it is also true that profound political and economic changes serving the interests of capital were carried out by the agencies of quasi-absolutist or military states. These *semi-revolutions from above* in France, Germany, Italy and Japan were the decisive events of the second half of the nineteenth century, and although Marx gave some recognition to them in his writings after 1859, it was Engels who dealt with them more extensively through the medium of his studies of the historical roles of Napoleon III and Bismarck.[79] In the case of Bismarckian Germany—which Engels characterized as a variety of Bonapartism—it was 'a strange destiny that Prussia would end up finishing towards the end of the century and under the more comfortable mantle of Bonapartism the German bourgeois revolution which had begun in 1808-13 and flickered briefly again in 1848.'[80] It is necessary to add that both Marx and Engels greatly underestimated the most important 'bourgeois revolution from above' of this entire epoch: the Italian Risorgimento. The struggle for national unification in Italy had unleashed incomparably more profound forms of popular, democratic mobilization than anything in Bismarckian Germany. Oddly, Engels overlooked this mass dimension of the Risorgimento to emphasize, instead, the limitations of its bourgeois leadership. 'The bourgeoisie, coming to power during and after national emancipation, has no desire to complete its victory. It has taken no initiative to

---

[79]'Einleitung zu den "Klassenkämpfen in Frankreich"', (1895) in Marx, *Ausgewählte Schriften*, Band II, Moscow 1934, p. 187. Also see Marx, 'Die Erfurterei im Jahre 1859', *Werke*, 13, p. 414. In 'semi-revolution from above' I include all those important structural transformations—social, economic and political—which are implemented by authoritarian state power in the interests of 'historic compromises' by new classes or dominant fractions (especially the bourgeoisie) with the old oligarchy. Because these changes occur with little or no authentic popular mobilization (indeed, often hand in hand with the crushing of the masses), they remain partial, unfinished and incomplete. As we shall see later, this phenomenon is scarcely limited to the nineteenth century.

[80]*La révolution démocratique bourgeois en Allemagne*, Paris 1951, p. 20.

destroy feudal remnants nor to reorganize national production on the model of modern capitalism.'[81]

It is unfortunate that this crucial block of European history did not command more sustained attention in the writings of Marx and Engels, and that the texts (expecially those of Engels) that did focus on the mode of socio-economic transformation represented by the Bismarkian programme or the Risorgimento deployed an array of concepts deriving from the 1848 Revolutions—particularly 'Bonapartism'—which were not entirely adequate to the specific contradictions involved. For it was these 'semi-revolutions' or 'passive revolutions' (as Gramsci termed them)—together with certain more limited 'bourgeois' reforms like the abolition of serfdom in Russia—that laid a basis for the European revolutions of the twentieth century. Precisely because these reforms from above were incomplete—leaving considerable feudal detritus and/or vestiges of the absolutist state, which the bourgeois would or could not destroy—they created the explosive contradictions that would allow the proletariat to raise the banner of democracy in its own name. In his 1874 Preface to *The Peasant War in Germany*, Engels ironically projected what the Germany of a generation later would look like: 'If all goes well, if everyone remains very tranquil and we should all live so long, then we might, perhaps, see in 1900 that the Prussian government has truly suppressed all the feudal institutions and that Prussia has finally arrived at the same point where France was at in 1792.'[82] However things went very differently, and the Prussia of Wilhelm II in 1900 was a long way away from the republican France of 1792. It required a workers' revolution in November 1918 to overthrow the monarchy and the power of the junker oligarchy. And it was clearly the cumulative retardation of reform that explained the wave of revolutionary explosions that rocked Germany, Austria, Hungary and Italy between 1918 and 1920: in other words, the inability of the bourgeoisie to lead bourgeois-democratic revolutions to their conclusion created the conditions for a revolutionary upsurge led by the proletariat itself.

---

[81]Marx and Engels, *Scritti italiani*, Milan and Rome 1955, p. 170.
[82]In *La révolution démocratique bourgeois en Allemagne*, p. 20.

2
Permanent Revolution in Russia

Trotsky's theory of permanent revolution was born in the revolutionary tumult of 1905-6 in Russia. Like the seminal texts of Marx and Engels in 1848-50, which first outlined a conception of revolution *en permanence*, Trotsky's works of this period—above all, *Results and Prospects*—were written from a standpoint of intense and impassioned engagement with the problems of a living revolution. Their interest, first and above all, is their originality. Trotsky's theses on the revolution of 1905 implied a radical break with the dominant beliefs of the Second International about the future of the class struggle in Russia. Since the death of Engels, it had become a universal, almost canonical assumption amongst 'orthodox' Marxists that the coming Russian revolution would be inevitably *bourgeois* in character. All factions of Russian social democracy took this assertion as their undisputed starting point; if they fought amongst themselves, it was over different interpretations of the role of the proletariat and its necessary class alliances in this bourgeois revolution. *Trotsky was the first and for many years the only Marxist to question this sacrosanct dogma.* To appreciate the qualitative originality of his approach, it is necessary to compare it with the ideas of his contemporaries in the Russian and international labour movements.

As we have seen, Marx and Engels were far from convinced that Russia was condemned to follow the same path as Western Europe, or that a socialist revolution was excluded in that country until the maturation of advanced industrial capitalism. It is, thus, impossible to attribute to them these doctrinaire assertions that would become hegemonic in Russian and Western Marxism until 1917. Their origins must be found elsewhere: especially in the writings of Georgi Valentinovich Plekhanov (1856-1918). It was he who developed for the first time in a coherent and systematic way an exclusively stagist conception of the Russian revolution, which, in turn, became a virtual paradigm for similar theorizations applied to other backward and underdeveloped countries. This does not mean, of course, that Plekhanov's interpretation could not claim legitimacy from certain texts of Marx and Engels; indeed, he repeatedly quoted certain passages from the 1859 Introduction and other essays. But what does set him aside from his mentors was his prodigious effort to transpose a rigid and one-sided version of the Western European 'model' of development on Russia. When Marx and Engels explicitly opposed this interpretation, criticizing Plekhanov's mechanical formalism (see the previously cited 1877 letter of Marx); he demonstrated his undeniable independence of mind by insisting all the more firmly that his position was more orthodox than (by inference) Marx's. Thus the irony that the 'Father of Russian Marxism' held views on Russia that diverged quite sharply from those of Marx himself.

Furthermore, one is inclined to ask whether Plekhanov's 'Marxism' did not differ from Marx in method and epistemology as well? In my opinion, a careful study of Plekhanov's writings reveals an approach very different from the revolutionary dialectics of Marx and Engels. It included certain closely related tendencies which might be characterized as *pre-dialectical*, and which constitute the methodological ground for his political theory:

(1) A tendency to underestimate the distance between Marx's new materialism and the older metaphysical materialism of Helvetius, La Mettrie, Feuerbach, etc. Plekhanov went so far as to write that Marx's *Theses on Feuerbach* 'did not reject the philosophy of Feuerbach; they only amended it. . . . The materialist conceptions of Marx and Engels had developed in the very sense indicated by the internal logic of Feuerbach's philosophy.'[1]

(2) A metaphysical naturalization of history leading to a fatalistic conception of the laws of social development is ubiquitous in his writings—as when he asserted that the programmatic aims of the labour movement would be achieved 'as certainly and surely as the rising of the sun in the morning.'[2]

(3) An 'objectivistic' economism that made the growth of the productive forces the exclusive foundation for social and political development: 'The degree of preparedness of a people for true democracy . . . depends on the degree of its economic development. . . . The development of productive forces brings us nearer to our goal and guarantees the victory of the proletariat.'[3]

[1]*Les questions fondamentales du marxisme*, Paris 1953, pp. 32-3.
[2]Quoted by A. Walecki, 'Le problème de la révolution russe chez Plekhanov', in *Histoire du marxisme contemporain*, Paris 1977, p. 87.
[3]'Nos controverses', *Oeuvres philosophiques*, Paris 1970, p. 286.

These general propositions were translated into Plekhanov's political analyses, which, in turn, became the central strategic axis for the constitution of Menshevism. The essence of the latter was the belief that Russia was a backward, 'Asiatic' and barbarous country requiring a long stage of industrialism and 'Europeanization' before its proletariat could aspire to power. Since Russia was only ripe for a bourgeois-democratic revolution, the task of the proletariat was to support the liberal bourgeoisie in overthrowing autocracy and establishing a 'modern' (i.e. 'European') constitutional state. Only after Russia had completely passed into this stage of advanced capitalism and parliamentary democracy would the requisite material and political conditions be available for socialist revolution.[4]

From his conversion to Marxism until his death in 1918 Plekhanov defended this orientation with an uncommon obstinacy and rigor, against all odds, and independently of changes in political conjuncture or the concrete historical situation. In a sense he had already written the last word in his political philosophy when he inscribed in his notebook in 1881: 'Russia stands at a crossroads on the way to capitalism and all other solutions are closed to her. In order to fight capitalism, only one way is left: to help it grow as fast as possible.'[5] This one-sided determinism and unflinching refusal to imagine any historical alternative to the capitalist road lay at the root of all of his political activity. This perspective first appears in 1883-4 when Plekhanov almost single-handedly founded Russian Marxism in a series of great polemical battles with populism. In his early pamphlets—*Socialism and Political Struggle* (1883) and *Our Controversies* (1885)—Plekhanov drew from a scientific analysis of the development of capitalism in Russia to demonstrate the errors and illusions of the populists. Yet, at the same time as he refuted the subjectivist fantasies of the Narodniks about the rural commune and Russian agrarian socialism, he also damned their more fertile and realistic intuitions: the idea of a specific road to socialism, the importance of the peasantry in the future revolution, and so on. Although he was justified in rejecting their slavophilic mysticism, he

---

[4]This conception was not contradictory with Plekhanov's occasional affirmation of the *hegemonic* role of the working class in the fight against Tsarism. In 1902, for example, Plekhanov wrote, 'Our party will take upon itself the task of the struggle against absolutism and indeed the hegemony in this struggle.' (*Sochinennya*, ed. Riazanov, vol. XII, Moscow 1923-7, pp. 101-2.) Yet at the same time he insisted that the future reserved for Russia 'the triumph of the bourgeoisie'. In other words, Plekhanov believed that the hegemonic role of the proletariat stopped short of the seizure of power: after the overthrow of Tsarism, the labour movement had to let the bourgeoisie rule alone in order to accomplish its historical tasks. See Perry Anderson, 'The Antinomies of Antonio Gramsci', *New Left Review* 100, January 1977, pp. 15-16.

[5]*Liternaturnie nasledie G. V. Plekhanova*, vol. I, Moscow 1939-40, pp. 206-7.

offered as a substitute only a narrow-minded eurocentrism which dogmatically asserted that Russia must reproduce Western forms of capitalist development and bourgeois power.

When, after 1903, Plekhanov assumed leadership of the Menshevik wing of the Russian Social-Democratic Workers Party (RSDLP), he revived the same arsenal of theses to combat a new *bête noir*: Bolshevism. Throughout the 1905 revolution Plekhanov and his Menshevik comrades maintained that 'it is now the turn of the bourgeoisie, and the proletariat cannot take history into its own hands and change it.'[6] Here is a precise formulation of a naturalistic and reified conception of history, in which socioeconomic stages and classes succeed each other according to a necessity as objective and inevitable as the succession of the seasons during the year. The idea of Marxist historicism—that people make their own history, but under given conditions—is replaced in Plekhanov's writings by a purely 'objective' conception, leaving no room for the revolutionary practice of the proletariat and its creative intervention in the political process. In the name of science, Plekhanov forbade the proletariat to take history into its own hands.

Finally, in 1917 at the most crucial moment in the history of the Russian workers' movement, Plekhanov clung stubbornly to his rigidly stagist doctrines. When Lenin published his famous *April Theses*, which broke decisively with traditional tenets and embraced a permanentist conception akin to Trotsky's, Plekhanov launched a virulent counter-attack: 'He who breaks off all contact with the interests of the bourgeoisie, is destroying the socialist revolution. . . . The attempt to precipitate a socialist revolution can be likened to the attempts of the anarchists of the International Congress in 1889, when the bourgeoisie had not yet matured. . . .'[7] Plekhanov's tragedy was that the more the proletariat radicalized itself and intensified its struggle against the bourgeoisie, the more the 'Father of Russian Marxism', in order to maintain the petrified and inflexible coherence of his theory, evolved towards moderate if not

---

[6]Letter to the Menshevik members of *Nachalo* (18 December 1905) quoted in Ella Feldman-Belfer, 'The Conflicts and Dilemmas of the Marxist Path of G. V. Plekhanov', Ph.D. thesis, Tel Aviv University, 1972, p. 222. Under such circumstances it is hardly surprising that Miliukov, the leader of the Kadets (the Constitutional Democratic Party: the principal political expression of the liberal bourgeoisie), hailed him with enthusiasm. 'If all G. V. Plekhanov's comrades understood what the most outstanding of their leaders understood, and if they were as little discomforted as he by the praises of the "liberal bourgeoisie", my God how that would simplify the explanation of our present political problems. . . .' (Ibid., p. 220).

[7]*Edinstvo*, 11 (12 April 1917) and 18 (20 April 1917), quoted in ibid., p. 365. The term 'maturity' that constantly appears in Plekhanov's writings is the shibboleth of a certain 'naturalization' of history.

conservative positions, insisting on the need to curtail socialist agitation and propaganda amongst the workers. He had so lost step with the real evolution of the Russian class struggle that on his deathbed in 1918 he could ask his old friend Leo Deutsch: 'Did we not start the Marxist propaganda too soon, in this backward, semi-Asiatic country?'[8] Clinging to his 'orthodox' interpretation of Marxism until the bitter end, Plekhanov seems to have come to the bizarre conclusion that such an interpretation could only triumph if Marxism remained unknown to the Russian toiling masses.

Of course, as has already been noted, the presupposition that the Russian revolution must necessarily be bourgeois-democratic in content was shared before 1917 by virtually every sector of Russian and international Marxism. Where Lenin and the Bolsheviks differed from Plekhanov and the Mensheviks was over which class would play the leading role in carrying out these bourgeois tasks. For the latter, the hegemonic class had to be the bourgeoisie itself, while for the former it would be an alliance of workers and peasants. Furthermore, we should recall that Lenin considered himself (until 1914 at least) as the philosophical disciple of Plekhanov, and his great epistemological opus—*Materialism and Empirico-Criticism*—was deeply influenced by the elder figure. In this phase Lenin accepted some of the fundamental premises of Plekhanov's pre-dialectical Marxism as well as their strategic corollary—the bourgeois-democratic character of the Russian revolution. Nevertheless he refused, unlike Plekhanov, to make a *tabula rasa* of the populist tradition. Although he also rejected the agrarian socialist dream, he did critically assimilate their insights on the roles of the intelligentsia and, especially, the peasantry (whom Plekhanov treated as an obscurantist and reactionary mass) in the revolutionary process. Moreover, from the very beginning, Lenin manifested a more radical concrete political orientation than that of the spirtual leader of Menshevism.

A close reading of Lenin's most important political text of this period, *Two Tactics of Social Democracy in the Democratic Revolution* (1905), reveals with extraordinary clarity the *tension* in Lenin's thought between his profound revolutionary realism and the limitations imposed by the straitjacket of so-called 'orthodox Marxism'. On one hand, this work contains an illuminating and penetrating analysis of the incapacity of the Russian bourgeoisie successfully to lead a democratic revolution, which, in fact, could be accomplished only by a worker-peasant front under proletarian hegemony. On the other hand, there are innumerable passages in the

---

[8]Quoted by Feldman-Belfer, p. 388.

pamphlet that categorically insist on the exclusively bourgeois character of the revolution and condemn as 'reactionary' the idea of 'seeking salvation for the working class in anything save the further development of capitalism'.[9] Lenin supported this latter thesis by appealing to the classical leitmotiv of pre-dialectical Marxism: 'The degree of Russia's economic development (the objective condition) and the degree of class consciousness and organization of the broad masses of the proletariat (the subjective condition, inseparably bound up with the objective condition) make immediate and complete emancipation of the working class impossible. Only the most ignorant people can close their eyes to the bourgeois nature of the democratic revolution which is now taking place.'[10] The objective determines the subjective, the economy is the condition of consciousness; here, in two phrases, is the quintessence of the materialist gospel of the Second International, whose dead weight overlay Lenin's rich and powerful political intuition.

'The Revolutionary Democratic Dictatorship of the Proletariat and the Peasantry': this formula was the shibboleth of pre-1917 'old Bolshevism', reflecting within itself all the ambiguities of the first Leninism. In contrast, the radically innovative dimension of Lenin's politics, which so sharply demarcated Bolshevism from Menshevism, was expressed by the far more flexible and realistic formula of 'Workers' and Peasants' Power'. As Trotsky later remarked, this last slogan had an 'algebraic' character in that the specific weight of each class was not determined *a priori* by some mechanistic principle. The apparently paradoxical term, 'democratic dictatorship,' on the other hand, revealed the limitations imposed by the schemas of the official Marxism of the Second International: the revolution cannot but be *democratic*, that is, *bourgeois*. This premiss, Lenin insisted, flowed from the 'elementary principles of Marxism'[11]—which is to say Marxism as conceived and taught by Plekhanov.

Another theme in the *Two Tactics* that testifies to the methodological obstacles created by the *analytical* (pre-dialectical) character of contempor-

[9]*Two Tactics of Social-Democracy in the Democratic Revolution, Collected Works* (henceforward CW), vol. 9, Moscow 1962, p. 49. See also p. 49: 'Marxists are absolutely convinced of the bourgeois character of the Russian revolution. What does this mean? It means that the democratic reforms that become a necessity for Russia, do not in themselves imply the undermining of capitalism, the undermining of bourgeois rule; on the contrary, they will, for the first time, really clear the ground for a wide and rapid, European and not Asiatic, development of capitalism; they will, for the first time, make it possible for the bourgeoisie to rule as a class.'
[10]Ibid., p. 28.
[11]Ibid., p. 49.

ary Marxism was the explicit rejection of the Paris Commune as a model for the Russian revolution. According to Lenin, the Commune failed because it was 'unable to distinguish·between the elements of democratic revolution and socialist revolution', and because it 'confused the tasks of fighting for a republic with those of fighting for socialism. Consequently, it was a government such as *ours* [the future provisional revolutionary government in Russia] should not be'.[12] As we shall see later, the return to the Paris Commune was to be one of the decisive steps in Lenin's drastic revision of the 'old Bolshevism' in April 1917.

It would not be fair to leave Lenin's writings on the revolution of 1905 without noting that there are some passages that seem to hint at the idea of an uninterrupted revolutionary development towards socialism. Particularly intriguing is an article on the peasantry written in September 1905 where Lenin asserts: 'From the democratic revolution we shall at once, and precisely in accordance with the measure of our strength, the strength of the class conscious and organized proletariat, begin to pass to the socialist revolution. We stand for uninterrupted revolution. We shall not stop half-way.'[13] Nonetheless this is an exceptional formulation which does not correspond to the orientation evinced in the overwhelming bulk of his writing in this period.[14]

It is quite characteristic of Lenin before 1914 that in his polemic against Plekhanov he evoked the authority of Kautsky. For instance, he saw in an article by Kautsky on the Russian revolution (1907) 'a direct hit against Plekhanov' and elsewhere he emphasized the coincidence between Kautskian and Bolshevik conception—'A bourgeois revolution, brought about by the proletariat and the peasantry in spite of the instability of the bourgeoisie—this fundamental principle of Bolshevik tactics is wholly confirmed by Kautsky.'[15] Indeed, Kautsky in his article, 'The Driving Forces and the Perspectives of the Russian Revolution' (1906), advanced some quite radical views which were (contrary to his later position in 1917) clearly antagonistic to Menshevism: 'As soon as the proletariat appears as an independent class with independent revolutionary aims, the bourgeoisie ceases to be a revolutionary class . . . the bourgeoisie therefore does not belong to the driving forces of the present revolutionary movement in Russia and to that extent one cannot designate it as a bourgeois one.' But at

---

[12]cw, vol. 9, pp. 80-81. This analysis of Lenin's views before 1914 draws on my article, 'From the Great Logic of Hegel to the Finland Station of Petrograd', *Critique* 6 (Spring 1976).

[13]cw, vol. 9, p. 237.

[14]See Norman Geras, *The Legacy of Rosa Luxemburg*, London 1976, pp. 92-3.

[15]cw, vol. 11, pp. 372-3. See also Massimo Salvadori, *Karl Kautsky and the Socialist Revolution, 1880-1938*, London 1979, pp. 100-8.

the same time he reaffirmed the orthodox dogma, categorically rejecting the possibility of socialist revolution. 'This does not at all permit us to write that this is a socialist movement. It will not lead in any case to a purely proletarian power, to its dictatorship. For this the Russian proletariat is too weak and underdeveloped.' However, Kautsky admits the possibility that social democracy might arrive in power with the support of other classes (especially the peasantry); but in this case 'it will not be able, as a victorious party, to go further in the implementation of its programme than as permitted by the interests of the classes which support the proletariat.' Like Lenin, Kautsky stresses, 'without the peasants we can not triumph in Russia. But we cannot expect that the peasants will become socialists.' Thus, it 'appears unthinkable that the present Russian revolution could lead to the introduction of a socialist mode of production, even if the revolution should temporarily put Social Democracy at the helm.'[16]

This hypothesis of a transitory workers power was also at the heart of Rosa Luxemburg's reflections on the Russian revolution of 1905. In 1906 in a polemical article against Plekhanov she tried to analyse the conditions and limits of such an experience. 'The proletariat, as the most revolutionary element, will perhaps take on itself the task of liquidating the old regime by "seizing power" in order to fight against the counter-revolution, in order to prevent the revolution from being blocked by a bourgeoisie which is by its nature reactionary. . . . Apparently, no social-democrat has any illusions about the possibility for the proletariat to remain in power; it could keep power, this would imply the domination of its class ideas, the implementation of socialism. But its forces are not sufficient for this at the present moment, because the proletariat, *strictu senso*, is only a minority of the society in the Russian Empire. . . . After the fall of Tzarism, power will pass into the hands of the most revolutionary section of society, the proletariat . . . but only as long as the power will not yet be in the hands legally designated to receive it.'[17] This legal power, for Rosa Luxemburg, had to be that of a democratically elected constituent assembly where the representatives of the majority of the Russian population—the peasantry and the petty-bourgeois democrats—would inevitably be dominant. This position is very reminiscent of Marx's warning in 1847 that a 'premature' taking of power by the proletariat would perforce be both temporary and constrained by the exigencies of the bourgeois nature of the revolution.

[16]*Neue Zeit* (25 Jahrgang), Stuttgart 1907, pp. 330-33 (my emphasis).
[17]'Blanquisme et social-démocratie', *Czerwony Sztander* 82 (June, 1906) translated in *Quatrième Internationale*, 2 (April, 1972), p. 55.

Even though her conception was more advanced than Plekhanov's—and even, to a certain extent, Lenin's—she did not question the most deeply rooted and 'self-evident' of social-democratic dogmas: the inevitably bourgeois character of the Russian revolution. At the same, however, she did in certain writings arrive at a premonition of the most crucial idea of the theory of permanent revolution—the historical combination and practical fusion between bourgeois and socialist revolutions. 'The present revolution in Russia goes far beyond the *content* of all previous revolutions. . . . It is then, both in method and in content, a radically new type of revolution. Bourgeois-democratic in form, proletarian-socialist in essence, it is also in content and form a *transitional* form between the bourgeois revolutions of the past and the proletarian revolutions of the future.' But in a later passage in the same essay Luxemburg again yielded ground to the traditional presupposition that the 'proletariat does not now place before itself the task of implementing socialism, but rather must first create the bourgeois-capitalist pre-conditions for the implementation of socialism.'[18]

The principal difference between the strategic viewpoints of Luxemburg and Lenin was over the question of the relationship between the proletariat and the peasantry. At the conferences of the Russian social democrats in 1907 and 1909, Luxemburg embraced the formulation first proposed by Trotsky in 1905: '*the dictatorship of the proletariat supported by the peasantry*'.[19] Although Lenin finally rallied to this slogan at the 1909 conference, there was still considerable distance between him and Luxemburg because she did not believe in the joint exercise of revolutionary power by workers and peasants; for her, only the concentration of all power into the hands of the proletariat could accomplish the tasks of the democratic revolution in Russia.[20] It was probably because of the coincidences between their formulations, that Trotsky later wrote in his autobiography that at the 1909 congress 'on the question of the so-called permanent revolution, Rosa took the same stand as I did'.[21] This is not quite true, for on the pivotal question of the bourgeois character of the programme to be enacted by the revolution, Luxemburg was still nearer to Lenin than to the theory of the permanent revolution. In a typical statement, combining ignorance and

---

[18]'Die russische Revolution (1649-1789-1905)', *Gesammelte Werke*, vol. 2, Berlin 1970, pp. 8-9.

[19]See Trotsky, *The Permanent Revolution* (1930), London 1962, p. 73.

[20] See 'Die Lehren der Drei Dumas', *Przeglad Socjaldemokratcyczny*, 3, (May 1908) in Luxemburg, *Internationalismus und Klassenkampf*, Luchterhand 1971, pp. 359-71.

[21]*My Life*, New York 1960, p. 203.

deliberate distortion, Stalin in 1931 attempted to contribute to the history of the theory of permanent revolution by claiming: 'Parvus and Rosa Luxemburg . . . invented the utopian and semi-Menshevik scheme of permanent revolution : . . subsequently, this semi-Menshevik scheme of permanent revolution was caught by Trotsky.'[22]

In fact, the first authors to use the term 'permanent revolution' in relation to the Russian revolution (before Trotsky himself) were Kautsky and Franz Mehring. Kautsky wrote in his most enthusiastic and radical article on the 1905 revolution that 'permanent revolution is . . . exactly what the proletariat in Russia needs'; but apparently for him this meant little more than that 'it is under revolutionary conditions that the proletariat . . . imprints its own stamp on state and society most profoundly, and obtains the greatest concessions from them'.[23] A few months later, in an article in *Neue Zeit* (November 1905) under the heading 'Die Revolution in Permanenz', Mehring emphasized the differences between the European upheavals of 1848 and the contemporary revolution in Russia. By refusing to lay down its arms and by accelerating the pace of popular mobilization, the Russian working class became the leading force in the revolution. Against the bourgeois slogan of 'order at any price', it opposed the defiant battle cry of 'the revolution in permanence'.[24] A close reading of Mehring proves that he cannot be considered a partisan of permanent revolution in the same sense as Trotsky in 1905-6 (or Marx in 1850);[25] but it is very likely that his article suggested to Trotsky the utilization of the term 'permanent revolution', otherwise virtually extinct in the vocabulary of the Second International. Indeed, in *The New Course* (1923) Trotsky recalled: 'Franz Mehring employed it for the revolution of 1905-7. The permanent revolution, in an exact translation, is the continuous revolution, the uninterrupted revolution.'[26] But Trotsky was wrong when he wrote that Mehring and Kautsky shared the 'viewpoint of permanent revolution'.[27] The vital kernel of the theory, its concept of the uninterrupted going-over of the democratic towards the socialist revolution, was denied by Mehring

[22]'Some Questions Concerning the History of Bolshevism', in *Leninism*, London 1940, p. 392. See the excellent analysis of the relationship between the strategic perspectives of Lenin, Luxemburg and Trotsky in Norman Geras, *op. cit.*, Chapter II.

[23]'Die Folgen des janpanischen Sieges und die Sozialdemokratie', *Neue Zeit*, XXIII, 1904-5, vol. 1, p. 462, quoted in Salvadori, *op. cit.*, p. 102.

[24]*Neue Zeit*, (24 Jahrgang), Band I 1904-5, pp. 169-71.

[25]See ibid., p. 171.

[26]*The New Course* (1923) in Trotsky, *The Challenge of the Left Opposition, 1923-1925*, New York 1975, p. 102.

[27]Preface (1922), *1905*, London 1971, p. viii.

(although he used the term) quite as much as by Kautsky. One cannot help but form the impression that Trotsky sometimes endeavoured to minimize the originality of his conception by claiming an identity of views with Luxemburg, Mehring, Kautsky and, to a certain extent, Lenin. Doubtless this was a retrospective attempt to play down the supposedly 'heretical' nature of the theory of permanent revolution. But Trotsky's contemporary polemical opponents had no illusions about the novelty of his ideas. For example, Mehring's article was immediately translated in 1905 in Trotsky's newspaper *Nachalo* in Petrograd and in the same issue the first article in which Trotsky probably used the term 'permanent revolution' appeared: 'Between the immediate goal and the final goal there should be a permanent revolutionary chain.' Martov, the Menshevik leader, in a work written many years later, recalled Trotsky's piece as a disturbing 'deviation from the theoretical foundations of the Programme of Russian Social-Democracy'. He clearly distinguishes between Mehring's article, which he considered acceptable, and Trotsky's essay, which he repudiated as 'utopian', since it transcended 'the historical task which flows from the existent level of productive forces'.[28]

If Trotsky's terminological source was Mehring, what was the theoretical source of the permanentist strategy? Parvus (Alexander Israel Helphand) is frequently mentioned as the true inspirer and mentor of Trotsky and some of the latter's enemies (such as Stalin) gave Parvus exclusive intellectual responsibility for the theory of permanent revolution.[29] Trotsky never attempted to hide his debt to Parvus. In many of his writings—particularly in *My Life*—he paid Parvus homage, emphasizing the 'extraordinary boldness of his thought' and recognizing his debt to him when he came to consider 'the conquest of power by the proletariat from an astronomical "final" goal to a practical task for our own day'.[30] As we shall see, however, Parvus—unlike Trotsky—never really crossed the Rubicon; his strategic conception did not break the established doctrinaire framework of a necessarily 'bourgeois' Russian revolution. But he contributed three central themes that laid a foundation for Trotsky's prophetic vision of Russia's

---

[28]*Die Geschichte der Russischen Sozialdemokratie*, Berlin 1926, pp. 164-5.
[29]See the discussion in L. Deutscher, *The Prophet Armed*, London 1954, pp. 102-3. The ulterior motive of this imputation was obviously to present Trotsky as the disciple of the 'renegade' Parvus, who became, after having been a dedicated member of the most extreme left wing of pre-war social democracy, a diplomatic agent of the German Kaiser during the First World War.
[30]*My Life*, New York, 1970, p. 167.

revolutionary future:

(1) In a series of articles on 'War and Revolution' published in *Iskra* in 1904, Parvus deployed the methodological category of *totality* towards an understanding of the world capitalist system as a whole. These articles had a great impact on Trotsky's thinking, and Parvus's biographers, Zeman and Scharlau, have correctly observed that: 'Helphand's thesis on the development of capitalism into a universal system, on the decline of the importance of the national state, and on the parallel extension of both the bourgeois and the proletarian interests outside the framework of these states, all this Trotsky took over *in toto*.'[31]

(2) An analysis of the peculiarities of the Russian social formation (partially inspired by the works of the liberal historian Miliukov): the semi-Asiatic character of the Russian state and society resulted in a very weak development of the towns, which were administrative-bureaucratic rather than economic centres; from this followed the weakness of the artisanate and of the petty-bourgeois strata which are the traditional social base for revolutionary democracy. The eventual development of an urban economy at the end of the nineteenth century was directly capitalist in character, with huge factories, a concentrated proletariat, and so on. Therefore, as Parvus put it, 'all that was negative for the development of petty-bourgeois democracy favoured the emergence of proletarian class consciousness in Russia'.[32]

(3) The idea that *the proletariat could and should take political power through the Russian revolution*. Parvus should probably be registered in the history of Marxism as the first thinker to envisage the possibility of a proletarian state in 'agrarian', 'backward' and 'Asiatic' Russia. He presented this idea for the first time in the 'Preface' to a collection of essays by Trotsky published under the title *Before the 9th January*: 'Only the workers can complete the revolutionary change in Russia. The revolutionary provisional government in Russia would be a government of workers' democracy. If social democracy stands at the head of the revolutionary movement of the Russian proletariat, then this government will be social-democratic.'[33] Although, as we have seen, both Trotsky and Luxemburg soon adopted this position, Lenin, in an article of March 1905, explicitly rejected it. 'This cannot be,

[31]Z. A. Zeman and W. B. Scharlau, *The Merchant of Revolution: The Life of Alexander Israel Helphand (Parvus) 1867-1924*, London 1965, p. 66.

[32]Preface to Trotsky's pamphlet, *Bis zum 9 Januar 1905 (Before the 9th January)*, in Zeman and Scharlau.

[33]Ibid., p. 358.

since only a revolutionary dictatorship, which is supported by a huge majority of the nation, can be of a certain duration. . . . The Russian proletariat, however, now forms only a minority of the nation.'[34]

Unfortunately, Parvus did not stay the course of the bold road that he opened with his brilliant essays and articles of 1904-5. He remained, in the last analysis, a prisoner of the immovable conviction of the Second International that the Russian revolution had to be non-socialist.[35] Thus his hypothetical workers' government was not supposed to take any directly socialist measures, but only to introduce progressive social legislation and reforms favourable to the working class within the limits of the capitalist mode of production, as according to the model of 'socialist' government that existed at that time in Australia.[36] In other words, Parvus wanted to change the locomotive of history, but not its rails.[37]

A summary of the different conceptions of the Russian revolution that were advanced by Russian Marxists from the end of the nineteenth century to 1917 will help to locate precisely Trotsky's specific theoretical innovation. Setting aside the ideas of pseudo-Marxist populists such as Nicolaion as well as, at the opposite pole, 'legal Marxists' such as Piotr Struve, who appropriated Marxist arguments to justify the progressive character of capitalism in Russia,[38] there remain *four clearly delimited positions* inside the social-democratic camp *strictu senso*:[39]

[34]Quoted in Zeman and Scharlau, *The Merchant of Revolution*, p. 79.

[35]See ibid., p. 358.

[36]'His prognoses indicated, therefore, not the transformation of the democratic revolution into the socialist revolution but only the establishment in Russia of a regime of workers' democracy of the Australian type, where on the basis of a farmers' system there arose for the first time a labour government which did not go beyond the framework of a bourgeois regime.' ('The Three Conceptions of the Russian Revolution' (1939), *Writings 1938-39*, New York 1969, p. 115.)

[37]See Brossat's excellent analysis of the differences between Parvus and Trotsky: 'Although Parvus possessed the concepts and historical understanding to grasp how the maturity of objective conditions on a world scale might lead to that apparent aberration implied by the possibility of proletarian revolution in backward Russia, he stopped at the threshold of his discovery, without doubt constrained by his adherence to the orthodox school of thought of German social democracy. Therefore Trotsky *alone* will cross the threshold of the new understanding of Marxism needed in this period, leaving Parvus behind him. . . .' (Brossat, p. 101.)

[38]Trotsky pointed out how Marxism, understood above all as a doctrine of the 'necessity and the historically progressive character of capitalist development' became at the end of the nineteenth century in Russia an ideology for the 'reconciliation of large strata of the intelligentsia with the role of intellectual servants of Capital'. ('Uber den Marxismus in Russland', *Neue Zeit*, XXVI, Band I, Stuttgart 1908, p. 8.)

[39]In his well-known essay, 'Three Conceptions of the Russian Revolution' (see note 36), Trotsky simplified the picture by ignoring one of these positions.

(1) The Menshevik view of the revolution as bourgeois by its nature and the motion of its driving force as an alliance of the proletariat with the liberal bourgeoisie.

(2) The Bolshevik conception also recognized the inevitably bourgeois-democratic character of the revolution, but it excluded the bourgeoisie from the revolutionary bloc. According to Lenin, only the proletariat and the peasantry were authentically revolutionary forces, bound to establish through their alliance a common democratic revolutionary dictatorship.

(3) The theory advocated by Parvus and embraced by Luxemburg which, while recognizing the bourgeois character of the revolution in the last instance, insisted on the hegemonic revolutionary role of the proletariat supported by the peasantry. The destruction of czarist absolutism could not be achieved short of the inauguration of a workers' power led by social democracy. At the same, however, such a proletarian government could not yet transcend in its programmatic aims the fixed limits of bourgeois democracy.[40]

(4) Finally, Trotsky's concept, which envisaged not only the hegemonic role of the proletariat and the necessity of its seizure of power, but also the possibility of a growing over of the democratic into the socialist revolution.

How was it possible for Trotsky alone to cut the gordian knot of the Marxism of the Second International and to grasp the revolutionary possibilities that lay beyond the dogmatic construction of a bourgeois-democratic Russian revolution which was the unquestioned problematic of *all* other Marxist theorizations?

Before 1905 Lev Davidovitch Bronstein's writings did not, in fact, go beyond the political horizon of his contemporaries. Indeed, in *Our Political Tasks* (1904), which contains his famous attack on the theses of Lenin's *What is To Be Done?*, he assumes a stance not very distinguishable from Menshevism: 'it is not yet possible for us to conduct a generalized political offensive against it [the bourgeoisie]. . . . Only in the future free Russia, in which we will obviously be obliged to play the role of the opposition party, and not that of a government, can the class struggle of the proletariat develop in all its fullness.'[41] It is true that the same essay contains

---

[40]Kautsky in his famous article on Russia in 1906 (see notes 15 and 16) would be located half-way between Lenin and Luxemburg. In 1917, of course, he adopted the traditional Menshevik viewpoint.

[41]*Nos tâches politiques*, Paris 1970, p. 120.

passages with a different ring that seem to announce an alternative perspective: 'As Communists, we neither can nor want to forget or repress our proletarian tasks. All our revolutionary tactics must be subordinated to these tasks, not only in the tedium of daily politics, but also on the eve of the revolutionary explosion and during the travail of the revolution itself.'[42] The tension in Trotsky's writing signalled his impending break with Menshevism. Only one month after finishing this work, with its dedication to 'My dear teacher: Pavel Borisovitch Axelrod', Trotsky abandoned his ephemeral alliance with the Mensheviks by refusing to endorse their campaign for the bourgeoisie's 'liberal banquets'. A few months later (December 1904) Trotsky launched a violent attack on bourgeois liberalism in his pamphlet *Before the 9th January*. In this work he defined the proletariat as the vanguard of the people and the leader of the national revolution, but he still limited the aims of the revolutionary movement to bourgeois-democratic tasks such as the establishment of a constituent assembly.[43]

It was during 1905, in the fire of the revolution, that Trotsky actually made that 'great leap forward' which, by formulating the first elements of his theory of permanent revolution, placed him in the ideological and political vanguard of European Marxism. In the preface (June) to the Russian edition of some of Lassalle's works on the 1848 Revolution, Trotsky for the first time advanced his perspective of a proletarian government in Russia, counterposing it to the views of the Bolsheviks. 'It is clear that the proletariat in order to fulfill its historical mission must rely—as the bourgeoisie in its time—upon the support of the peasantry and the petty-bourgeoisie. It leads the village and draws it into the movement. . . . The leading force is the proletariat itself. This is not a "dictatorship of the proletariat and the peasantry", but rather the dictatorship of the proletariat supported by the peasantry.'[44] Later that summer he began to formulate his chief heresy: the possibility of the democratic revolution uninterruptedly unfolding, without fixed stages, into the socialist revolution. From his

[42]Ibid., p. 44.
[43]Excerpted as 'The Proletariat and the Revolution', in I. Deutscher, *The Age of Permanent Revolution: A Trotsky Anthology*, New York 1964, pp. 42, 44, 49. In my opinion Brossat is wrong to consider this text as the pivotal transition—'the complex, uncertain and contradictory process of a break or a changing of ground'—toward a permanentist perspective. (Brossat, pp. 87, 90.) Actually the key concept of the pamphlet, the hegemonic role of the proletariat, was common to Russian Marxism, especially to Lenin and the Bolsheviks. The real novelty was rather the preface by Parvus, which advanced for the first time the conception of a *workers' government* in Russia.
[44]Preface to Lassalle, *Rech Pered Sudom Prisyarnikh*, St. Petersburg 1905, p. 27.

retreat in Finland, between July and October 1905, he wrote an article declaring: 'The revolutionary foreground is already occupied by the proletariat. Only the Social Democracy, acting through workers, can make the peasantry follow its lead. This opens to the Russian Social Democracy the prospect of capturing the power before that can possibly take place in the countries of the west. The immediate task of the Social Democracy will be to bring the democratic revolution to completion. But once in control, the proletarian party will not be able to confine itself merely to the democratic programme; it will be obliged to adopt socialist measures. How far it will go in that direction will depend not only on the correlation of forces in Russia itself, but on the entire international situation as well.'[45] Previously we noted that Lenin refused to take the Paris Commune as a model because it 'confused' the democratic-republican revolution with the socialist. But Trotsky in December 1905 made the Commune an exemplary reference precisely for this reason. In his preface to a Russian edition of Marx's writings on the Commune, he prophesized that the future workers' government in Russia would be forced, like the Communards in 1871, 'by the very logic of its situation, to go over to a collectivistic practice'.[46]

Why did the other exponents of Marxism in Russia regard these bold theses of Trotsky as so utopian and adventuristic? The difference in revolutionary generations may have been partly responsible for the hostile reception to the first version of permanent revolution. Plekhanov, Axelrod and Zasulich belonged to the first generation of Russian Marxists, who had to wage an arduous struggle against the influence of populism by criticising its 'socialist' utopias and the mystique of Russian exceptionalism. To use Lenin's favourite metaphor, they 'bent the stick' very far to demonstrate the inevitability of capitalist development in Russia. Trotsky, on the other hand, was twenty-five years younger and, finding the ideological battle more or less won, could permit himself to take a more nuanced view of the Narodniks (Lenin occupies in this respect an intermediate position). He was less obsessed than his predecessors and mentors by the need to prove at any price that Russia could not escape the same fate as Western Europe.[47] Yet this hardly suffices as an explanation for the difference in vision, since

[45]Quoted in *My Life*, pp. 171-2.
[46]Preface to Marx, *Parizskaya Kommuna*, St Petersburg 1906, p. xx.
[47]See Denise Avenas, *Economie et politique dans la pensée de Trotsky*, Paris 1970, p. 7. Writing on the role of generations in the process of knowledge, Mannheim has argued that each generation 'eliminates from the beginning a great number of possible ways and means of experiencing, thinking, feeling and acting, and restricts the space of expression of the individual to certain limited possibilities.' (Karl Mannheim, *Wissensoziologie*, Neuwied 1964, p. 528.)

Mensheviks such as Martov or Bolsheviks such as Kamenev were also contemporaries of Trotsky, but scarcely shared his theories.

Indeed, a careful study of the roots of Trotsky's political boldness and of the whole theory of permanent revolution reveals that Trotsky's views were informed by a specific understanding of Marxism, an interpretation of the dialectical materialist method, distinct from the reigning orthodoxy of the Second International. This methodological specificity, which differentiated Trotsky from the dominant trends of Russian Marxism, may have owed something special to the thinker whose works first tutored the young Trotsky in the foundations of historical materialism—namely, Antonio Labriola. In his autobiography Trotsky recalled the 'delight' with which he first devoured Labriola's essays during his imprisonment in Odessa in 1893.[48] His initiation into 'materialist dialectics', thus, took place through an encounter with perhaps the least orthodox of the major theoretical figures of the Second International. As Gramsci once pointed out, Labriola occupied a very special place in the panorama of pre-war European Marxism as 'the only man who has attempted to build up the philosophy of praxis scientifically'.[49] Formed in the Hegelian school, Labriola battled relentlessly against the neo-positivist and vulgar-materialist trends that proliferated in Italian Marxism (Turati, for example). He was one of the first to reject the orthodox economistic interpretation of Marxism by attempting to restore the concept of *totality* and by defending historical materialism as a self-sufficient and independent theoretical system, irreducible to other trends.[50] Moreover, he rejected scholastic dogmatism and the talmudic cult of the textbook, criticizing explicitly all attempts to 'reduce the doctrine to a kind of vulgate or recipe for the interpretation of the history of all times and all places . . . Marxism . . . is not and cannot be confined to the writings of Marx and Engels. . . . Since this doctrine is *critical*, it cannot be developed, applied and corrected except *critically*'.[51]

Trotsky's starting-point, therefore, was this critical, dialectical and anti-dogmatic understanding of Marxism that Labriola had inspired. 'Marxism is above all a method of analysis—not analysis of texts, but analysis of

---

[48] *My Life*, p. 119.

[49] *Prison Notebooks*, London 1971, p. 387.

[50] "Those who designate the new materialist conception of history as an economic interpretation of history are wrong. . . . It is rather an organic conception of history. In it *the totality and unity of social life* are reflected. The economy itself . . . is dissolved into the flow of a process . . . and is historically conceived.' (Antonio Labriola, *La concepción materialista de la historia* [1897], Havana 1970, p. 115.)

[51] Ibid., p. 243.

social relations.'[52] In his polemics against the Mensheviks, who always used quotations from Marx to prove that 'the time for the proletariat had not yet arrived', Trotsky attacked them as 'scholasticists who regard themselves as Marxists only because they look at the world through the paper on which Marx's works are printed'.[53] In *Results and Prospects* he did not hesitate to criticize a well-known text of Engels (at that time wrongly attributed to Marx) in which the historical backwardness of the German bourgeoisie and proletariat were intimately linked—'Like master, like man'. Textual orthodoxy did not worry him too much; as we shall see, the essential part of his argumentation was based on a careful analysis of the Russian social formation. Indeed, the only passage from Marx quoted by Trotsky in support of the thesis of permanent revolution is the paragraph of the *Communist Manifesto* where Marx asserted that the German bourgeois revolution would be the immediate prelude to proletarian revolution.[54]

Trotsky's attitude towards the founding fathers testifies to his intellectual independence and originality, but it is nonetheless surprising that he did not utilize more of the texts of Marx that manifestly paralleled and prefigured his own problematic, particularly the *Address of March 1850* and the writings on Russia from 1877 to 1882. In the case of the former text, the only possible explanation is that Trotsky simply did not know of its existence at the time (1905-8) (the old re-edition of 1885 in Zurich was not well known in Russia and a new German edition was only issued in 1914); so it was through Mehring's 1905 article that he discovered the term 'permanent revolution'. But in the case of the Russian writings, such as the Preface to the Russian edition of the *Manifesto*, which he could not have been ignorant of, the probability is that he preferred not to use them because of their affinity with certain populist ideas, especially the role of the *obshtchina*. Even the slightest concession to the Narodniks would have aggravated his isolation inside Russian social democracy and laid him open to his adversaries.

Whatever Trotsky failed to borrow from the text of Marx was more than compensated for by his fidelity to the Marxist *method*, however. And however heavily the works of Plekhanov and the Mensheviks may have relied upon exegetical authority, they fundamentally lacked the *dialectical* approach so evident in Trotsky's work. Let us focus on *five* of the most important and distinctive features of the methodology that underlies the

[52]*Results and Prospects*, London 1962, p. 196.
[53]'The Proletariat and the Russian Revolution', in *1905*, p. 295.
[54]*Results and Prospects*, pp. 217-8.

original version of Trotsky's theory of permanent revolution:

(1) From the vantage point of a dialectical comprehension of the unity of opposites, Trotsky criticized the Bolsheviks' rigid division between the socialist dictatorship of the proletariat and the 'democratic dictatorship of workers and peasants' as a 'logical, purely formal operation'. This abstract logic is even more sharply attacked in his polemic against Plekhanov, whose whole reasoning can be reduced to the 'empty syllogism': our revolution is bourgeois, therefore we should support the Kadets. Moreover, in an astonishing passage from a critique of the analysis of the Menshevik Cherevanin, he explicitly condemned the *analytic* (i.e., abstract-formal, pre-dialectical) character of Menshevik politics. 'Tscherewanin constructs his tactics as Spinoza did his ethics, that is to say, geometrically.'[55] Of course Trotsky, unlike Lenin was not a philosopher and almost never wrote specific philsophical texts, but this makes his clear-sighted grasp of the methodological dimension of his controversy with stagist conceptions all the more remarkable.

(2) In *History and Class Consciousness*, Lukács stressed that the category of totality was the essence of Marx's method, indeed the very principle of revolution within the domain of knowledge.[56] Trotsky's thinking is an exceptionally significant illustration of this Lukácsian thesis. Indeed, one of the essential sources of the superiority of Trotsky's revolutionary theory is the fact that he adopted *the viewpoint of totality*, visualizing capitalism and the class struggle as a world process. In the Preface to the aforementioned Russian edition of *Lassalle*: 'Binding all countries together with its mode of production and its commerce, capitalism has converted the whole world into a single economic and political organism. . . . This immediately gives the events now unfolding an international character, and opens up a wide horizon. The political emancipation of Russia led by the working class . . . will make it the initiator of the liquidation of world capitalism, for which history has created all the objective conditions.'[57] Only by posing the problem in these terms—at the level of the 'maturity' of the capitalist system in its *totality*—was it possible to transcend the traditional perspec-

---

[55]'The Proletariat and the Russian Revolution', p. 289; see also in *1905*, 'Our Differences', pp. 306-12. One can hardly take seriously the superficial and ludicrous idea advanced in a recent pamphlet of the British communists that the difference between Trotsky and the Mensheviks was 'not theoretical, but a very specific tactical-political difference'. (Loizos Michail, *The Theory of Permanent Revolution*, London 1977, p. 28.)

[56]London 1971.

[57]*Rech Pered Sudom Prisyarnich*, p. 27 (partly quoted in *Results and Prospects*, p. 240).

tive that saw the socialist-revolutionary 'ripeness' of Russia exclusively in terms of *national* economic determinism.[58]

(3) Trotsky explicitly rejected the *economism* (the tendency to reduce, in a non-mediated and one-sided fashion, all social, political and ideological contradictions to the 'economic infrastructure') which was one of the hall-marks of the Plekhanovian interpretation of Marxism. Indeed, Trotsky's break with economism was one of the decisive steps towards the theory of permanent revolution. A key paragraph in *Results and Prospects* defined with precision the political stakes entailed in this rupture: 'To imagine that the dictatorship of the proletariat is in some way automatically dependent on the technical development and resources of a country is a prejudice of "economic" materialism simplified to absurdity. This point of view has nothing in common with Marxism.'[59]

However some of Trotsky's modern critics, such as Nicolas Krassó, have maintained that behind his rejection of economism lurked another, equally profound 'deviation': 'We may call this, for the sake of convenience, "Sociologism". Here it is not the economy, but *social classes*, which are extracted from the complete historical totality and hypostasized in an idealistic fashion as the demiurges of any given political situation. . . . In his [Trotsky's] writings, mass forces are presented as constantly dominant in society, without any political organizations or institutions intervening as necessary and permanent levels of the social formation.'[60] In his reply to Krasso, Ernest Mandel has shown quite clearly how this imputation of 'sociologism' is totally irrelevant in relation to Trotsky's post-1917 writings (for example, his famous analysis of the political conjuncture in Germany in the early 1930s). I would extend his caveat and assert that Krassó's charge is not valid for the young Trotsky of *Results and Prospects* (1906) either. As Krassó himself honestly recognizes, 'Trotsky shows a great awareness of the *state* as a bureaucratic and military apparatus.'[61] Now is not the state an 'institution intervening as [a] necessary and permanent level of the social formation'? In fact, the only correct argument that Krassó can advance to prove his thesis is the underestimation of the role of the party in Trotsky's views on the revolution of 1905—an error which Trotsky himself later designated as the main weakness of his political thought in

---

[58]See Avenas, pp. 12-15.
[59]*Results and Prospects*, p. 195.
[60]Krassó, p. 22.
[61]Ibid., p. 17. Some pages later Krassó seems to forget this assertion, writing without hesitation that 'Trotsky's indifference to political institutions divided him from Lenin before the October Revolution' (p. 89). Would the state be a non-political institution to Krassó?

this period. Granting this, I would still challenge the accuracy of Krassó's statement that 'indeed, when Trotsky writes of the political struggle in Russia he never simply refers to the role of revolutionary organizations—he only speaks of social forces.'[62] If Krassó had only read *Results and Prospects* more carefully, he would have encountered several passages where Trotsky emphasized the leading role of the revolutionary party in the capture and maintenance of proletarian power. 'Collectivism will become not only the inevitable way forward from the position in which the party in power will find itself, but will also be a means of preserving this position with the support of the proletariat.'[63]

(4) Trotsky's method is resolutely *historical*. The historical specificity of the Russian social formation is a central theme in Trotsky's writings. Moreover, his historicism is an *open* historicism, a rich and dialectical conception of historical development as a contradictory process, where at every moment alternatives are posed; it has nothing in common with the impotent fatalism that pervaded Menshevik thinking, where the dead ruled the living and the past determined the future. The task of Marxism, according to Trotsky, is precisely to 'discover the "possibilities" of the developing revolution by means of an analysis of its internal mechanism'.[64] In *Results and Prospects*, as well as in later essays (see, for example, his 1908 polemic against the Mensheviks, 'The Proletariat and the Russian Revolution' in *1905*), he tended to see the process of permanent revolution towards socialist transformation as an *objective possibility*, legitimate and realistic, whose outcome depended on innumerable subjective factors as well as unforeseeable events—and not as an inevitable necessity whose triumph (or defeat) was already assured. It was this recognition of the open character of social historicity that gave revolutionary praxis its decisive place in the architecture of Trotsky's theoretical-political system from 1905 on.

(5) At the height of its engagement with populism, Russian Marxism, and especially the Mensheviks, insisted on the unavoidable similarity between the socio-economic development of Western Europe and the future of Russia. Every particularity of Russia was denied or overlooked, and the 'universal' laws of capitalist accumulation were extended, pure and simple, to the Czarist Empire. One of Trotsky's chief merits was his success in achieving, to an impressive degree, a dialectical synthesis of the particular and the universal, of the specificity of the Russian social formation and of

[62]Ibid., p. 17.
[63]*Results and Prospects*, p. 212.
[64]Ibid., p. 168.

the general tendencies of capitalist development. Thanks to his dialectical orientation, he was able to simultaneously transcend-negate-preserve (*Aufhebung*) the contradiction between populism and Menshevism, and to develop a new perspective, which was both more concrete and less unilateral. In a remarkable passage in the *History of the Russian Revolution* (1930) Trotsky explicitly formulated the viewpoint that was already implicit in his 1906 texts: 'In the essence of the matter the Slavophile conception, with all its reactionary fantasticness, and also Narodnikism, with all its democratic illusions, were by no means mere speculations, but rested upon indubitable and moreover deep peculiarities of Russia's development, understood one-sidedly however and incorrectly evaluated. In its struggle with Narodnikism, Russian Marxism, demonstrating the identity of the laws of development for all countries, not infrequently fell into a dogmatic mechanization discovering a tendency to pour out the baby with the bath.'[65]

It was the combination of all these methodological innovations that made *Results and Prospects*—a pamphlet written in jail in 1906—so unique.[66] This first systematic exposition of the theory of permanent revolution begins with an analysis (inspired by Parvus and Miliukov) of the genesis of the Russian social formation and its peculiarities—an analysis which Trotsky would continue to develop and enrich in his subsequent works between 1906 and 1908 (a number of essays from this period are included in the volume *1905*). Trotsky contrasts the differential character of the urban economy in Russian and Western history: whereas towns in Western Europe were the nuclei of commercial and artisanal production, in Russia they remained, well into the nineteenth century, mere fortresses and administrative centres. When, at the end of the nineteenth century, European capital began to pour into Russia, it suffocated the seeds of a Russian artisanate and thereby destroyed the social basis for a bourgeois-democratic mass movement of a Western type: the plebian and petty-bourgeois urban layers. Furthermore, heavy industry in Russia did not develop, as in the West, 'organically' from small crafts and manufacturing, but was to a large extent directly implanted by foreign (German, French, Belgian and

---

[65]Vol. 1, London 1965, p. 427.

[66]'Whether one reads his message with horror or hope, whether one views him as the inspired herald of a new age surpassing all history in achievement and grandeur, or as the oracle of ruin and woe, one cannot but be impressed by the sweep and boldness of his vision. He reconnoitred the future as one who surveys from a towering mountain top a new and immense horizon and points to vast, uncharted landmarks in the distance.' (*The Prophet Armed*, p. 161.)

English) capital. This foreign and very modern origin of the dominant sections of Russian industrial capital was a principal cause of both the weakness of the native Russian bourgeoisie and of the relative socio-political weight of the young Russian working class. 'The proletariat immediately found itself concentrated in tremendous masses, while between these masses and the autocracy there stood a capitalist bourgeoisie, very small in numbers, isolated from the "people", half-foreign, without historical traditions, and inspired only by the greed for gain.'[67]

Trotsky showed how the concentration of workers in Russian industry had attained truly gigantic proportions, even by the standards of the advanced capitalist countries. Indeed he would later demonstrate that the percentage of the labour force employed in very large factories was much higher in Russia [38.5%] than in Germany [only 10%].[68] In this analysis it is possible to see the emergence of the first sketch of the *theory of unequal and combined development*. Later, in his book *1905* (written between 1905 and 1909) he filled in this sketch with more elaborated concepts; stressing, for example, that Russian society comprised an articulation of 'all stages of civilization' from the most primitive and archaic agriculture to the most modern large-scale industry. He criticized the Mensheviks for their inability to grasp the complex and contradictory interpenetration of world capitalism and the Russian social formation. 'Today they fail to see the unified process of world capitalist development which swallows up all the countries that lie in its path and which creates, out of the national and general exigencies of capitalism, an amalgam whose nature cannot be understood by the application of historical clichés, but only by materialist analysis.'[69]

Trotsky's interpretation of Russian reality was intertwined with a broad and original conception of the world-historical movement. Comparing 1789, 1848 and 1905, he periodized the modern class struggle into three important phases: *first*, when the revolutionary bourgeoisie leads the rebellion of the plebeian masses against despotism; *second*, when the bourgeoisie is no longer revolutionary, but the proletariat is still too weak; and *third*, when the proletariat becomes the leading force in the struggle against the autocracy. (The Russian bourgeoisie was more afraid of the armed Russian proletariat than of the Cossacks; it therefore betrayed the revolutionary

---

[67]*Results and Prospects*, p. 183.

[68]*1905*, pp. 21-2. Comparing the number of workers in big factories (more than a thousand workers), Trotsky showed that backward and semi-Asiatic Russia had three times more workers (in absolute numbers) in this category than Germany (1,115,000 versus 448,731)! (pp. 291-92)

[69]Ibid., p. 54.

ideals of its youth, ideals of which the proletariat had become the inheritor.)[70] Trotsky's historical schema can also be used to elucidate the difference between his theory of permanent revolution and Marx's; Marx's conceptions of a permanentist strategy remained unconsolidated because he was, so to speak, trapped in the epoch of transition between the ages of bourgeois and socialist revolution. Trotsky, on the other hand, entered the workers' movement at the advent of the era of the proletarian revolution. He was one of the first to grasp in its universal-historical significance.[71] The practical conclusion of this whole socio-historical analysis, at the level of political action, was the famous formula that Trotsky advanced after 1905: 'the dictatorship of the proletariat supported by the peasantry'. This slogan, of course, was considered heretical by most Russian Marxists, especially the Mensheviks, for whom the role of the proletariat could not but be the direct expression of the level of industrial development; it implied, therefore Trotsky's rejection of economism and his comprehension of the relative autonomy of the political sphere.[72]

What were the principal divergences between the views of Trotsky and Lenin on the social nature of the Russian revolution? Trotsky agreed with Lenin that the revolutionary power to be established in Russia must be some sort of coalition between the proletariat and the peasantry, but he insisted that the proletariat should necessarily be the *hegemonic* force in this alliance. In support of this thesis, he advanced three different arguments: (1) the inevitable subordination of the country to the town as a result of industrialization; (2) the peasantry's incapacity to play an independent political role and its necessary dependence upon the leadership of one of the urban classes; (3) that since Russia lacked an authentic revolutionary bourgeoisie, the peasantry would, therefore, be forced to support the power of workers' democracy—'it will not matter much even if the peasantry does this with a degree of consciousness not larger than that with which it usually rallies to the bourgeois regimes.'[73] Lenin polemicized vigorously against this last thesis, stressing, not without reason, that 'the proletariat

---

[70]*Results and Prospects*, pp. 186, 193.

[71]See Brossat, p. 16.

[72]'Between the productive forces of a country and the political strength of its classes there cut across at any given moment various social and political factors of a national and international character, and these displace and even sometimes completely alter the political expression of economic relations. In spite of the fact that the productive forces of the United States are ten times as great as those of Russia, nevertheless the political role of the Russian proletariat . . . [is] incomparably greater than in the case of the proletariat of the United States.' (*Results and Prospects*, p. 197.)

[73]Ibid., p. 205.

cannot count on the ignorance and prejudices of the peasantry as the powers that be under a bourgeois regime, count and depend on them, nor can it assume that in time of revolution the peasantry will remain in their usual state of political ignorance and passivity.'[74] But in the last analysis, his disagreement with Trotsky was not so deep, since he too insisted on the need for proletarian hegemony in the revolutionary movement.[75] For example at the 1908/1909 conference of the RSDLP, Lenin, after proposing the formula 'the proletariat which carries behind it the peasantry', finally rallied to the motto advanced by Trotsky and Luxemburg—'the dictatorship of the proletariat supported by the peasantry'—explaining that the conception behind this different slogan was still the same.

As a matter of fact, Trotsky's perspective of a workers' government in Russia was shared by Parvus, Luxemburg and, more intermittently, by Lenin as well. *The radical novelty of the theory of permanent revolution was located less in its view of the class nature of the future revolutionary power than in its conception of its historical tasks.* Trotsky's decisive contribution was the idea that the Russian revolution could transcend the limits of an extensive democratic transformation and begin to take anti-capitalist measures with a distinctively socialist content. How did Trotsky justify this iconoclastic hypothesis? The linchpin of his argument was the belief that 'the political domination of the proletariat is incompatible with its economic enslavement.' Why—Trotsky asked—would the proletariat in power, and controlling the means of coercion, continue to tolerate capitalist exploitation? And even if the working class attempted to restrict itself to an implementation of the demands of its minimum, democratic programme, would not 'the very logic of its position . . . compel it to pass over to collectivistic measures'? For example, if the state gave aid to strikers, it would probably provoke a reaction by the employers in the form of widespread lock-outs. Confronted by the challenge of a 'strike by capital', the proletarian power would be obliged to take over factories and organize production. To put it in a nutshell, 'the barrier between the "minimum" and the "maximum" programme disappears immediately the proletariat comes to power.'[76] (It should be noted that the workers' power to which Trotsky refers has nothing to do with the participation in government by reformist workers' parties in the framework of the bourgeois state—as with Jaurès and the French socialists at the turn of the century.)

Trotsky's conception of the *permanent* character of the revolutionary pro-

[74]CW, 15, p. 374.
[75]See Geras, p. 75.
[76]*Results and Prospects*, pp. 232-4.

cess, then, follows logically from an extrapolation of the dynamics of class struggle in a 'revolutionary democratic dictatorship'. Moreover, it is rooted in a deep understanding of how, in the conjuncture of revolutionary transition, the political sphere becomes dominant: the political power of the proletariat immediately becomes a social and economic power, a direct threat to bourgeois domination in the factories. Under such conditions lock-outs and various forms of economic sabotage (curtailment of investment, flight of capital, hoarding, etc.) are the logical and almost inevitable response of a bourgeoisie confronted with the break-down of institutional (state) guarantees of private property and the great danger of working-class power. In other words, the contradiction between the political domination of the proletariat and the economic power of the bourgeoisie is unbearable for both classes; such a highly unstable and ephemeral situation must rapidly be resolved in favour of one or the other antagonists. Finally, Trotsky also argued that this same process of uninterrupted revolution would also be enacted in the countryside; the dictatorship of the proletariat would necessarily be forced to take socialist measures—such as the organization of cooperative production or state farms—because the division of the great estates would be an unimaginable economic and political regression.

This last thesis—so squarely contradicted by the experience of the October Revolution—leads us to the most debatable feature of his 1905-6 conception of permanent revolution: namely, the nature of the relationship between the proletariat and the peasantry in the course of revolutionary struggle. For Trotsky, the alliance between the two classes, and particularly the support of the whole peasantry for the proletarian dictatorship, was a transitory factor that would endure only until the abolition of feudalism and absolutism. After that a new phase would open, with the workers' government necessarily implementing measures favouring the rural proletariat which would then, incur the hostility of the rich peasant stratum. Meanwhile the proletariat could count on little more than the indifference or passivity of the mass of the peasantry, which would remain socially too undifferentiated and petty-minded to grasp the historical stakes of the socialist transition. Thus, Trotsky drew the starkly pessimistic conclusion that 'the more definite and determined the policy of the proletariat in power becomes, the narrower and more shaky does the ground beneath its feet become.'[77] Under such conditions how could the dictatorship of the proletariat survive? The only solution that Trotsky can envision is

---

[77]Ibid., pp. 208-9.

the extension of the revolution to Europe. 'Left to its own resources, the working class of Russia will inevitably be crushed by the counter-revolution the moment the peasantry turns its back on it. It will have no alternative but to link the fate of its political rule, and, hence, the fate of the whole Russian revolution, with the fate of the socialist revolution in Europe.'[78] Thus the real obstacle to the implementation of a socialist programme by a workers' government in Russia would not be economic so much—that is, the backwardness of the technical and productive structures of the country—as *political*: the isolation of the working class and the inevitable rupture with its peasant and petty-bourgeois allies. Only international solidarity could save the socialist Russian revolution: 'Without the direct state support of the European proletariat the working class of Russia cannot remain in power and convert its temporary domination into a lasting socialistic dictatorship.[79]

These two, interconnected predictions—the impossibility of preserving the worker-peasant alliance after the establishment of proletarian power, and the dependence of this power upon socialist revolutions in Western Europe—were the objects of frequent criticism by Trotsky's adversaries. Who was ultimately proved more correct? It is difficult to give a clear-cut answer to such a question. It is, of course, true that during the 1920s the alliance with the peasantry collapsed and violent confrontation took its place. But was this inevitable, as Trotsky saw in 1906, or was it rather the result of the disastrous policies of Stalin-Bukharin in 1924-7 (support to the kulaks) and of Stalin alone in 1928-30 (forced collectivization)? Trotsky's own fight at the head of the Left Opposition against these policies obviously presumed the possibility of an alternative orientation. On the other hand, it was also true that workers' democracy in Russia was not able to survive long after the defeat of the European revolution (1923); although its decline did not lead, as Trotsky had feared in 1906, to bourgeois restoration, but rather to the rule of a bureaucratic stratum which largely originated from within the working class itself. It must be observed also that both series of events were deeply interrelated, because the contradictions between the workers and peasants help to facilitate the emergence of the bureaucracy as an all-powerful arbitrator, while the repression of the peasantry in the late 1920s accelerated the growth of the monstrous power of the GPU. Thus, although Trotsky's prognostics of 1906 grasped the crucial connection between the weakening of the worker-peasant alliance and the fate of the international revolution, they could scarcely anticipate

[78]Ibid., p. 247.
[79]Ibid., p. 237.

the importance or relative autonomy of the political struggle *within* the proletarian party in shaping the ultimate outcome.

Results and Prospects remained for a long time a forgotten book. It seems that Lenin did not read it—at least before 1917[80]—and its influence over contemporary Russian Marxism was desultory at best. Like all forerunners, Trotsky was in advance of his time, and his ideas were too novel and heterodox to be accepted, or even studied, by his party comrades. But during the bitter period of revolutionary low-tide and reactionary stability (1907-16), Trotsky did not abandon his vision of Russia's revolutionary future. There was a moment, however, in the wake of the defeat of 1906 and in the face of his comrades' incomprehension, when Trotsky attempted to moderate his views closer to 'orthodox' party positions. Both in his speech before the London congress of the RSDLP in 1907 and in the pamphlet *In Defence of the Party*, published in the same year, he contented himself with re-affirming the necessity of a workers' government to assure the victory of the democratic revolution, but without advancing the perspective of a permanentist transition towards socialist revolution.[81] But during the next year he rapidly returned to his whole programme of permanent revolution in the course of a series of polemics both against the Mensheviks and the Bolsheviks. In a critical review (published in 1908 in *Neue Zeit*) of a book on 1905 by Cheravanin, he once again argued that the transformation of the democratic into a socialist revolution was an *objective possibility* that could not be excluded *a priori* by abstract and formal reasoning (the so-called 'geometrical' arguments). The social and economic conditions of Russia would lead to a potential historical situation in which the victory of a bourgeois revolution would be possible only through a proletarian revolutionary power. 'Does the revolution therefore stop being a bourgeois one? Yes and no. The answer does not depend on formal definitions but on the further progress of events. If the proletariat is overthrown by a coalition of bourgeois classes, including the peasantry whom the proletariat itself has liberated, then the revolution will retain its limited bourgeois character. But if the proletariat succeeds in using all means to achieve its own political hegemony and thereby breaks out of the national confines of the Russian revolution, then that revolution could become the

---

[80]*Permanent Revolution*, p. 42.

[81]*1905*, p. 294 ('A government supported directly by the proletariat and, through it, by the revolutionary peasantry does not yet mean a socialist dictatorship.') See also Trotsky, 'Zur Verteidigung der Partei' (1907), in *Schriften zur revolutionären Organisation*, Hamburg 1970, p. 154.

prologue to a world socialist revolution. The question as to what stage the Russian revolution will reach can, of course, be answered only conditionally.'[82] In the same period, in an article published in a Polish review edited by Rosa Luxemburg (*Przeglad Social-demokratyczny*) Trotsky criticized the Bolsheviks for what he termed their 'class asceticism': that is, the idea that the proletariat in power would have to adhere to the limits and borders of bourgeois democracy. As in *Results and Prospects*, he stressed that a workers' government could not refrain—except by betraying its own class—from supporting strikes and struggles against unemployment; in the face of fierce resistance from the bourgeoisie, it would be forced to undertake socialist measures to avoid economic chaos.[83]

With the outbreak of the First World War and the crisis of the Second International, Trotsky continued to defend his permanentist perspective. In a series of articles in his paper *Nashe Slovo* he explained how changes in Russia since 1905 had only reinforced his view of the central class dynamics of the Russian revolution. 'The period of reaction and economic crisis saw the further 'Europeanization' of Russian industry . . . leading to a further deepening of the social contradictions which prevent the proletariat and bourgeoisie from fighting together against the regime. The proletariat grows in numbers, class consciousness and organization . . . thus enlarging the social base of the revolution and strengthening its socialist aims.'[84] In this period, however, he was tempted to develop his conceptions in a one-sided way, going as far as to deny the possibility of a revolutionary alliance of the workers with the petty-bourgeois intellectuals and the peasantry. 'The experience of 1905 teaches us not to count on the eventual participation of the peasantry . . . the workers can rely only on the semi-proletarian rural labourers, not on the peasants. The revolutionary movement will acquire more of a *class*, and less of a *national*, character than in 1905.'[85] Although this formulation was not characteristic of Trotsky's global political orientation, it did reveal his habitual mistrust of the peasantry (about which he would write an unequivocal self-criticism in 1930[86]).

---

[82]*1905*, p. 289.

[83]'Our Differences', in ibid., pp. 314-6.

[84]'Catastrophe militaire et perspectives politiques', *Nashe Slovo* (September, 1915), in Trotsky, *La Guerre et l'Internationale*, Paris 1974, pp. 166-9.

[85]Ibid., p. 167.

[86]'In the twelve years (1905-17) of my revolutionary journalistic activity, there are also articles in which the episodic circumstances and even the episodic polemical exaggerations inevitable in struggle protrude into the foreground in violation of the strategic line. Thus, for example, articles can be found in which I expressed doubts about the future revolutionary role

If, during the war years, Trotsky stood fast by his conception of permanent revolution, the challenge of organizing an internationalist opposition to the mass slaughter changed his views on party organization; and, shortly after the February revolution, led him to join the Bolshevik party (May 1917). Trotsky's reconciliation with the Bolsheviks was reciprocated by a profound shift in Lenin's views on the nature of the coming revolution. To understand how the theory of permanent revolution became the action programme of the Bolsheviks, it is necessary to survey briefly the evolution of Lenin's strategic thought between the outbreak of the war and his famous April Theses, which signalled his adoption of a permanentist perspective.

On 4 August 1914 German social democracy voted war credits while Kautsky called upon the German proletariat to defend the fatherland. At the same moment, that other patriarch of 'international' socialism, Plekhanov, was rousing the Russian toilers to fight for their motherland. The Second International, the supposedly impregnable fortress of proletarian internationalism, had broken down. It was probably the trauma of these events that moved Lenin to seek a critical revision of 'orthodox' Marxism *from its very foundations*. Perhaps he also had a lucid intuition that the methodological Achilles heel of the Second International's politics was the absence of dialectics. Whatever the precise reason, he began in September 1914 to study Hegel's *Science of Logic*; in the course of which he wrote what later became known as the *Philosophical Notebooks*. This collection of glosses, comments and brief digressions amounted to nothing less than a sketch of a new understanding of the Marxist method, radically opposed to the one developed by Kautsky and Plekhanov. The most significant elements of Lenin's methodological break-through were: (1) a vigorous critique of metaphysical materialism, which Lenin characterized as 'stupid', 'crude', 'dead' and in most respects inferior to the 'intelligent' idealism of Hegel; (2) a clear distinction between vulgar evolutionist and dialectical conceptions of development (only the last being capable of 'giving us the key to the leaps and . . . to the breaks in continuity'); (3) the dissolution of the 'solid and abstract opposition' between the subjective and the objective; (4) the critique of the absolutization and fetishism of the concept of law; (5) the understanding of the category of totality—'the development of the entire ensemble of the moments of reality'—as being the essence of dialectical knowledge; and (6) a dialectical view of opposites which transcended

---

of the peasantry *as a whole, as an estate*, and in connection with this refused to designate, especially during the imperialist war, the future Russian revolution as "national". . . .' (*Permanent Revolution*, pp. 47-8).

their metaphysical petrification and grasped their transformation in one another.[87]

Lenin's methodological break with pre-dialectical Marxism prepared the way for his break with its *political corollary*: the dogma that the material and objective conditions in Russia were not 'mature' enough for a socialist revolution. In other words, the *Philosophical Notebooks* were a kind of philosophical prolegomena to the *April Theses* of 1917: from a conversion of opposites into one another, to the transformation of the democratic into the socialist revolutions; from the critique of vulgar evolutionism, to the 'break in continuity' in 1917; and so on. But even more important, Lenin's critical reading of Hegel helped deliver him from the straitjacket that the Plekhanovian philosophical orthodoxy had imposed on his thinking (and which was still so visible in his other great philosophical meditation: the 1909 *Materialism and Empirio-criticism*). It permitted him to cross the forbidden threshold and to develop in April 1917 the 'concrete analysis of the concrete situation' which he proposed to the Bolsheviks as the perspective of a struggle for a proletarian and socialist power in Russia. In the meantime Lenin had also written his *Imperialism, the Highest Stage of Capitalism*, which, situating capitalism in its concrete totality as a world system, allowed him to approach the question of the Russian revolution in a new light. In particular, it led to the theory of the 'weakest link', which postulated that revolutionary 'maturity' had to be adjudged in the framework of the international system of imperialism, and not exclusively at the level of an isolated country.

It is only, however, after the eruption of the February revolution that Lenin's new methodological departures and theory of imperialism were synthesized within an explicitly permanentist conception of the revolutionary process. In March, while the majority of the Bolsheviks in Petrograd were still conceiving of the new revolution as limited to bourgeois tasks, Lenin sent from exile his 'Letters from Afar', which envisioned *socialist measures* as already being on the order of the day.[88] At the moment of his return to Russia on 3 April, he made an extraordinary speech at the Finland Station to the mass of workers, soldiers and sailors. 'You must struggle for the socialist revolution, struggle to the end, till the complete victory of the proletariat. Long live the socialist revolution!'[89] These words, and the

---

[87] *Philosophical Notebooks*, CW, vol. 38, pp. 151, 157-9, 179, 187, 260, 276-7 and 360. See also my essay, 'From the Great Logic of Hegel to the Finland Station in Petrograd', *Critique*, 6 (Spring 1976).

[88] 'Letters from Afar', CW, vol. 21, p. 34.

[89] Stenographic notes by the Bolshevik Bonch-Bruevitch in G. Golikov, *La révolution d'octobre*, Moscow 1966.

central political slogan proposed by Lenin—'All power to the soviets!'—resounded, according to the testimony of the Menshevik Sukhanov, 'like a thunderclap from a clear blue sky', which 'stunned and confused even the most faithful of his disciples'. On 8 April *Pravda*, the official organ of the Bolsheviks, published an editorial signed by Kamenev, stressing that 'as for the general scheme of comrade Lenin, it seems to us unacceptable, in that it starts from the assumption that the bourgeois-democratic revolution is ended and counts upon an immediate transformation of this revolution into a socialist revolution.' According to Sukhanov, the Mensheviks greeted *Pravda*'s position with glee, 'it seemed that the Marxist rank and file of the Bolshevik party stood firm and unshakable, that the mass of the party was in revolt against Lenin to defend the elementary principles of the scientific socialism of the old days; alas, we were mistaken!'[90] As a matter of fact, Lenin's new theses did imply a profound break with the 'scientific socialism of the old days' and with a certain way of understanding the 'elementary principles' of Marxism, inspired by Plekhanov and Kautsky, which had been the common wisdom of Bolsheviks and Mensheviks alike. In a critical commentary on Sukhanov's book written in 1923, Lenin emphasized the methodological roots of this break: people like Sukhanov 'call themselves Marxists, but. . . . They completely failed to understand what is decisive in Marxism, namely, its revolutionary dialectics.'[91]

Faced with almost unanimous condemnation of his heretical views, Lenin for the moment moderated his propositions: the *April Theses* did not speak of socialist revolution, although they implied it by evoking the Commune-state of 1871 as a model for the Soviet Republic. The Paris Commune was traditionally understood, as a result of Marx's analysis in *The Civil War in France*, as an example of the dictatorship of the proletariat; moreover, Lenin himself had previously criticized the Commune (in his *Two Tactics*) from a stagist perspective for having confused the tasks of the democratic and socialist revolutions. So to advance the proposal for a 'Commune-state' was, in the last analysis, to struggle for the dictatorship of the proletariat in Russia and for a revolution combining democratic and socialist tasks. As E. H. Carr has put it, 'Lenin's powerful argument . . . implied the transition to socialism, though he stopped short of explicitly proclaiming it.'[92] But the Bolsheviks did not have to wait long for Lenin to make the point explicitly; before the end of April, he was battling within the party for the abandonment of the traditional slogan of a 'democratic

[90]N. Sukhanov, *La révolution russe de 1917*, Paris 1964, pp. 139-43.
[91]'Our Revolution', CW, vol. 33, p. 476.
[92]*The Bolshevik Revolution*, vol. 1, London 1950, p. 82.

dictatorship of the proletariat and the peasantry'. In his eyes, those who still clung to the old formula (Kamenev, for example) had 'in effect *gone over* to the petty bourgeoisie against the proletarian class struggle,' and 'should be consigned to the archive of "Bolshevik" pre-revolutionary antiques (it may be called the archive of "old Bolsheviks")'.[93] Later, in a series of articles in the newspaper *Volna*, which summarized in question-and-answer form the positions of the different Russian political parties, he gave this answer to the question 'What is their [Bolsheviks'] attitude towards socialism?'—'For socialism. The Soviets must immediately take all possible practicable steps for its realization.'[94]

Over the last half-century, generations of Stalinist and 'post-Stalinist' ideologues have toiled to prove that Lenin's conceptions in 1917 had nothing in common with Trotsky's theory of permanent revolution, and that they were merely an 'amended and improved' version of the strategy he had formulated back in 1905. The touchstone of this laborious argumentation is the thesis that the Soviet of Workers' and Soldiers' Deputies, established in February 1917 alongside the Provisional Government, was the materialization of the 'democratic dictatorship of workers and peasants'.[95] But it is impossible to bend the events of 1917 to fit the neat schemas of 1905. In the first place, if Lenin did consider the Petrograd Soviet as a 'democratic dictatorship . . .', it was only 'to a certain extent . . . with a certain number of highly important modifications'; namely the fact that this institution—dominated in the beginning by the Mensheviks and the Social Revolutionaries—'voluntarily gave up its power to the bourgeoisie.'[96] This, in turn, deprived it of the capacity to implement its historical tasks; the most important of which was the revolutionary solution of the agrarian question through *the expropriation of the landowners*. But an even more fundamental point is overlooked by the different Stalinist and neo-Stalinist theoreticians: while in his *Two Tactics* Lenin is still convinced that the Russian revolution can only 'clear the ground for a wide and rapid, European and not Asiatic, development of capitalism',[97] in March/April 1917 he made the decisive transition to a perspective that stressed the immediacy of anti-capitalist, socialist-revolutionary measures. In 1905 he believed that 'the degree of Russia's economic development . . . make[s] immediate and complete emancipation of the working class impossible;'[98]

[93]'On Tactics', CW, vol. 24, p. 45.
[94]'Political Parties in Russia and Tasks of the Proletariat', CW, vol. 24, p. 97.
[95]Cf. Monty Johnstone, 'Trotsky—Part One', *Cogito*, 5, pp. 11-2; and Michail, pp. 31-40.
[96]'Letters on Tactics', pp. 43-8.
[97]*Two Tactics*, p. 48.
[98]Ibid., p. 28.

but in 1917 he advanced a strategy that aimed at nothing less than this 'complete emancipation'. How, then, is it possible to deny the deep affinity and evident convergence of his *April Theses* with Trotsky's conception of permanent revolution?

The events of 1917 dramatically confirmed Trotsky's predictions twelve years earlier. First, the Russian bourgeoisie (and its political allies: the Mensheviks, moderate populists, and so on) proved incapable of completing the democratic revolution, especially of satisfying the revolutionary aspirations of the peasantry. Second, the crucial democratic tasks were, therefore, only completed after the seizure of power by the proletariat, who emerged as the real emancipator of the peasantry. As Lenin later observed, 'it was the Bolsheviks . . . who, thanks only to the victory of the proletarian revolution, helped the peasants to carry the bourgeois democratic revolution really to its conclusion.'[99] Third, once in power the working class was unable to confine itself to merely democratic reforms; the dynamic of the class struggle forced it—as Trotsky had prophesized—to undertake explicitly socialist measures. Indeed, in the face of the economic boycott conducted by the propertied classes and the growing menace of a general paralysis of production, the Soviets were led—much sooner than he forsaw—to expropriate capital when, in June 1918, the Peoples' Council of Commissars decreed the socialization of the principal branches of industry.[100] Thus the revolution of 1917 underwent a process of *uninterrupted* development from its (unfinished) bourgeois-democratic phase in February to its proletarian-socialist phase which began in October. With the support of the peasantry, the Soviets *combined* democratic tasks (the agrarian revolution) with socialist tasks (the expropriation of the bourgeoisie), opening a 'non-capitalist road' for the transition to socialism. But the Bolshevik party, with Lenin and Trotsky at its head, could only

[99]CW, vol. 28, p. 314. See also *The Permanent Revolution*, p. 109: 'The gist of the matter lay in the fact that the agrarian question, which constituted the basis of the bourgeois revolution, could not be solved under the rule of the bourgeoisie. The dictatorship of the proletariat appeared on the scene not *after* the completion of the agrarian democratic revolution but as the necessary *prerequisite* for its accomplishment.'

[100]See Marcel Liebman, *The Russian Revolution*, New York 1970, p. 324: 'During the same period, the government ordered the nationalization of a number of individual enterprises without, however, evincing any desire to extend this measure to the entire economy. In each case, they were motivated by the departure or the hostile attitude of the proprietors, or by the particular importance of these enterprises. . . . the Bolshevik Government was forced to reconsider its relatively moderate policy which depended on some measure of co-operation by the industrialists, who became more obstructive as the Civil War drew nearer. . . . And when the Civil War could no longer be averted, and the production of arms had to be stepped up, centralization became a matter of life and death for the new regime'.

take the leadership of this gigantic social movement that 'shook the world', because of the radical strategic re-orientation that Lenin had initiated in April 1917 along lines congruent with the theory of permanent revolution.

The 'orthodox' Marxists of the Second International condemned the October Revolution for its defiance of the 'iron laws of history'. In a 1921 *Pravda* article on the 'Fourth Anniversary of the October Revolution', Lenin brilliantly summed-up the theoretical-political gulf between stagist and permanentist conceptions of revolution. 'The Kautskys, Hilferdings, Martovs, Chernovs, Hillquits, Longuets, MacDonalds, Turatis and other heroes of "Two-and-a-Half" Marxism were incapable of understanding *this* relation between the bourgeois-democratic and the proletarian-socialist revolutions. The first develops into the second. The second, in passing, solves the problems of the first. The second consolidates the work of the first. Struggle, and struggle alone, decides how far the second succeeds in outgrowing the first.'[101] Of course, the Mensheviks and their supporters in European social democracy did attempt to base their critique of Bolshevism on a consistent Marxist argument: the establishment of socialism requires the existence of a high level of the development of the productive forces. But Lenin and Trotsky did not dispute this premise, but rather the false reasoning which the Mensheviks attempt to deduce from it. In his memoirs the Menshevik historian Sukhanov asked, 'How to reconcile this economic backwardness, this peasant and petty-bourgeois structure of society, with socialist transformation. . . ?'[102] In a review of Sukhanov's book, Lenin responded as follows. 'You say that civilization is necessary for the building of socialism. Very good. But why could we not first create such prerequisites of civilisation in our country as the expulsion of the landowners and the Russian capitalists, and then start moving towards socialism? Where, in what books, have you read that such variations of the customary historical sequence of events are impermissible or impossible?'[103]

In the light of the experience of the Russian revolution, Lenin and the Third International attempted to outline a global strategy for the backward, underdeveloped, colonial or semi-colonial societies. Here, also, Lenin deeply modified and revised his pre-war views. For example, in a 1912 article on China, he had polemicized against Sun Yat-sen (not without, first, praising his revolutionary-democratic sincerity), attacking his populist ideology and his 'dream' that China could somehow 'avoid the

[101]CW, vol. 33, p. 54.
[102]Sukhanov, p. 14.
[103]'Our Revolution?' CW, vol. 33, p. 480.

capitalist road'. At that time Lenin believed that the concept of a non-capitalist road in China was nothing more than another version of the 'theory of petty-bourgeois reactionary "socialism"', which Russian Marxism had fought against so long and hard in the form of Narodnikism. Moreover, he predicted that within fifty years China would have many towns like Shanghai: 'that means, great centres of capitalist wealth and proletarian poverty and misery'.[104] Eight years later, at the Second Congress of the Communist International, Lenin undertook a radical reformulation of his views on the prospects for national liberation movements in the colonial world. After a series of extended discussions and debates (in 1920 the Comintern was still an organization where dissent and debate were considered both healthy and normal), the two main strategic orientations—those of Lenin and of the Indian communist, M. N. Roy—had converged in a certain consensus or compromise. Both agreed that the fundamental strategic aim in 'Oriental' countries (a term which, in reality, designated all the colonial and semi-colonial nations) must be the struggle for the establishment of a soviet-based workers' and peasants' power, which would, in turn, open a non-capitalist road of socialist transition.[105] Disagreement remained over the *tactics* to be adopted toward bourgeois nationalism: Lenin envisaged the possibility of 'temporary alliances with bourgeois democracy in colonial and backward countries',[106] while Roy, Sultan-Zade and others were more reserved about such possible coalitions.[107] Ultimately, a common agreement was reached on the need to distinguish between bourgeois-democratic reformism and popular-revolutionary movements for emancipation in the colonies and semi-colonies.[108]

[104]'Democracy and Narodism in China', CW, vol. 18, p. 163-9.

[105]Lenin, 'The Report of the Commission on the National and Colonial Questions' (26 July, 1920), in *Lenin on the National and Colonial Questions*, Peking 1967, p. 35: 'The question was posed as follows: Are we to accept as correct the assertion that the capitalist stage of development of the national economy is inevitable for those backward nations which are winning liberation. . . ? We replied in the negative. If the victorious revolutionary proletariat conducts systematic propaganda among them, and the Soviet governments come to their assistance with all the means at their disposal—in that event it would be wrong to assume that the capitalist stage of development is inevitable for the backward peoples. With the aid of the proletariat of the advanced countries, the backward countries can pass over to the Soviet system and, through definite stages of development, to communism, without going through the capitalist stage.'

[106]Ibid., p. 27.

[107]See Henri Carrière d'Encausse and Stuart Schram, *Le marxisme et l'Asie*, Paris 1965, pp. 44-5, 205-22.

[108]'Preliminary Draft Theses on the National and Colonial Questions', *Theses, Resolutions and Manifestos of the First Four Congresses of the Third International*, London 1980, pp. 76-81.

On the central question of the peasantry, however, Lenin's views remained ambiguous, if not actually contradictory. On the one hand, he proposed the constitution of *peasant soviets*, even in countries with precapitalist agrarian structures; while, on the other hand, he proclaimed, 'there is not the slightest doubt that every national movement can only be a bourgeois-democratic movement, for the overwhelming mass of the population in backward countries consists of peasants who represent bourgeois-capitalist relations.'[109] This typically 'Europeanist' conception of the peasantry—shared by Trotsky—did not take into account sufficiently the historical specificity of the rural class structures and ideologico-cultural matrices in the colonial and semi-colonial countries. In particular, it greatly underestimated the peasantry and rural poor's potential as a *socialist* revolutionary force under the leadership of a Marxist-proletarian vanguard, as manifested on a world scale repeatedly in this century. (We shall return to this question in relation to Trotsky.)

The 'Theses on the Eastern Question' of the Fourth Congress of the Comintern (December 1923) developed and complemented those of the Second. While again recognizing that 'temporary agreements with bourgeois democracy are acceptable and indispensable', they stressed that 'the objective tasks of the colonial revolution transcend the framework of bourgeois democracy' and that 'the moment the proletarian and peasant masses incorporate themselves into the revolutionary movements in the colonies, the elements of the great bourgeoisie and of the landowning bourgeoisie draw back from it.' The strategic perspective of the Congress was that of the establishment of a soviet-like power in the East; a power of workers' and peasants' councils that would spare countries the stages of capitalist development and exploitation.[110] Although the principal interest of the Third International was in the Asian bloc of colonial/semi-colonial countries, other regions of imperialist domination were not forgotten. Although there were no specific Congress resolutions, a number of other documents and appeals of the Executive Committee of the Comintern sketched a permanentist strategy—unifying the anti-imperialist struggle, agrarian emancipation and socialist revolution—for Latin America. For example, in a January 1921 text, the Executive Committee asserted that only a revolutionary movement expressing the interests of the proletariat and the peasantry could liberate Latin America from the oppression of both its national exploiters and American imperialism. Moreover, after a remarkable analysis of the Mexican revolution, the document concluded with

[109]*Lenin on the National and Colonial Questions*, p. 32.
[110]Cf. *Theses, Resolutions and Manifestos*, pp. 409-18.

the necessity of an *anti-capitalist* alliance between the proletariat and peasantry.[111] There was no question in this or similar Comintern statements of the 1921 to 1923 period of a specific 'bourgeois-democratic stage' or of the revolutionary role of the national bourgeoisie in Latin America. Indeed, there was no mention even of a possible alliance of the workers and peasants with bourgeois democracy.

A detailed analysis of the Comintern's policies on the 'national and colonial question' during its Leninist period—the first four congresses 1919-22—is beyond the scope of this work. It suffices to note that the general orientation of most documents and resolutions of the congresses and of the Executive Committee advocated a struggle in the colonial and semi-colonial countries for a soviet-type power of the workers and peasants, under proletarian hegemony, with a programme combining democratic, national and anti-capitalist (socialist) revolutionary measures: in other words, a strategy which had the same general orientation as the theory of permanent revolution. The question that remained open and subject to debate was over the nature of the tactics to be employed relative to bourgeois-nationalist currents. If the idea of 'temporary alliance' was more or less accepted by the entire Comintern leadership, the concrete implementation of it in each country was more controversial.[112]

How did Trotsky's ideas on permanent revolution develop during the first years after the victory of the October Revolution? As one would expect, Trotsky considered that the revolution thoroughly confirmed his conceptions and forecasts of 1905-6. In a preface written in 1919 to the re-issue of *Results and Prospects*, he wrote: 'The final test of a theory is experience. Irrefutable proof of our having correctly applied Marxist theory

---

[111]'The Mexican case is at the same time both typical and tragic. The agrarian workers rebelled and made a revolution only to see the fruits of their victory stolen by the capitalists. . . . The revolutionary union of the poor peasantry and the working class is indispensable; only in this way can the proletarian revolution liberate the peasantry by smashing the power of capital, and only in this way can the proletarian revolution be safeguarded from being crushed by the counter-revolution'. ('Sur la révolution en Amérique, Appel à la classe ouvrière des deux Amériques', *L'Internationale Communiste*, 15 [January, 1921], pp. 321-2. See also 'Aux ouvrièrs et paysans de l'Amérique du sud', *La correspondance internationale*, 2 [20 January, 1923], pp. 26-7).

[112]This was particularly the case with the entrance of the Chinese communists into the Kuomintang in 1923. 'I personally was from the very beginning, that is from 1923, resolutely opposed to the Communist Party joining the Kuomintang. . . . Up to 1926 I always voted independently in the Political Bureau on this question, against all the others'. (Letter to Max Schachtman, 10 December, 1930, in Trotsky *On China*, New York 1976, p. 490.) However this must be qualified by Trotsky's admission to Radek (Letter of March 1927) that before 1925 he had been willing to concede that joining the Kuomintang for one or two years 'would have, perhaps, been admissible'. (Ibid., p. 122.)

is given by the fact that the events in which we are now participating, and even our methods of participation in them, were foreseen in their fundamental lines some fifteen years ago.'[113] A similar viewpoint was expressed in 1922 in another preface (to a new edition of *1905*) and again, a year later, in *The New Course*, where he answered the first wave of criticism that claimed that the permanent revolution was an 'un-Leninist theory'. 'I persist in considering that the thoughts I developed at that time (1904-5), taken as a whole, are much closer to the genuine essence of Leninism than much of what a number of Bolsheviks wrote in those days. . . . The theory of permanent revolution led directly to Leninism and in particular to the April 1917 Theses.'[114] But as the pressure increased, and the attacks on the permanent revolution became an increasingly important element of the 'troika's' (Zinoviev, Kamenev and Stalin) campaign against him, Trotsky was backed into a more and more defensive stance. In *Our Differences* (written in November 1924, but never published), for example, he claimed that the formula of permanent revolution only 'reflected a stage in our development that we have long since passed through'.[115] Later, in a January 1925 letter to the Central Committee of the Party, he went so far as declaring that 'the formula "permanent revolution" . . . applies wholly to the past. . . . If at any time after October I had occasion, for private reasons, to revert to the formula "permanent revolution", it was only a reference to party history, i.e. to the past, and had no reference to the question of present-day political tasks.'[116]

On the other hand, it is interesting to consider briefly Trotsky's views, in the five years after October, on the revolution's significance for other peripheral capitalist countries. To what extent could the theory of permanent revolution be generalized to zones of belated capitalist development or to the regions of colonial oppression? Certainly at the beginning of the 1920s the colonial revolution was far from the centre of his interests, since he was preoccupied with the fate of the revolutionary left in Western and Central Europe. Nevertheless, Trotsky's relatively rare pronouncements on the 'Eastern question' suggest a quite negative attitude towards the role of the native bourgeoisie in the dominated countries. In a speech to the Third World Congress of the International (1921), he attempted to apply the lessons of the Russian revolutionary experience to the struggle for national

---

[113]*Permanent Revolution*, p. 164; and *1905*, p. 8 ('Despite an interruption of twelve years, this analysis has been entirely confirmed.')
[114]*Challenge of the Left Opposition*, pp. 101-2.
[115]Ibid., p. 299.
[116]Ibid., p. 305.

liberation in Asia. 'The basis for the liberationist struggle of the colonies is constituted by the peasant masses. But the peasants in their struggle need leadership. Such a leadership used to be provided by the native bourgeoisie. The latter's struggle against foreign imperialist domination cannot, however, be either consistent or energetic, inasmuch as the native bourgeoisie itself is intimately bound up with foreign capital. Only the rise of a native proletariat strong enough numerically and capable of struggle can provide a real axis for the revolution. In comparison to the country's entire population, the size of the Indian proletariat is, of course, numerically small, but those who have grasped the meaning of the revolution's development in Russia will never fail to take into account that the proletariat's revolutionary role in the Oriental countries will far exceed its actual numerical strength.'[117] Although this passage clearly provides an indication of the theory of permanent revolution's applicability to other national contexts, it would be incorrect to conclude that Trotsky already possessed in the early 1920s a global, coherent and precise conception of the dynamics of revolution in the colonial and dependent countries. Only after the tragedy of the Chinese revolution of 1926-7 and in the midst of his struggle against Stalin's doctrine of 'socialism in one country' did Trotsky attempt to systematically generalize the theory of permanent revolution as a theory of world revolution.

---

[117]'Report on the World Economic Crisis and the New Tasks of the Communist International' (23 June, 1921), in *The First Five Years of the Communist International*, vol. 1, New York 1972, p. 223.

3

The Emergence of the General Theory

Trotsky elaborated the international implications of the theory of permanent revolution in the course of fierce theoretical and political confrontations with Stalinism in the late 1920s. Three distinct polemical phases can be distinguished: (1) the struggle against the neo-Menshevik doctrine of socialism in one country (1925-9); (2) the debate on the Second Chinese Revolution of 1926-7; and (3) the appearance of Trotsky's book *Permanent Revolution* in 1928.

Historians have frequently been bewildered by the confused and abstract character of the debate on socialism in one country. Heinz Brahm has complained that it is 'as senseless as the medieval ruminations on how many angels could stand on the head of a pin', while even Isaac Deutscher denounced the 'bizarre irrelevancy' of the whole controversy on occasion.[1] But behind the abstruseness and the almost ritualistic character of the polemics (with every side piously collecting as many quotations as possible from Lenin) critical political questions, decisive for the future of the world labour movement, were being debated.

The doctrine of 'socialism in one country' was without any doubt the original creation of Stalin, first elaborated in the year after Lenin's death. Indeed, its appearance can be dated with some precision. For as late as May 1924 Stalin still defended (in *Foundations of Leninism*) the traditional Bolshevik view on the question: 'For the final victory of socialism, for the organization of socialist production, the efforts of one country, particularly of a peasant country like Russia, are insufficient; for that the efforts of the proletariat of several advanced countries are required.'[2] But a few months

---

[1] H. Brahm, *Trotskijs Kampf um die Nachfolge Lenins, die ideologische Auseinandersetzung, 1923-26*, Cologne 1964, p. 211; I. Deutscher, *Stalin*, London 1949, p. 288. Trotsky himself recognized that the debate appeared on the surface as academic or scholastic. See 'Socialism in One Country', in *The Revolution Betrayed*, New York 1965, p. 292.

[2] Stalin, *On the Opposition* (1921-7), Peking 1975, p. 156.

later (December 1924), in his pamphlet *The October Revolution and the Tactics of the Russian Communists*, he suddenly declared that the USSR possessed favourable conditions 'for pushing on with the organizing of a socialist economy'.[3] Why this change? In *Concerning Questions of Leninism* (January 1926) Stalin explained it in characteristic terms: the first formulation was directed against certain assertions of the Trotskyists, and 'to that extent—but only to that extent—this formulation was then (May 1924) adequate and *undoubtedly it was of some service*.' Subsequently, however, as new questions came to the fore, this formula 'became obviously inadequate, and *therefore incorrect*'.[4] This is a truly striking example of the almost purely opportunistic nature of theoretical constructions in Stalin's writing: truth or error are not defined in relation to facts, but instrumentally according to their being or not being 'adequate' or 'of some service' to polemical employment. Thus a theory becomes 'incorrect' not because the objective situation has changed or become better understood, but only because the needs of the ideological struggle have changed.

If this doctrine of socialism in one country was summoned forth as a weapon against Trotsky, it owed its inception also to its immediate affinity with the spontaneous nationalistic ideology of the emerging bureaucratic strata. In 1926 Stalin openly admitted an even more compelling *raison d'être* for the theory: 'Can it (our country) remain the mighty centre of attraction for the workers of all countries that it undoubtedly is now, if it is incapable of achieving victory at home over the capitalist elements in our economy, the victory of socialist construction? I think not. But does it not follow from this that disbelief in the victory of socialist construction, the dissemination of such disbelief, will lead to our country being discredited as the base of the world revolution?'[5] As we shall see this is, in fact, the real political role of the doctrine in its global implications: to guarantee the prestige of the USSR, its 'central position' and its hegemony over the world communist movement. In other words, the ideology of socialism in one country was needed by Stalin and the bureaucratic ruling strata to justify the subordination of the international class struggle to the requirements of 'building socialism' in the USSR. As Stalin would have put it, the doctrine was 'adequate, and undoubtedly of some service. . . .'

If the debate over socialism in one country tended to become obscure, it was because two different sets of questions were frequently conflated: first, the possibility of an isolated workers' state surviving for some extended

[3]Ibid., p. 318.
[4]Ibid.
[5]Ibid., p. 330.

historical period; and, second, the potentiality for achieving a completed socialist society in a single country. As regards the survival of a workers' state, we have already seen how in 1906 Trotsky asserted that without the rapid reinforcements of a triumphant revolution in Europe, the working class could scarcely hope to remain in power in Russia. He continued to defend this idea through the 1920s, sometimes insisting on the danger of imperialist military intervention, sometimes of an economic collapse of the USSR.[6] Further, there can be little doubt that Lenin shared Trotsky's view on this point, and all later efforts of Stalin to discover a contradiction between them were in vain.[7] As time passed, however, and no intervention or collapse occurred, Trotsky continued to speak of a 'breathing-space' or an 'undated moratorium' for the USSR.[8] Finally by the 1930s it had become obvious that the course of events cóntradicted, at least in the direct sense, this perspective of imminent danger. In the *Revolution Betrayed* (1936), he recognized that 'to be sure, the isolation of the Soviet Union did not have those immediate dangerous consequences which might have been feared. . . . The "breathing spell" proved longer than a critical optimism had dared to hope. . . . But a more malign product of isolation and backwardness has been the octopus of bureaucratism.'[9] Nevertheless, Trotsky continued to defend his 1906 position as correct in the medium-range. '*Without a more or less rapid victory of the proletariat in the advanced countries*, the workers' government in Russia will not survive. Left to itself, the Soviet regime must either fall or degenerate. More exactly it will first degenerate and then fall. I myself have written about this more than once, beginning in 1905.'[10] In fact, at that time (1937), the workers' government in Russia had already degenerated, and the bureaucracy had politically expropriated the proletariat.[11] So in a certain sense Trotsky had been

[6]Cf. *Permanent Revolution*, pp. 142-3; and *The Third International After Lenin*, New York 1936, pp. 64-5.

[7]To take one of innumerable examples: 'Anglo-French and American imperialism will *inevitably destory the independence and freedom of Russia if* the world socialist revolution, world Bolshevism, does not triumph.' ('The Valuable Admissions of Pitirim Sorokin' [November 1918], CW, vol. 28, p. 188.)

[8]*Permanent Revolution*, p. 143.

[9]*Revolution Betrayed*, p. 300.

[10]*Stalinism and Bolshevism*, London 1956, p. 9.

[11]At first Trotsky wàs reluctant to admit the full extent of this expropriation, and continued through 1936 to consider the USSR a 'degenerated form of the dictatorship of the proletariat'. After the Moscow Trials, however, he discarded this concept. Although he maintained until his death that the Soviet Union was a 'workers' state' (principally because of its planned economy), he now characterized the political regime as a 'dictatorship of the bureaucracy', stressing that the state apparatus 'was transformed from the weapon of the working class into a weapon of bureaucratic violence against the working class'. (See *The Transitional Programme* [1938], London n.d., p. 43.)

correct all along: in the isolated USSR the workers were not able to keep power. But it was a bureaucracy—not the bourgeoisie or imperialism—that wrested power from them and physically destroyed the Bolshevik old guard in the purges of 1936-8. In that sense Trotsky was wrong, the degeneration of the regime was not equivalent to its 'fall'—that is, to a capitalist restoration.

The other problem implied in the controversy over socialism in one country and frequently confused with the first, is the possibility of building a 'complete socialist society' within the limits of one nation, specifically the USSR. As previously noted, much of the discussion of this question has revolved around talmudic exegeses of Lenin's writings. Without delving into the scholastic detail, it should simply be noted that the overwhelming bulk of Lenin's texts which at all touch on this question deny its possibility. [12] Indeed, the *only* text that Stalin could adduce to support his position was a short paragraph in the 1923 article 'On Cooperation', where Lenin argues that the USSR has 'all that is necessary and sufficient' to build a socialist society. Trotsky's answer was that Lenin meant by this only the *political*, not the material conditions for the realization of socialism. [13] At any event, this rather arid debate over quotations is scarcely the crux of the matter.

Trotsky's most serious argument was based on the assumption that socialism was by definition a system economically superior to capitalism and could not therefore represent a regression in relation to the international level already attained by the development of the productive forces under capitalism. 'The productive forces of capitalist society have long ago outgrown the national boundaries. . . . In respect of the technique of production socialist society must represent a stage higher than capitalism. To aim at building a *nationally isolated* socialist society means, in spite of all passing successes, to pull the productive forces backwards even as compared with capitalism.' [14] From this perspective, Russia's economic backwardness (the predominance of peasant agriculture, the low level of productivity,

---

[12] See, for example, his well-known declaration during the 1918 Congress of Soviets: 'The complete victory of the socialist revolution in one country alone is inconceivable and demands the most active cooperation of at least several advanced countries, which do not include Russia'. ('Speech on the International Situation' (8 November 1918), CW, vol. 28, p. 151.)

[13] *Third International After Lenin*, pp. 31-4.

[14] *Permanent Revolution*, p. 22. See also *Third International After Lenin*, pp. 52-3: 'Socialism, however, must not only take over from capitalism the most highly developed productive forces but must immediately carry them onward, raise them to a higher level and give them a state of development such as has been unknown under capitalism. The question arises: how then can socialism drive the productive forces back into the boundaries of a national state which they have violently sought to break through under capitalism?'

and so on) was not the decisive aspect, since even in *England*, according to Trotsky, it would be impossible to build an isolated 'national socialist' economy.[15] What was all important was the extension of the revolution to several or more advanced countries. Needless to say, authors who have attributed to Trotsky the belief that there is within the USSR a contradiction between its 'socialist economy and un-socialist state' completely misunderstand his thesis. While considering that the planned state economy of the USSR was a conquest of the October Revolution that had to be defended at all costs, Trotsky never identified this with socialism.[16]

In contrast, the partisans of 'socialism in one country', Stalin and Bukharin, defined socialism as synonymous with social forms of property. Bukharin even wrote about a 'backward socialism' in Russia, implying by 'socialism' the predominance of the national (state) economy and co-operatives over private capital.[17] Of course anyone is entitled to define 'socialism' as they please. But it is obvious that for Marx and Engels a 'backward socialism' would have been a contradiction in terms, since socialism meant to them precisely a superior level of the development of the productive forces that are ultimately limited and constrained within capitalist relations of production. Moreover, such a socialist economy could not at all be reduced, in their view, simply to social property in the means of production. In his *Critique of the Gotha Program* Marx explicitly indicated that in the *first stage* of socialist society, commodity production, money and the law of value would disappear.[18]

This controversy over the meaning of socialism was, in turn, subsumed within an even broader struggle. The concrete, political stake of the debate over 'socialism in one country' was ultimately nothing less than whether or not the world class struggle was to be subordinated to the 'building of socialism in the USSR'. In other words, Stalin's doctrine was an ideological rationalization (with the usual dimension of self-mystification involved) for the submission of the international communist movement to the economic, political, diplomatic and military needs of the USSR as understood by its

[15]'Great Britain . . . being no doubt a highly developed capitalist country, it has *precisely because of that* no chance for successful socialist construction within the limits of its own island. Great Britain, if blockaded, would simply be strangled in the course of a few months.' (*Third International After Lenin*, pp. 57-8.)

[16]Even a rigorous thinker like Cludín commits this error, attributing to Trotskyism the thesis that 'the system of production is socialist but not the political superstructure.' (Fernando Claudín, *Eurocommunism and Socialism*, London 1978, p. 61.)

[17]Bukharin, *Le socialisme dans un seul pays*, Paris 1974, pp. 185-6.

[18]In Marx and Engels, *Selected Works*, Moscow 1968, pp. 320-1. See also Engels, *Anti-Dühring*, Moscow 1959, pp. 386-9.

bureaucratic leadership. Trotsky clearly perceived this implication and made it the central object of his critical writings in the late 1920s. 'The new doctrine proclaims that socialism can be built on the basis of a national state *if only there is no intervention*. From this there can and must follow . . . a collaborationist policy towards the foreign bourgeoisie with the object of averting intervention, that is to say, will solve the main historical question. The task of the parties in the Comintern assumes, therefore, an auxiliary character; their mission is to protect the USSR from intervention and not to fight for the conquest of power. It is, of course, not a question of the subjective intentions but of the objective logic of political thought.'[19]

Although Lenin and other Soviet leaders had shown an avid interest during the early 1920s in the anti-imperialist movements of the East, the fact that the next great revolutionary upheaval after October 1917 (and after the defeats in Hungary and Germany in 1919-23) took place in Asia came as a great surprise to the Bolshevik and Comintern leadership. The five-month long general strike of the Canton—Hong Kong workers in 1925 (under communist leadership and backed by a workers' militia) was the first dramatic sign of the rising tide; and when the 'Northern Expedition' of the Kuomintang Army led by Chiang Kai-shek in 1926 was followed by a vast wave of peasant rebellions, workers' strikes and insurrections in the warlord-controlled regions, it was clear that a major revolutionary process was unfolding.

Initially there appeared to be a kind of consensus amongst the Soviet leadership that China was still too backward a country and its proletariat too small to allow anything like a re-enactment of the October Revolution. Even Trotsky, as we shall see, retreated in the beginning to a position similar to Lenin's strategy of 1905 (a 'workers' and peasants' democratic dictatorship'). But Stalin and Bukharin very quickly regressed to a neo-Menshevik stand, comparable although not identical to the positions of Dan and Martynov in 1905. As a matter of fact, the Second Chinese Revolution of 1925-8 provided the catalyst for Stalin's second great ideological contribution (with the help of collaborators like Martynov!): the doctrine of revolution by stages and of the bloc of four classes. These new conceptions were destined to become the strategic line advanced by the Comintern in all the backward, colonial and semi-colonial countries. They became so strongly rooted in the thinking of non-Western communist parties that, after Stalin's dissolution of the Comintern in 1943, they

[19]*The Third International After Lenin*, p. 61.

remained accepted in theory even by those communists such as Mao and Ho who departed from them in practice. Indeed the evolution of this strategic line is the key to understanding the history of communism in Asia.

The first document to elaborate these two interlinked tenets of stagism and a four-class bloc was the *Thesis on the Situation in China*—directly inspired by Stalin and Bukharin—approved in December 1926 by the Seventh Plenum of the Executive Committee of the Communist International (ECCI). This document stated that 'in its present stage, the Chinese revolution is historically a revolution of a bourgeois-democratic nature.' Therefore, 'the proletariat allied with the peasants struggling for their rights, with the urban petty-bourgeoisie and a section of the capitalist bourgeoisie. This combination of forces finds its political expression in the Kuomintang and the Canton government.'[20] Although both the Second (1920) and the Fourth (1922) Congresses of the Comintern had envisaged 'temporary alliances' with bourgeois forces, the idea of a *strategic bloc* with them—including a coalition government—and of a separate bourgeois-democratic stage was a new departure. The change appears even more striking if one considers Stalin's speech at the Seventh Plenum of the ECCI on 30 November 1926. Whereas Lenin had earlier insisted (during the Second Congress in 1920) that the Comintern emphasize the priority of building *peasant soviets* in the colonial and semi-colonial countries, Stalin now opposed this strategy in the Chinese countryside—'to speak of soviets now would be running too far ahead.' Moreover, in place of the Comintern's original stress on the importance of fighting every form of bourgeois influence over the popular anti-imperialist movements, he specifically urged that Chinese youth (student, working-class and peasant) be 'subordinated to the ideological and political influence of the Kuomintang'.[21]

Stalin's evolving orientation clearly implied that the Bolshevik strategy of the October Revolution had no direct relevance to the struggle in China. As a matter of fact, even the 'old Bolshevik' line of 1905 ('the revolutionary dictatorship of the proletariat and the peasantry') was no longer considered a suitable precedent, since it was based on the intransigent refusal of

---

[20]'Thèses sur la situation en Chine', in Pierre Broué, *La question chinoise dans l'Internationale Communiste*, Paris 1976, pp. 69, 71.

[21]'Prospects of Revolution in China', in Stalin, *On the Opposition*, pp. 509, 515. Actually Stalin had first floated this conception back in May 1922 when he severely criticized the 'deviation' which consisted in 'underestimating the alliance of the working class with the revolutionary bourgeoisie against imperialism'. He considered as guilty of such a dangerous deviation those communist parties of Asia that had launched the slogan of soviet power. ('Des tâches politiques de l'Université des Peuples de l'Orient', in Stalin, *Le Marxisme et la question nationale et coloniale*, Paris 1937, pp. 252-3.)

strategic alliances or pacts with the liberal bourgeoisie. This rejection of traditional Bolshevik conceptions was first explicitly recognized in February 1927 by A. S. Martynov, a former leading Menshevik who joined the RCP in 1923 and was soon afterwards promoted by Stalin as a principal spokesman for the Comintern's positions on the Chinese revolution. According to Martynov, 'in its attitudes towards the national government and the leadership of the revolutionary army, the Chinese Communist Party could not confine itself to merely copying the Bolsheviks' tactics toward the Russian liberal bourgeoisie in 1905.' Although the official goal of the struggle was still a 'democratic dictatorship of the proletariat and peasantry', the road leading to this dictatorship was not the same as that of the Bolsheviks in 1905. Indeed, it could only be achieved by the Chinese communists fully supporting—not opposing—the revolutionary work being undertaken by the national government [Kuomintang] and its revolutionary army under bourgeois command.'[22]

What did this policy of support for the Kuomintang mean in 1927 at the very moment when everywhere in China the peasants and workers surged forth against the landlords and the capitalists? In order to remove any doubts about his position, Martynov explicitly argued that 'what was now being resolved via workers' strikes and spontaneous movements of the peasants should instead be resolved by government legislation and commissions of arbitration.'[23]

Of course, it would be both incorrect and ahistorical to simply equate Stalin's doctrine of revolution by stages with Menshevism *tout court*. But the affinity between their strategic conceptions is undeniable, despite Stalin's ritualistic evocations of Bolshevik tradition. Thus, it was no accident that it was precisely the same Martynov who had twenty years before so vehemently defended Menshevik stagism who became an official mouthpiece for Comintern policy, while the exiled Menshevik leader Dan wholeheartedly supported him from afar. Writing in a bulletin of the expatriate Mensheviks published in Switzerland, Dan commented: 'On April 10, Martynov, in *Pravda*, most effectively and, despite the obligatory

[22]Martynov, 'Le rôle du PC chinois' (1927), in Broué, pp. 116-7. In 1902-3 Martynov was one of the leaders of the so-called 'economist' wing of Russian Social Democracy which Lenin attacked in *What Is To Be Done?* He was also the author of a Menshevik pamphlet in 1905 (*The Two Revolutions*) which also fell under Lenin's severe polemical censure for its advocacy of an alliance with the bourgeoisie. He may, thus, be considered as one of the most coherent advocates of the Menshevik doctrine of the bouregois-democratic stage in Russia. He joined the Communist Party after the initiation of the NEP and immediately joined the polemic against Trotsky and the Left Opposition.
[23]Ibid., p. 118.

abuse of the Social Democracy, in a quite "Menshevik manner" showed the "left" Oppositionist Radek the correctness of the *official* position, which insists on the necessity of retaining the "bloc of four classes", on not hastening to overthrow the coalition government in which the workers sit side-by-side with the big bourgeoisie, not to impose "socialist tasks" upon it prematurely.'[24]

On March 21 1927 the communist workers of Shanghai seized power and opened the city to the 'Northern Expedition' of Chiang Kai-shek. There were insistent rumours of an impending alliance between Chiang and the reactionary warlords against the communists. Yet on March 30 the official bulletin of the ECCI in Moscow declared: 'A split in the Kuomintang and hostilities between the Shanghai proletariat and the revolutionary soldiers are absolutely excluded right now. . . . A revolutionist like Chiang Kai-shek will not ally himself, as the imperialists would like one to believe, with the counter-revolutionary Chang Tso-lin to struggle against the emancipation movement.'[25] Was this just a propaganda manoeuvre by the Comintern for external consumption, or did its leadership actually believe this? At a meeting of functionaries in the Hall of Columns in Moscow on April 5, Stalin argued: 'Why drive away the Right [of the Kuomintang] when we have the majority and when the Right listens to us? . . . When the Right is of no more use to us, we will drive it away. At present, we need the Right. It has capable people, who still direct the army and lead it against the imperialists. Chiang Kai-shek has perhaps no sympathy for the revolution but he is leading the army and *cannot do otherwise than lead it against the imperialists.*'[26] According to the testimony of Chen Tu-hsiu, at that time the General Secretary of the Chinese Communist Party, the Comintern sent him a telegram instructing the Party to bury the weapons of the workers in Shanghai before the arrival of Chiang's troops in order to avoid possible confrontations.[27] When Chiang entered Shanghai on April 12, he immediately allied with the warlord Chang Tso-lin to crush the revolutionary workers. In a reign of terror thousands of trade unionists and communists were executed; some by being thrown alive into

---

[24]*Sotsialistichesky Vestnik*, 23 April 1927, p. 4, quoted by Trotsky, 'The Chinese Revolution and the Theses of Comrade Stalin' (7 May 1927), in *Leon Trotsky On China*, New York 1976, p. 165.

[25]*Inprekorr*, 30 March 1927, quoted by Harold Isaacs, *The Tragedy of the Chinese Revolution*, Stanford 1961, p. 160—my emphasis.

[26]Quoted by Isaacs p. 162—my emphasis.

[27]Ibid, p. 163. One can find an interesting literary presentation of the debates between a Comintern emissary (Vologin) expressing Stalin's views and some revolutionary Chinese communists in André Malraux, *Man's Estate*, Harmondsworth 1961, pp. 126-48.

the boilers of the army's locomotives. It was the beginning of the end of the Second Chinese Revolution.

A few weeks after Chiang's April Coup, the 'left wing' of the Kuomintang under the leadership of Wang Chin-wei seceded and set up a coalition government with communist participation in Wuhan. Stalin doggedly insisted on the necessity of the Chinese communists remaining within the ('Left') Kuomintang while denying the feasibility of launching workers' or peasants' soviets in China. By advancing the slogan of soviets, he proclaimed, Trotsky 'has confused a bourgeois-democratic revolution with a proletarian revolution. He has "forgotten" that, far from being completed, far from being victorious as yet, the bourgeois-democratic revolution in China is only in its initial stage of development.'[28] Stalin denied that the Bolshevik strategy of 1917 had any relevance for China, since 'Russia at that time was facing a proletarian revolution while China now is facing a bourgeois-democratic revolution.'[29] 'How then', Stalin asked, was '. . . the formation of Soviets of workers' deputies in Russia in 1905 to be understood? Were we not then passing through a bourgeois-democratic revolution?' His answer was quite interesting, revealing with particular acuity the qualitative differences between the new doctrine and the Bolshevik tradition (of 1905 as well as 1917). 'It is possible that there would have been no Soviets in Russia in 1905 if there had been at that time a broad revolutionary organization in Russia, similar to the Left Kuomintang in China today. . . . The Left Kuomintang is performing approximately the same role in the present bourgeois-democratic revolution in China as the Soviets performed in the bourgeois-democratic revolution in Russia in 1905.'[30] Indeed the only historical precedent that Stalin evoked to defend his policy of communist participation in (and subordination to) the Wuhan government was the example of Marx's attitude toward the German liberal bourgeoisie at the *beginning* of the 1848 revolution.[31] Again it is hard to deny the striking resemblance between Stalin's positions and the historical policies of Menshevism. And once again the similarity was ratified by the exiled Menshevik paper, which on May 9 1927 endorsed Stalin's view of the Chinese Revolution: 'If we strip the envelope of words that is obligatory

[28]'The Revolution in China and the Tasks of the Comintern' (24 May 1927), in *On the Opposition*, p. 714.

[29]Ibid., p. 713.

[30]Ibid., p. 715.

[31]'I might refer to the example of Marx himself in 1848, at the time of the German revolution, when he and his supporters joined the bourgeois-democratic league in Germany.' (Stalin, 'Talk with Students of the Sun Yat-sen University' (13 May 1927), in *On the Opposition*, p. 671.)

for the theses of a communist leader, then very little can be said against the essence of the "line" traced there. As much as possible to remain in the Kuomintang, and to cling to its left wing and to the Wuhan government to the last possible moment. . . .'[32]

The tragic course of events that followed is well-known: A few months later, in July 1927, the 'Left' Kuomintang of Wang Chin-wei, which was supposed to play 'approximately the same role' as the 1905 Soviets, and the Wuhan government, which Stalin considered as the 'centre of the revolutionary movement in China' (Speech of May 24 1927), broke with the communists and quickly achieved reconciliation with Chiang. Once again thousands of revolutionary workers and peasants were massacred. How did Stalin and the Comintern leadership explain such a catastrophic defeat? Absolving himself and the ECCI of all blame, Stalin declared that 'the task was to make the Wuhan Kuomintang the centre of the fight against counter-revolution. . . . Was that policy correct? The facts have shown that it was the only correct policy. . . .'[33] Responsibility for the defeat was shifted, instead, exclusively onto the Chinese communists; the official proclamation of the ECCI castigated the 'opportunist errors of the Central Committee of the Chinese Communist Party'.[34] According to all surviving testimony, however, the Chinese communist leadership did nothing more than to faithfully execute the very precise instructions which they received from Comintern delegates and Russian advisors. Moreover, these instructions repeated the same insistent themes: 'Submit to the Kuomintang. Don't divide the "anti-imperialist" bloc.' According to Chen Tu-hsiu, when the Chinese communists in 1926 wanted to keep five thousand rifles from the Soviet shipments to Chiang's troops to arm workers' militias, the Comintern delegate flatly refused and added, 'the present period is a period in which the communists should do the coolie service for the Kuomintang.'[35]

What were Trotsky's views on the correct strategic orientation for the Second Chinese Revolution (1926-7)? Already in the period before Chiang's coup of April 1925, a number of clear-cut differences opposed Trotsky to the dominant Stalin-Bukharin-Martynov line.

(1) *The alliance with the Kuomintang*: As we have already seen, Trotsky voted against the Chinese communists joining the Kuomintang in 1923. In 1926

---

[32]*Sotsialistichesky Vestnik*, 9 May 1927, in *On China*, pp. 196-7.
[33]'Plenum of the CC of the CPSU(B)' (1 August 1927), *On the opposition*, p. 788.
[34]Quoted by Isaacs, pp. 266-7.
[35]Ch'en Tu-hsiu, 'Appeal to All the Comrades of the Chinese Communist Party' (10 December 1929), Appendix to *On China*, p. 601.

he again reiterated the necessity for the full political and organizational independence of the Chinese Communist Party.[36]

(2) *The national bourgeoisie*: Trotsky had no illusions about the 'revolutionary' nature of the Chinese national bourgeoisie; in his opinion, 'the section of the Chinese bourgeoisie which still participates in the Kuomintang' was, in the last analysis, 'an auxiliary detachment of the compradorian bourgeoisie and of the foreign imperialists.'[37] Moreover, he rejected the Stalin-Martynov theory of a national-bourgeois stage under Kuomintang leadership as a typically Menshevik conception.

(3) *The question of soviets*: For Trotsky the struggle for workers, peasants and soldiers soviets was the correct alternative to dependence upon the Kuomintang. In a letter to the Politbureau on March 31 1927, he stressed that the task of 'forming soviets of the working and exploited masses . . . cannot be postponed any longer'.[38]

(4) *The immediate danger of a right-wing coup by the Kuomintang leadership*: Trotsky repeatedly warned against any illusions about the Nationalist military top brass. In his letters to the Politbureau, he emphasized that in the Kuomintang's National Army 'the officer cadre . . . is characterized by bourgeois and landlord origins and by sympathies tending to favour these same classes.' He pointed to the impending danger of a Bonapartist military coup: 'Will anyone wish to deny that in the staff of the Kuomintang its own Pilsudski will be found? They will. Candidates can already be designated.'[39] At the same time he reminded the Russian leadership that 'there is no more effective measure for countering such dangers than the establishment of soldiers sections of the soviets.' In the absence of such revolutionary measures, he predicted with uncanny precision (March 22 1927) the collapse of the Comintern's opportunist strategy: 'The concept is Menshevik through and through. . . . And of course, we will fall flat on our face at the very first turn. This turn will in all likelihood be the occupation of Shanghai.'[40] A bare three weeks later, on April 12, the 'turn' took place as Chiang's legions slaughtered the Shanghai workers.

[36]*On China*, pp. 113-20. The editors show (pp. 22-3) that authors such as Isaac Deutscher and E. H. Carr have been mistaken in suggesting that Trotsky did not consistently oppose the Kuomintang alliance until March or April 1923.
[37]'Class Relations in the Chinese Revolution' (3 April 1927), in *On China*, p. 145.
[38]Ibid., p. 134.
[39]Ibid., pp. 134, 144.
[40]Ibid., p. 126.

Subsequently, after the establishment of the coalition government between Communists and the 'Left' Kuomintang in Wuhan (Hankow), Trotsky delivered another prophetic warning to the Plenum of the ECCI (May): 'The leading Kuomintang people in Hankow, the likes of Wang Ching-wei and Company, are beginning to become involved with the bourgeoisie, holding back the agrarian movement, and the workers movement, and if they do not succeed in holding these back, they will unite with Chiang Kai-shek against the workers and peasants. Those who, under these conditions, oppose soviets and are for subordination to the Kuomintang, i.e. to Wang Ching-wei, are preparing the way for a new, perhaps even more serious defeat for the Chinese revolution.'[41] Two months later, as we have seen, Wang unleashed a new white terror against the Chinese communists and the popular movement.

Trotsky's foresight, the accuracy of his predictions and the strategic truth of his warnings are unquestionable. But at the same time he did not yet have an adequate understanding of the class dynamics and historical character of the Chinese revolution. His break with the stagist conceptions of Stalin and the ECCI remained incomplete; as late as March 1927, for example, he still considered that 'in China what is occurring is a national-democratic revolution, not a socialist one', and that soviet power in China would not be 'an instrument of proletarian dictatorship, but of revolutionary national liberation and democratic unification of the country'.[42] He still conceived the future popular power in China in accordance with the 'old Bolshevik' slogan (which he had rejected in 1905 as inapplicable for Russia) of the 'democratic dictatorship of the proletariat and the peasantry'. Although he did not totally exclude the hypothesis of socialist revolutionary development in China, he argued—in a very one-sided and awkward formulation—that 'the possibility of the democratic revolution growing over into the socialist revolution—depends completely and exclusively on the course of the World revolution, and on the economic and political successes of the Soviet Union.'[43]

Now, Trotsky could not consistently, nor for a long time, advocate ideas that were so blatantly opposed to the perspective he had developed since 1905 to characterize the revolutionary process in Russia. And indeed a few months later, in September 1927, he clearly abandoned any remnant of a stagist framework in regard to China: '. . . for us it is no longer a question of the democratic dictatorship of the proletariat and the peasantry, but of

[41]'Statement to the Plenum of the ECCI' (May 1927), in *On China*, p. 217 (see also p. 248).
[42]*On China*, p. 135.
[43]'Class Relations in the Chinese Revolution', in *On China*, p. 143.

the dictatorship of the proletariat supported by the inexhaustible masses of urban and rural poor—a dictatorship that poses for itself the objective of solving *the most* urgent and vital problems of the country and its working masses, and in the process inevitably passes over to the path of making socialist inroads on property relations.'[44] This new formulation, explicitly permanentist, was beyond the theoretical and political horizon of most of the leadership of the Left Opposition, some of whom, like Preobrazhensky, reproached Trotsky for ignoring the extreme backwardness of China's economic development. In reply, Trotsky, evoking the precedent of Lenin's polemic against Sukhanov, stressed the methodological implications of the debate. 'The gist of the matter lies precisely in the fact that although the political mechanics of the revolution depend in the *last analysis* upon an economic base (not only national but international) they cannot, however, be deduced with abstract logic from this economic base.'[45]

While the policies imposed by Stalin were leading the Chinese urban proletariat to disaster, a young and unknown communist leader, Mao Tse-tung, was organizing—largely in defiance of Comintern directives—a radical peasants' movement in Hunan province. It is interesting to note the attitude of the Left Opposition to his new and promising beginning. Under the heading, 'The Sure Road', Trotsky wrote an article in May 1927 on the Hunan movement, where he observed that 'the workers and peasants of Hunan are showing the way out of the vacillations, and by that, the road to save the revolution.'[46] And a few months later, Victor Serge, a leading oppositionist and friend of Trotsky's, wrote an enthusiastic review of Mao's article on the Hunan peasant movement: 'I have read many things on the Chinese revolution, but I have found nothing in communist analysis more impressive than that of a young and unknown militant, Mao Tse-tung. . . . If the other leaders of the Chinese revolutions had been inspired by as clear a conception as his of the class struggle, than all victories would have been possible. Alas!'[47]

After 1927 the doctrine of revolution by stages and of the bloc of four classes were generalized and applied in different forms and variants, to all backward, dependent, colonial or semi-colonial countries. But its first 'universal' formulation—in the 1928 *Draft Programme* of the Comintern—was not very typical because it was elaborated as part of the Comintern's 'Third Period' (1928-33) turn toward mechanical leftism, and, therefore,

[44]'New Opportunities for the Chinese Revolution' (September 1927) in *On China*, p. 266.
[45]'Third Letter to Preobrazhensky' (March-April 1928), in *On China*, p. 286.
[46]*On China*, p. 208.
[47]Victor Serge, *La révolution chinoise, 1927-29*, Paris 1977, pp. 75-6.

had a radical tone which would disappear after the middle 1930s. Even Trotsky in his severe critique of the *Draft* (which Bukharin had written) described it as 'eclectic through and through' rather than as completely opportunist.[48] Indeed, compared to the quasi-Menshevik categories that the ECCI had applied to China in 1927, the *Draft* appeared as a partial return to Bolshevism *circa* 1905: the struggle for workers' and peasants' soviets, the democratic dictatorship of the proletariat and the peasantry, the denunciation of the treason of the national bourgeoisie of the colonial countries, etc. Yet a careful reading of the document reveals the persistence of an underlying stagist conception and its inherent continuity with the 1927 line. First of all, the *Draft Programme* denied the validity of '1917 Bolshevism' (i.e. of the *April Theses*) for the colonial and semi-colonial countries. The rationalization for this distinction was principally *economic*: the 'unequal maturity of capitalism in the different countries'. Thus Russia before 1917 was classified as a country with 'half developed capitalism' and a 'minimum of industry', conditions which permitted a 'quick transformation of the bourgeois-democratic revolution into a socialist revolution'. By contrast, in colonial and semi-colonial nations such as India and China, where 'feudal-medieval relations predominate in the economic life of the country as well as in its political super-structure', 'the passage to the dictatorship of the proletariat is possible only by a series of preparatory stages. . . .'[49]

Not only was this thesis about the predominance of feudal relation of production in countries such as India or China highly debatable on purely empirical grounds, but it also revealed something essential about the method of Bukharin and Stalin. It testified to the resurgent *economism*, which, in a manner reminiscent of Plekhanovite-Menshevik Marxism, attempted to deduce directly the capacity of the proletariat to seize power from the degree of industrialization and the 'maturity' of capitalism.[50] Thus the *Draft Programme* seemed to believe that the formula of the 'democratic dictatorship of the proletariat and the peasantry' flowed necessarily from the level of economic and industrial development; while, at the same time, through its ambiguity it opened the door for alliances with bourgeois forces rebaptized as 'peasant parties' (like the Kuomintang in 1926). As a matter of fact, the *Draft Programme* admitted the possibility of 'temporary

[48]*The Permanent Revolution*, p. 157.

[49]*Projet de programme de l'Internationale Communiste*, 1928, Supplement of *Internationale Communiste* (15 June 1928), pp. 27-8.

[50]Althusser is correct to stress that economism was one of the decisive tenets of Stalinism, but wrong to consider Stalinism as a primarily ideological 'deviation'. See *Essays in Self-Criticism*, London 1976, p. 88-9.

agreements' with the national bourgeoisie in colonial and semi-colonial countries 'insofar as the bourgeoisie does not obstruct the revolutionary organization of the workers and peasants and wages a genuine struggle against imperialism'.[51]

With the adoption of the popular front strategy in the mid-1930s, and the discarding of Third Period rhetoric, the stagist character of the Comintern's strategic policy in the dependent capitalist countries became gloriously explicit. From the Seventh World Congress (1935) through the dissolution of the Comintern (1943) until the present day, this 'general line' has gone through various 'left' and 'right' turns, and assumed various forms (popular front, national union, democratic alliance, etc.), but the basic strategy has remained the same. To chart the application of this strategy in different national contexts is beyond the scope of this book; besides, most of the national experiences and theorizations do not add anything decisively new to the doctrine elaborated in the late 1920s. The exceptions, of course, (which I will consider later) are those communist parties who in practice—and to a certain extent in theory—departed from the 'general line' and forged autonomous revolutionary paths: China, Vietnam, Yugoslavia and Cuba.

In his 1928 book, *The Permanent Revolution*, Trotsky presented his views on the dynamics of social revolution in the colonial and semi-colonial countries for the first time in a systematic, coherent and rigorous way as a theory that encompassed global historical developments and claimed a *universal*—and not only Russian or Chinese—significance and validity. Nevertheless, this text has some undoubted shortcomings in its form of exposition. First, it was an answer to a 'non-book' by Radek: a 'non-book' in the double sense that it was never published and was known only to a very small circle of Russian oppositionists, and that it did not contain any theoretical insights that justified such an extended polemical response. Second, Trotsky's main critical thrust was directed against the formula of the 'democratic dictatorship of the proletariat and the peasantry'—a slogan that was soon abandoned by the Stalinized Comintern. Third, the book gave far more attention to the Russian experience (and to an exhaustive exegesis of Lenin's views) than to the concrete problems of the revolution in the colonial and semi-colonial world (which became central only in the last section). These flaws notwithstanding, however, *The Permanent Revolution* remains one of the most seminal and consequential works of Marxist political thought in

---

[51]*Projet de Programme de l'IC*, p. 38. A similar formula had been employed by Lenin in 1920.

the twentieth century. But to attain a full and accurate understanding of the many facets of Trotsky's theory, one needs to 'complete' the theses of *The Permanent Revolution* with ideas and arguments developed in other writings—contemporary or posterior—concerning the problems of class struggle in areas of peripheral capitalism.

It is noteworthy that after the end of the 1920s Trotsky never really *systematically* returned to the subject again. To understand why not, one has to remember that after the defeat of the second Chinese revolution in 1927-8 there were no further *major* upheavals on an equivalent scale in the colonial world during Trotsky's lifetime. Certainly the Vietnamese soviets and the Chinese Long March of the 1930s were important events, but they were not processes with a global impact and, thus, never impinged commensurately on Trotsky's political awareness. As a result, Trotsky probably never felt the political exigency to produce a further theorization of permanent revolution in the colonial theatre. Instead his subsequent writings were principally focused on either the USSR or the imperialist countries of the West (Germany, France, Spain[52] and the United States). But one can find, scattered here and there in his later texts, commentary on events in China, India, and Mexico which afford some valuable suggestions that enrich and extend the concepts of the 1928 book.

It is most likely that Trotsky's generalization of the theory of permanent revolution to the entire colonial and semi-colonial (or ex-colonial) world was catalysed by the dramatic upsurge of the Chinese class struggle in 1925-7, much as his original formulation of the theory was prompted by the Russian revolution of 1905. Already in June 1928, in the chapter on 'Summary and Perspectives of the Chinese Revolution' of his book *The Third International After Lenin*, he argued that the lessons from China were significant for all the countries of Asia (Africa and Latin America were still outside his range of interest). In his view the Chinese events confirmed the conclusions drawn from the two Russian revolutions and revealed the fundamental similarities between Russia, China and the other 'Oriental' (i.e. colonial and semi-colonial) countries: the indissoluble dependence of the national bourgeoisie upon imperialism and the landowners, the political weight of the proletariat (disproportionate to its actual numerical strength), the impossibility of the peasantry playing an autonomous politi-

---

[52]The Spanish revolution of the 1930s was an intermediate case: it could have been analysed from the angle of permanent revolution as well as within the context of the debate over the Popular Front. Trotsky's writings on Spain contain a few illuminating remarks on the dialectics between democratic (or national, as in Catalonia) struggle and socialist revolution, but his main focus was on the problematic of the Popular Front.

cal role, etc. Moreover, the very *historical reality* of the Russian revolution had become, in his opinion, an enormously powerful stimulant toward a permanentist course, since it encouraged the indigenous proletariat to follow the example of October and, one could add, simultaneously reinforced the conservative tendencies of the local bourgeoisie and its fear of popular mobilization.

However, Trotsky's universalization of the theory of permanent revolution was not only the result of an inductive reasoning from the Russian and Chinese experiences. It was also grounded on a general theory of the socioeconomic dynamics of the historical process (the law of uneven and combined development) and on a rather condensed analysis of the role of the main classes in the colonial and semi-colonial societies which he developed between 1928 and 1930.

Unquestionably the most general historical-theoretical foundation of the theory of permanent revolution was the *law of uneven and combined development*. Although, as we have seen, this conception was already implicit in the theses of *Results and Prospects*, its full, explicit elaboration awaited the first chapter of the *History of the Russian Revolution* (1930). A new understanding of human history is the point of departure for the formulation of the law: with the appearance of capitalism as a world system, world history becomes a (contradictory) concrete *totality* and the conditions of socioeconomic development undergo a qualitative change. 'Capitalism . . . prepares and in a certain sense realizes the universality and permanence of man's development. By this a repetition of the forms of development by different nations is ruled out. Although compelled to follow after the advanced countries, a backward country does not take things in the same order.' Backward societies are allowed, or rather compelled, to adopt some advanced features, skipping intermediate stages: 'Savages throw away their bows and arrows for rifles all at once, without travelling the road which lay between those two weapons in the past. . . . The development of historically backward nations leads necessarily to a peculiar combination of different stages in the historic process.' This more complex perspective enabled Trotsky to transcend the evolutionist conception of history as a succession of rigidly predetermined stages, and to develop a dialectical view of historical development through sudden leaps and contradictory fusions. 'Unevenness, the most general law of the historic process, reveals itself most sharply and complexly in the destiny of the backward countries. Under the whip of external necessity, their backward culture is compelled to make leaps. From the universal law of uneveness thus derives another law which, for the lack of a better name, we may call the law of *combined development*—by which we mean a drawing together of the different stages of the journey, a combining of separate steps, an amalgam of archaic with more contemporary forms.'[53] (Once again one can see the central place that the methodological category of *totality* occupied in Trotsky's theoretical constructions and in his interpretation of historical materialism.)

There is little need to stress the obvious political and strategic conclusions that flow from the law of uneven and combined development: the articulation of modern industry with traditional (pre-capitalist or semi-capitalist) rural conditions, creating the objective possibility for the leading role of the proletariat at the head of the rebellious peasant masses. Thus the amalgam of backward and advanced socio-economic conditions becomes the structural foundation for the fusion or combination of democratic and socialist tasks in a process of permanent revolution.[54] Or, to put it in a different way, one of the most important political consequences of uneven and combined development is the unavoidable persistence of unresolved *democratic tasks* in the peripheral capitalist countries. Despite the claims of his critics, Trotsky never denied the democratic dimension of revolution in backward countries nor did he ever pretend that the revolution would be 'purely socialist'; what he did repudiate, however, was the

---

[53]*History of the Russian Revolution*, vol. I, pp. 22-3.

[54]A coherent and rigorous stagist conception of revolution in backward countries implies, therefore, a critical confrontation with Trotsky's theory of uneven and combined development. Such an attempt has been made recently by David J. Romagnolo, an advocate of Mao's (and Stalin's) doctrine of alliance with the national bourgeoisie during the democratic, anti-imperialist stage of revolution. (See his essay, 'The So-called Law of Uneven and Combined Development', *Latin American Perspectives*, II, 4 [Spring 1975].) According to Romagnolo, Trotsky's theory of the global extension of capitalism was, indeed, based on Marx's writings. But he argues that whereas it was true in Marx's lifetime that capitalism in its competitive phase can and does begin to develop in backward areas', after Marx's death, imperialism as an outgrowth of monopoly capitalism, 'arrests' or 'retards' the development of capitalism in colonial and semi-colonial nations (pp. 23-4, 27). Since no sources are mentioned, one wonders where Romagnolo obtained the extraordinary impression that capitalism had developed less in countries such as Brazil or Argentina (to take two examples) during the twentieth century (the era of imperialism) than during the nineteenth (the era of competitive capitalism). According to the author, 'like merchant capital, finance capital comes to backward countries from the outside and exploits its primitive forms through trade and large scale money-lending' (p. 26). This way of defining imperialism is very peculiar since it ignores the central role of foreign *investment*. Of course, it is necessary to ignore productive industrial investment if one wishes to prove, like Romagnolo, that imperialism is 'retarding the extensive as well as intensive development of capitalism in colonial and semi-colonial countries', or that 'far from innundating the oppressed areas with capitalist relations of production, imperialism sustains the primitive forms of exploitation' (p. 27). His reasoning is a perfect example of an undialectical methodology. Either the forms of exploitation are 'primitive' or they are capitalist; he obstinately refuses to consider the possibility of a fusion or combination between 'primitive' and capitalist forms. Thus his thoroughly dualistic approach is the logical consequence of his rejection of the law of uneven and combined development.

dogma of bourgeois-democratic revolution as a *separate historical stage* that *has to be completed before the proletarian struggle for power can commence*. The democratic tasks solved by the advanced capitalist countries of Europe and North America are well-known: abolition of autocracy, liquidation of feudal (or pre-capitalist) survivals in the agrarian relations of production, the establishment of parliamentary democracy based on universal (male) suffrage, national unification and/or liberation. The democratic tasks in backward and dependent countries of the twentieth century are similar, but not identical, since the existence of imperialism creates a new historical configuration. According to Trotsky—if one tries to systematize his scattered remarks on the question—these tasks comprise above all:

(1) *The agrarian democratic revolution*: The bold and definitive abolition of all residues of slavery, feudalism and 'Asiatic despotism'; the liquidation of all pre-capitalist forms of exploitation (*corvée*, forced labour, etc.); and the expropriation of the great landowners and the distribution of the land to the peasantry.[55]

(2) *National liberation*: the unification of the nation and its emancipation from imperialist domination; the creation of a unified national market and its protection from cheaper foreign goods; the control of certain strategic natural resources; etc.[56]

(3) *Democracy*: for Trotsky this included not only the establishment of democratic freedoms, a democratic republic and the end of military rule, but also the creation of the social and cultural conditions for popular participation in political life by the reduction of the working day to eight hours and through universal public education.[57]

Since it must solve these problems, the revolutionary process in countries of dependent or peripheral capitalism can be defined, to a certain extent, as democratic or even bourgeois-democratic, since these demands do not transcend the limits of bourgeois society. But this in no way entails the leading role of the bourgeoisie in the democratic struggle nor does it prevent the revolution from going beyond capitalism—'I never denied the *bourgeois* character of the revolution in the sense of its immediate tasks, but only in the sense of its driving forces and its perspectives.'[58] Indeed, it was

[55]Trotsky, 'Sobre el segundo plan mexicano de seis anos' (1939), in Trotsky, *Sobre la liberación nacional*, Bogata 1976, pp. 109-11.
[56]The main examples mentioned by Trotsky are China in the 1920s and Mexico in the 1930s. Cf. *On China*, p. 299 and *Writings 1938-39*, New York 1969, pp. 84-99.
[57]*Writings 1930-1*, New York 1973, pp. 31-2, 136.
[58]*The Permanent Revolution*, p. 56.

precisely the question of the 'driving forces' of the revolution that first drove Trotsky into such radical opposition to the reborn stagism of the Comintern from 1926 onwards. According to Trotsky, the postulation of a 'revolutionary' bourgeoisie in the colonial countries, which is at the root of the strategy of the 'bloc of four classes', only 'reproduces inside out the fundamental error of Menshevism, which held that the revolutionary nature of the Russian bourgeoisie must flow from the oppression of feudalism and the autocracy'.[59] In reality uneven and combined development tends to lead to the contradictory combination/articulation of the international and national, modern and traditional, ruling classes. For example, in China, 'while at the bottom, in the agrarian base of the Chinese economy, the bourgeoisie is organically and unbreakably linked with feudal forms of exploitation, at the top it is just as organically and unbreakably linked with world finance. The Chinese bourgeoisie cannot on its own break free either from agrarian feudalism or from foreign imperialism.'[60] This did not mean that there could not exist contradictions either between the national bourgeoisie and imperialism, or the bourgeoisie and the landlords. Certainly the Chinese bourgeoisie in 1925-7, for instance, was interested in enlarging its domestic markets through moderate land reforms and in achieving greater economic autonomy *vis-a-vis* imperialism. But, as Trotsky added, one must never for an instant forget that 'its conflicts with the most reactionary feudal militarists and its collisions with the international imperialists always take second place at the decisive moment to its irreconcilable antagonism to the poor workers and peasants.'[61] Needless to say, this is a rule that transcended the Chinese case.

The democratic revolutionary victory over imperialism and the landowners could only come about through a mass upheaval, immense popular mobilization and violent explosions—all of which would soon seem menacing to the national bourgeoisie. Confronted with such a threat to its privileges, the indigenous bourgeoisie would tend to opt for a more moderate and conciliatory policy towards foreign capital and domestic reaction. Rather than a popular revolution, the bourgeoisie would always prefer '*the Bismarckian way*', a non-revolutionary path for satisfying its class aspirations.[62] It must be emphasized that Trotsky never denied that such a route might allow the national bourgeoisie, in collaboration with imperial-

[59]*On China*, p. 295.

[60]Ibid., p. 403.

[61]Ibid., pp. 299, 403.

[62]Ibid., pp. 297-8. Trotsky refers to bourgeois attitudes during the 1848-71 period as an example of such an orientation.

ism, to achieve a certain degree of industrialization,[63] or that the bourgeoisie was *a priori* incapable of implementing *any* of the democratic tasks. What he did insist upon, rather, was the limited, half-hearted and frequently *ephemeral* character of such 'progress'. Reforms in this mode would be 'wretched, unstable and niggardly' like the Kuomintang's nationalism in China, they would achieve only 'very partial results', and eventually the 'revolution' would be halted and reversed like the 1906-7 aftermath in Russia.[64] In other circumstances a national bourgeoisie might be forced to wage a war of national liberation against colonial or imperialist occupation, but characteristically it would only do so at the service of another, more flexible imperialist power—as, for example, in the 1930s. 'Chiang Kai-shek struggles against the Japanese violators only within the limits indicated to him by his British or American patrons.'[65] In short: a *complete and genuine* solution to the national and democratic tasks in the countries of peripheral capitalism would be impossible under the leadership of the national bourgeoisie.[66]

Once again, this did not imply that the national bourgeoisie could not, under intense popular pressure, move to the left (generally followed by sharp turns to the right and brutal repression against the workers and peasants) and that purely tactical agreements with it for precise and limited aims might not be useful to the popular movement. What Trotsky clearly rejected was the perspective of long-term (strategic, programmatic or governmental) agreements, or 'class blocs', even if limited, as in the *Draft Programme* of the Comintern, by the condition that the national bourgeoisie 'does not obstruct the revolutionary organization of the workers and peasants, and wages a genuine struggle against imperialism'. In contrast, Trotsky asserted that the main 'condition' for limited and temporary agreements with bourgeois forces was 'in not believing for an instant in the

[63]See for instance his remarks on the possibility of industrial development in India: 'In the near future the antagonism between the Indian masses and the bourgeoisie promises to become sharper as the imperialist war more and more becomes a gigantic commercial enterprise for the Indian bourgeoisie. By opening up an exceptionally favourable market for raw materials it may rapidly promote Indian industry.' ('Manifesto of the Fourth International on the Imperialist War and the Proletarian World Revolution' [1940], in *Writings 1939-40*, p. 39.)
[64]*The Permanent Revolution*, p. 132.
[65]*On China*, p. 585.
[66]See *Permanent Revolution*, p. 152. Sometimes Trotsky formulated this idea in a very sharp and one-sided manner, as, for example, when he wrote that 'the independence of a backward state inevitably will be semi-fictious and its political regime, under the influence of internal class contradictions, and external pressure, will unavoidably fall into dictatorship against the people—such is the regime of the 'People's' Party in Turkey, the Kuomintang in China; Gandhi's regime will be similar tomorrow in India' (Trotsky, 'Manifesto of the Fourth International', *Writings 1939-40*, p. 39.)

capacity or readiness of the bourgeoisie either to lead a *genuine* struggle against imperialism or *not to obstruct* the workers and peasants'.[67]

In 1938, after his arrival in Mexico and during the presidency of Lazaro Cardenas, Trotsky found himself confronted with a new phenomenon: the Bonapartist and semi-Bonapartist regimes in backward or dependent countries, which can have a relatively progressive policy in relation to the agrarian and national questions for a limited period of time. For him, this development did not contradict the idea of the weakness and unrevolutionary character of the national bourgeoisie, but was, in fact, an expression of it: the relationship of forces between classes in the dependent countries 'creates special conditions of state power. The government veers between foreign and domestic capital, between the weak national bourgeoisie and the relatively powerful proletariat. This gives the government a Bonapartist character *sui-generis*. . . . It raises itself, so to speak, above classes.'[68] This conception of Bonapartism although insufficiently developed, was probably one of Trotsky's most fruitful intuitions and an important contribution to grasping the specificity of a series of 'national-populist' regimes, which have emerged, especially after the Second World War, in Africa and Latin America. (We shall return to this in the last chapter.) As a revolutionary tactic in relation to such regimes, Trotsky proposed to support any *direct* fight against imperialism and the landowners and any *concrete* step against them (expropriations, etc.) without giving any political support to the national bourgeoisie or the government, and without ceasing for one moment to struggle atainst them for leadership of the popular (peasant) masses.[69]

Refusing to recognize the national bourgeoisie as a revolutionary class, Trotsky insisted that only the proletariat and the peasantry could act as the driving forces of a democratic revolution. What would the respective roles and position of the two classes be? One of the most typical accusations of

[67]*On China*, p. 292. For Trotsky, 'purely practical agreements, such as do not bind us in the least and do not oblige us to anything politically, can be concluded with the devil himself if that is advantageous at a given moment. But it would be absurd in such a case to demand that the devil should *generally* become converted to Christianity, and that he use his horns not against workers and peasants but exclusively for pious deeds. In presenting such conditions we act in reality as the devil's advocates. . . .' (Ibid., pp. 292-3).

[68]'Nationalized Industry and Worker's Management' (1938), *Writings 1938-39*, p. 87.

[69]See 'A Discussion with Trotsky on Latin American Questions', *Intercontinental Press* (12 May 1975), p. 668.

Stalin and his followers against Trotsky was his supposed 'denial', 'ignorance' or 'neglect' of the peasantry. Already in 1924 Stalin had proclaimed *urbi et orbi* that Trotsky 'simply forgot all about the peasantry as a revolutionary force and advanced the slogan of "no Tsar, but a workers' government", that is the slogan of a revolution without the peasantry.'[70] By simply showing that he had, in fact, never proposed such a slogan (which in reality had been coined by Parvus) and that he had consistently emphasized in all his earlier writings the necessity of a workers' and peasants' alliance (whatever his misgivings on the future of such an alliance in power, Trotsky had little difficulty in refuting this criticism.[71] When he universalized the theory of permanent revolution in the late 1920s as a strategy for all the areas of peripheral capitalism, Trotsky continued to stress the decisive role of the peasantry in any real revolutionary process. 'Not only the agrarian, but also the national question assigns to the peasantry—the overwhelming majority of the population in backward countries—an exceptional place in the democratic revolution. Without an alliance of the proletariat with the peasantry the tasks of democratic revolution cannot be solved, nor even seriously posed.'[72] What Trotsky denied was not the crucial weight of the peasantry in the revolution, but its capability of playing an independent political role and of becoming an independent ruling class. In his view the intermediate character and social heterogeneity of the peasantry (and the petty-bourgeoisie) compelled it ultimately to choose between either the bourgeoisie or the proletariat—a choice that usually polarized the upper and lower strata of the peasant 'estate'.[73] Since the national bourgeoisie was incapable of implementing a genuine revolutionary democratic solution of the national and agrarian questions, it became possible for the proletariat, through fierce political struggle against the bourgeoisie, to win over the bulk of the peasant masses and with their support establish a proletarian dictatorship.

As we shall see this conception contained a very deep *political* truth, but if understood in directly *sociological* terms, it was contradicted by the actual course of historical development in China and other dependent countries. For instance, some of Trotsky's writings, particularly the texts on China, conceive of the strategic idea of proletarian hegemony in its immediate

---

[70]*Problems of Leninism*, in *Works*, vol. 6, p. 382.

[71]*Permanent Revolution*, p. 99.

[72]Ibid., pp. 152-3.

[73]Ibid., pp. 69-70, 153-4. This, as we have seen, was a principal divergence between Trotsky and Lenin in 1905-6, which was finally settled by events in 1917.

social meaning as being the urban struggle of the working class, the locomotive of history drawing behind it the insurgent peasantry. Thus, at the very moment when the Chinese communists were establishing a red army and a soviet government in the Kiangsi countryside (1930), Trotsky wrote: 'Only the predominance of the proletariat in the decisive industrial political centres of the country creates the necessary basis for the organization of a red army and for the extension of a soviet system in the countryside.' It is clear that he was transposing the 'classic' paradigm of Russia in 1917 and not grasping the fact that a radically new form of revolutionary process was unfolding in the wake of the 1927-8 defeats of the Chinese proletariat. Indeed, he went so far as to recommend that the Chinese communists should 'not scatter their forces among the isolated flames of the peasant revolt. . . . The communists must concentrate their forces on the factories and the shops and in the workers districts. . . . Only through the process of activating and uniting the workers will the Communist Party be able to assume leadership of the peasant insurrection, that is, of the national revolution as a whole.'[74] This is one of the few instances where Trotsky's views can rightly be adjudged guilty of the error of 'sociologism', and it prevented him from understanding the dynamics of the Chinese revolution after 1928.

This error became even more visible a few years later in his analysis of the *political* nature of the Chinese red army, which he attempted to deduce directly from its *social* composition: 'the fact that individual communists are in the leadership of the present armies does not at all transform the social character of these armies, even if their communist leaders bear definite proletarian stamp . . . the majority of the rank-and-file communists in the red detachments unquestionably consists of peasants, who assume the name communist in all honesty and sincerity but who in actuality remain revolutionary paupers or revolutionary petty proprietors. In politics he who judges by denominations and labels and not by social facts is lost.'[75] In fairness, however, it should be noted that in other writings Trotsky avoided this sociologistic reductionism and interpreted the concept of proletarian leadership in more specifically political terms as the leadership of a *proletarian organization*. For example, in the 'Basic Postulates' that sum up the contents of *The Permanent Revolution* he advanced the idea that 'the realization of the revolutionary alliance between the proletariat and

---

[74]'Manifesto of the International Left Opposition' (1930), *On China*, pp. 480-1.
[75]'Peasant War in China and the Proletariat' (1932), in *On China*, pp. 480-1.

the peasantry is conceivable only under the political leadership of the proletarian vanguard organized in the Communist Party.'[76]

Integral, of course, to this whole discussion of the workers' and peasants' alliance was the question of the precise socio-political nature of the peasant movement. Trotsky's attitudes towards the Chinese peasantry were somewhat ambivalent: on the one hand, he clearly perceived the manifest anti-bourgeois dimension of the peasant insurgency;[77] but on the other hand, he still considered it as a fundamentally petty-bourgeois democratic movement—even when it was led by the Communist Party in the form of the red army.[78] Even more importantly, he did not envisage the possibility of large sections of the peasantry attaining a socialist consciousness before the victory of the proletarian revolution. These questionable assumptions of Trotsky's explain why he almost totally neglected the significance of the red army in his articles on China during the late 1930s and why he did not appreciate the originality of the historical process taking place in the rural areas controlled by the Communist Party. At the same time, it is interesting to note that the Comintern leadership, despite their criticisms of Trotsky for underestimating the role of the peasantry, had a very similar attitude towards the developments in China during the 1930s. For example, the ECCI resolution on China in August 1931 forcefully insisted on 'the need to radically ameliorate the social composition of the party', transforming it into a 'proletarian party not only by its political line but by its composition'. It imperatively proclaimed that 'the party has the obligation to re-establish as soon as possible the lost links with the party groups in the factories', and that 'the best functionaries of the party must be detached to the factory cells.'[80] Even Mao Tse-tung, although empirically prioritizing rural guerrilla warfare, as late as 1930 still insisted that the principal task of

---

[76]*Permanent Revolution*, p. 153.

[77]'The peasants revolt in China, much more than it was in Russia, is a revolt against the bourgeoisie. A class of landowners as a separate class does not exist in China. The landowners and the bourgeoisie are one and the same'. ('Manifesto of the International Left Opposition', in *On China*, p. 482.)

[78]'While we refuse to identify the armed peasant detachment with the red army as the armed power of the proletariat and have no inclination to shut our eyes to the fact that the communist banner hides the petty-bourgeois content of the peasant movement, we on the other hand, take an absolutely clear view of the tremendous revolutionary democratic significance of the peasant war.' ('Peasant War in China', in *On China*, p. 530.)

[79]'Under a proletarian regime, more and more masses of peasants become re-educated in the socialist spirit. But this requires time, years, even decades' (ibid., p. 524).

[80]Helène Carrière d'Encausse and Stuart Schram, *Le Marxisme et l'Asie 1853-1964*, Paris 1965, pp. 342-4.

the Party was its implantation in the factories, the red army and the rural soviets being merely auxiliary elements to the struggle in the cities(!)[81]

It is, thus, possible to see that Trotsky's error was not the result of any particular tendency on his part to 'ignore the peasantry', so much as a result of the classical Marxist view of the peasantry as an atomized and petty-bourgeois class. This conception, of course, had been articulated most vividly by Marx in his writings on France (especially the *Eighteenth Brumaire*), where the peasantry was seen as a 'sack of potatoes', incapable of independent self-organization or social hegemony. Trotsky's mistake—as well as that of most other Western Marxists—was to generalize this conception to the peasantry of the colonial and semi-colonial nations, which had quite different structural characteristics, for example communal or collectivist village traditions, massive uprootedness resulting from capitalist penetration, very high rates of demographic growth, proletarian or semi-proletarian status of rural labourers on the great plantations or haciendas, etc. Moreover, for Russian Marxists especially, the denial of the socialist-revolutionary potential of the peasantry was deeply ingrained since it had been the key issue in the earlier ideological battles with the populists. It was therefore not surprising that Trotsky should have been less perceptive of the specificity of the rural class structure of the non-Western nations than he was of other features of their historical evolution. Nevertheless, in one of his last works—*The Three Conceptions of the Russian Revolution* (1939)—he considered the revision of this traditional Marxist conception of the peasantry: 'The Narodniks saw in the workers and peasants simply "toilers" and the "exploited" who are equally interested in socialism. Marxists regarded the peasant as a petty bourgeois who is capable of becoming a socialist only to the extent to which he ceases materially or spiritually to be a peasant. . . . Along this line occurred for two generations the main struggle between the revolutionary tendencies of Russia. . . . It is, of course, possible to raise the question whether or not the classic Marxist view of the peasantry has been proven erroneous. This subject would lead us far beyond the limits of the present review. Suffice it

---

[81]'The most important organizational tasks of our party are the creation of a proletarian base and the organization of factory cells in the urban centres. At the same time, however, the development of the struggle in the countryside, the creation of small soviet zones and the birth and growth of a Red Army, are also conditions which can aid the struggle in the cities and contribute to the growth of the revolution. This is why it would be a very great error to renounce the struggle in the towns and to relapse into the mentality of rural guerrillas.' (In Stuart Schram, *Mao Tse-tung*, Paris 1963, p. 233. Schram published the original version of this document (a report to the Central Committee of the CCP, 5 April 1929, which differs considerably from its 'official' 1951 abridged re-edition.)

to state here that *Marxism had never invested its estimation of the peasantry as a non-socialist class with an absolute and static character.*[82]

Trotsky's analysis of the social motive forces of revolution in backward countries was complemented by a theory of how the political perspectives of the revolutionary process were also shaped by the action of uneven and combined development. Indeed, as we have already seen, the uninterrupted and combined character of the revolution—its fusion/articulation/overlapping of democratic and socialist tasks—was related to the uneven and combined character of the social relations of production. Writing about China in 1928, Trotsky repeatedly referred to the ties between urban capital and landownership, which determined that 'the agrarian revolution is . . . as much anti-bourgeois as it is anti-feudal in character'.[83] This did not imply, however, that Trotsky mechanically deduced political strategy from the economic structure; on the contrary, he insisted on the specificity and autonomy of the socio-political level. In a letter to Preobrazhensky in 1928, for example, he emphasized that the political process could not be related 'with abstract logic' to the economic base since 'the class struggle and its political expression, unfolding on the economic foundations also *have their own* imperious logic of development.'[84] And it is precisely this 'imperious logic' which drives the national bourgeoisie toward reactionary positions and produces a profound social polarization to divide the intermediate layers. Thus, according to Trotsky, 'between Kerenskyism and the Bolshevik power, between the Kuomintang and the dictatorship of the proletariat, there is not and cannot be any intermediate stage, that is, no democratic dictatorship of the workers and peasants.'[85] The experience of 1917 definitively bolted the door against the slogan of 'democratic dictatorship'. 'With his own hand, Lenin wrote the inscription on the door: No Entrance—No Exit.' During the second Chinese revolution 'the Comintern picked up a formula discarded by him only in order to open the road to the politics of Plekhanov.'[86]

---

[82] In *Writings 1938-39*, pp. 113-4—my emphasis.

[83] 'Summary and Perspectives of the Chinese Revolution' (1928), in *On China*, p. 303.

[84] 'Three Letters to Preobrazhensky', in *On China*, p. 288—my emphasis. Trotsky also insisted that the political dimension was not identical with its class base. This distinction emerged clearly in his critique of Radek's idea that the fundamental issue in the 'democratic dictatorship' was the class correlation and not political institutions. 'Radek has abstracted himself so violently from "political institutions" that he forgets "the most fundamental thing" in a revolution, namely who leads it and who seizes power. A revolution, however, is a struggle for power. It is a political struggle which the classes wage *not* with bare hands but through the medium of "political institutions" (parties, etc.)' (*Permanent Revolution*, p. 80).

[85] *Permanent Revolution*, p. 154.

[86] Ibid., p. 114; and *On China*, p. 587.

The central thesis of stagism as advanced by Stalin, Martynov and the ECCI—'the idea of fixing an order of succession for countries at various levels of development by assigning them in advance cards for different rations of revolutions'—was attacked by Trotsky as a vulgar *evolutionism*, to which he counterposed the dialectical articulation of phases in a process of permanent revolution.[87] While not denying that there could be various episodic stages at the beginning of a revolution, Trotsky stressed that there could be no separate and complete democratic stage, since 'the victory of the democratic revolution is conceivable only through the dictatorship of the proletariat which bases itself upon the alliance with peasantry.' This proletarian power first of all addresses the exigencies of democratic revolution, but very quickly it will be forced to make deep inroads into bourgeois property relations—'the democratic revolution grows over directly into the socialist revolution and thereby becomes a *permanent* revolution'.[88] From a metaphysical, abstract logical viewpoint it might be possible to distinguish two separate stages; but in the actual logic of the revolutionary process they will be organically combined as a dialectical totality.[89] As Trotsky wrote in his Preface to Isaacs' book on China, 'revolutions, as has been said more than once, have a logic of their own. But his is not the logic of Aristotle, and even less the pragmatic semilogic of "common sense". It is the higher function of thought: the logic of development and its contradictions, i.e. the dialectic.'[90] In summary, Trotsky's theory contains two sets of closely interlinked propositions:[91]

(1) A proletarian revolution may take place sooner in a backward than in an advanced country; this proletarian revolution, moreover, will not *follow* the completion of the democratic revolution, but *precede* it and/or combine with it. Under proletarian (communist) leadership and with the support of

---

[87]*Permanent Revolution*, pp. 115, 124.

[88]Ibid., pp. 153-4.

[89]Ibid., pp. 107, 114.

[90]*On China*, p. 581.

[91]For Trotsky, 'the conquest of power by the proletariat does not complete the revolution but only opens it', both on a national and international scale. Moreover, this permanent character of the socialist revolution, this continuity of the revolutionary process after the seizure of power, is valid for the backward as well as for the advanced countries. (See *Permanent Revolution*, pp. 8-9.) Unfortunately, this highly fruitful and suggestive hypothesis is not emphasized or developed by him to the same extent as the other two dimensions of the theory, and it remains quite marginal in his *The Permanent Revolution*. Yet it can be argued that this conception implicitly runs through *The Revolution Betrayed* (1936) where Trotsky examines how the bureaucratic degeneration in Russia paralysed the process of socialist transformation and how the doctrine of socialism in one country became the ideological rationalization of this reactionary practice by proclaiming that socialism had already become established.

the peasantry the democratic revolution will grow over into a socialist revolution.

(2) A radical and consistent democratic revolution is not possible under a non-proletarian (non-communist) leadership. The peasantry and/or the petty bourgeoisie are not capable of pursuing a truly independent policy and cannot therefore assume leadership of the democratic revolution. On the other hand, under the leadership of the national bourgeoisie a *complete* and *genuine solution of the democratic tasks is impossible.*

In Part Two we will discuss the extent to which the history of the twentieth century has confirmed or contradicted these two hypotheses, which constitute the core of the theory of permanent revolution.[92]

[92]There are two other meanings of 'permanent revolution' attributed to Trotsky by his, mainly but not exclusively Stalinist, critics: first, the idea that the revolution is possible at any moment everywhere (a 'permanent possibility' *hic et nunc*); and, second, the principle that the revolution must occur simultaneously all over the world. There is no need to stress that nothing in Trotsky's writing bears the faintest resemblance to these fantastic theses.

4
Conclusions

The idea of permanent revolution only appears in chrysalis in the writings of Marx and Engels: as a series of brilliant but unsystematized intuitions that were largely ignored in the codification of the Marxism of the Second International. It remained for Trotsky in his *Results and Prospects* to develop the first coherent and operational conceptualization of a permanentist problematic that was rigorously grounded in a sweeping historical theory and socio-economic analysis. Trotsky's perspective, as we have seen, was a major theoretical and political breakthrough. In particular, it offered a radical alternative to the economistic and vulgar-evolutionist interpretation of Marxism that was hegemonic in the pre-1917 socialist movement, and whose mechanical and pre-dialectical strategic corollary was the theory of stages. This permanentist strategy prevailed only during the revolutionary high tide of 1917-23 when it informed the practical activities of the Bolshevik Party and the Comintern. After Lenin's death, however, a new variety of stagism became official doctrine because of its congruence with the shortsighted *realpolitik* that increasingly dominated the thinking of the Soviet bureaucracy. In its consistent and thorough application, Stalin's variant of stagism invariably produced tragic defeats for the labour movement; and only those communist parties who in practice went beyond the official limits and pursued an implicitly permanentist line were able to triumph. For their part, those forces that programmatically embraced Trotsky's theory of permanent revolution remained too small to compete as real alternatives in the eyes of the popular masses. (A history of the Fourth International founded by Trotsky in 1938 and its efforts to win the masses in the colonial and semi-colonial countries lies outside the scope of this book.)

The disasters of stagism, it could be argued, provide very significant 'negative tests' for the theory of permanent revolution. While we cannot undertake a systematic historical analysis of all the conjunctures in which Stalinist stagism played a destructive role, it may be useful to attempt a brief résumé of some of the most salient examples.

In inter-war Europe, Spain was perhaps the country that reproduced most the structural features of late Romanov Russia: semi-feudal relations of production in the countryside, oppressed national minorities, an authoritarian state apparatus, and a concentrated, combative proletariat in the big urban centres (Madrid, Seville and Barcelona) and the mining regions (Asturias). However, from 1931 the Comintern insisted upon the necessarily 'bourgeois-democratic' character of the impending Spanish revolution, while denouncing the 'petty-bourgeois anarchism' of sections of the Spanish working class that was 'expressed in a tendency to ignore the stage of bourgeois-democratic revolution'.[1] In 1936 the Comintern further declared that the Popular Front was the concrete expression of this struggle for the completion of the bourgeois-democratic revolution. In a remarkable essay on this period, Fernando Claudin, a former leader of the PCE, shows how the 'hard Comintern team established in Spain' (Togliatti, Codovilla, Geröe, etc.) together with 'the equally hard team of military advisers and Soviet politicians' had the very difficult task of 'nothing less than forcing the proletarian revolution back into the bourgeois democratic framework it "should not have" left. . . . For a start, it was necessary to deny the anti-bourgeois reality of the revolution, so that action aiming to restore bourgeois reality could appear to be something other than what it was.'[2] As is well known, the Soviet-Comintern team, with the help of the PCE, was only too successful in carrying out this arduous mandate. By the end of 1937 'bourgeois reality' had been restored, and all the partisans of a socialist revolution—Trotskyists, left communists of the POUM, anarchists of the CNT and *Caballeristas* in the PSOE—had been politically defeated (and, in some cases, physically liquidated). One year and a few months later, Franco's legionnaires entered Madrid. . . .

Other examples of the disasters of stagism can be found in Latin America; indeed, in no other continent did the communist movement so strictly apply the stagist 'general line' of the Stalinist Comintern. Yet at the same time, rigid and sycophantic adherence to Stalinist doctrine was achieved relatively late; and during the 1920s and early 1930s some of the most

---

[1] Togliatti ('Ercoli'), 'Sulle particularita della rivoluzione spagnola' (1936), in *Sul movimento operaio internazionale*, Rome 1964, p. 196.
[2] Fernando Claudin, 'Spain—The Untimely Revolution', *New Left Review* 74 (July-August 1972), p. 16.

important Latin American communist leaders refused to accept the new orthodoxy and even sympathized with the Left Opposition. For example, José Carlos Mariategui, founder of the Peruvian Communist Party (1928) and one of the most original of Latin American Marxist theoreticians, wrote in 1927: 'There does not exist in Peru, nor has there ever existed, a progressive bourgeoisie with a nationalist sensibility.'[3] Although he did not dispute the adequacy of the Comintern's strategy in China, he refused to apply the same orientation in the Americas. He was, in fact, convinced that 'against capitalist, plutocratic and imperialist North America, one can effectively oppose only a socialist Latin (or Iberian) America. . . . The Latin American countries came too late in the capitalist competition . . . [and] the fate of these countries in the capitalist order is that of simple colonies. . . . The Latin American revolution will be . . . purely and simply a socialist revolution. To this term you may add, according to the circumstances, all the adjectives you wish: "Anti-imperialist", "agrarian", "revolutionary nationalist". Socialism implies, precedes and incorporates all of them.'[4] Similar views were held in the same period by Julio Antonio Mella, the founder of the Cuban Communist Party and its principal ideologue until his murder by henchmen of the Cuban dictator Machado in 1929. Mella argued that 'a complete national liberation will only be obtained by the proletariat through a workers' revolution', and he refused to make alliances with the national bourgeoisie ('this classical betrayer of all national movements for true emancipation').[5] Furthermore, these conceptions did not remain merely theoretical: they provided the strategic impulse for the 1932 revolutionary uprising in El Salvador—the only mass armed insurrection under Communist Party leadership in Latin American history. The aim of the movement, according to the documents and manifestoes of the Party, was the establishment of a government of workers',

---

[3] *Siete ensayos de interpretacion de la realidad peruana* (1928), Santiago de Chile 1955, p. 29.

[4] Mariategui, 'Carta colectiva del grupo de Lima' (1929), in *El proletariado y su organizacion*, Mexico 1970, pp. 119-20. The similarity between Mariategui's and Trotsky's views is striking. Mariategui did not openly support Trotsky against Stalin, but in an article written in 1928, when Trotsky had already been expelled from the party and exiled in Central Asia, he referred to his defeat as 'temporary' and spoke of him as 'one of the most open-minded and clear-sighted critics of our time'. (See Mariategui, 'Trotsky y la opposición comunista' (1928), in *El Proletariado*, p. 33).

[5] Julio Antonio Mella, 'Que es el ARPA?' (1928), in *Ensayos revolucionarios*, Havana 1960, p. 23-4. Exiled in Mexico, Mella joined the Communist Party in that country, but had troubles with its leadership, who accused him of Trotskyist tendencies. See Bernardo Claraval, *Cuando fui communista*, Mexico 1944, p. 49.

soldiers', and peasants' soviets in order to pursue the 'relentless destruction of the national bourgeoisie and imperialism'.[6]

However after the mid-1930s there were no longer dissidents in the leadership of any Latin American communist parties, and a monolithic adherence to the 'general line' was implemented throughout the continent. The most important historical experience that resulted from this orientation was probably the Chilean Popular Front, a governmental coalition between the Communist, Socialist and Radical parties that lasted almost a decade (1938-47). According to Carlos Contrera Labarca, General Secretary of the CPC, the Front was made possible because the Party had abandoned its sectarian leftist position of 1932 which had expressed itself 'in premature slogans that attempted to leap over the bourgeois-democratic stage of the revolution'. He defined the 1938 Popular Front as a 'broad alliance of classes', including 'certain sectors of the Chilean bourgeoisie which can and must be won for national liberation by a progressive and democratic policy'; moreover, he emphasized that the Front should, if possible, also be extended to 'important sectors of the political parties of the right which have had moments of vacillation . . . inviting them to enter the popular movement with assurances of the satisfaction of their desires for order, progress and democracy.'[7] During the ten years of the Popular Front, the Radical Party, firmly controlled by large landowners and sections of the bourgeoisie, maintained its hegemony by playing off the other parties against one another. Finally in 1947 the communists were expelled from the government and the CPC was formally outlawed, with hundreds of members imprisoned. What assessment can be made of the achievements of this 'broad class alliance'? According to James Petras, the Popular Front created an industrial infrastructure and increased the government's role in the development process, but 'these changes tended to enrich the upper and middle class in status, wealth and power, at the expense of the workers and peasants. Popular Front politics weakened the left. . . . At the end of a decade of working class—middle class coalition, the Rightist parties were politically, socially and economically stronger than ever.'[8]

[6]Cf. Roque Dalton, 'Miguel Marmol: El Salvador 1930-32', *Pensamiento Critico*, 48 (January 1971), p. 102; and T. P. Anderson, *Matanza, El Salvador's Communist Revolt of 1932*, Lincoln, Nebraska 1971, p. 68.

[7]Carlos Contreras Labarca, 'The People of Chile Unite to Save Democracy', *The Communist*, XVII, (11 November 1938), pp. 1037-8.

[8]James Petras, *Politics and Social Forces in Chilean Development*, Berkeley and Los Angeles 1970, p. 132. The demoralization of the labour movement can be gauged by the fact that when the Socialist and Communist parties finally decided to stop quarrelling and unite in an

In the other countries of Latin America no real Popular Front was within reach of the communist parties. Nonetheless they persisted in defending its strategic primacy. In a 1936 speech, for example, Cuban communist leader Blas Roca quoted Stalin's warning of 1925 against the underestimation of the importance of the alliance between the working class and the 'revolutionary' bourgeoisie. Roca stressed that in Cuba 'all the layers of our population from the proletariat to the national bourgeoisie, fraternally united by the common interest of liberating our country, can and should constitute a broad popular front against the foreign oppressor.'[9] Who was to be the political representative of this progressive national bourgeoisie? After some years of hesitation, the Cuban communists decided that it was a certain Colonel Batista, and they established a political alliance with him that lasted from 1939 to 1944.

It is also important to understand that the stagist orientation of the Latin American communists was continuous through the various tactical turns ordered by the Comintern and Soviet leadership. Indeed it is instructive to compare the underlying immunity of the strategic framework to 'right' and 'left' shifts at a tactical level. Consider the following examples of 'moderate' and 'radical' stances:

(1) The end of the Second World War was a highpoint of communist 'moderation' and class collaboration. Thus in November 1945, the official newspaper of the Mexican Party proposed the following thesis: 'The goal of developing capitalism in Mexico is a revolutionary aim, because it means the development of a national economy . . . the disappearance of semi-colonial vestiges and the conclusion of the agrarian reform, the democratic and general development of the country as far as it can be developed by an agrarian anti-imperialist revolution.' According to this article, the measures proposed by the Communist Party 'are, like the agrarian reform, bourgeois measures that correspond to the goal of allowing the development of a Mexican capitalism, that can industrialize the country and free it from imperialist intervention. . . .'[10] This conception, as well as analogous ideas advanced by other Latin American communist parties, is scarcely even Menshevik in its essence; it evokes, in fact, the so-called 'Legal

[9]Quoted by Saverio Tutino, *L'ottobre cubano*, Milan 1968, p. 148.
[10]Carlos Sanchez Cardenas, 'La révolucion mexicana y el desarrollo capitalista de Mexico', *La Voz de Mexico* (20 November 1945), p. 1.

electoral front in 1952, their common candidate, Salvador Allende, received merely 6 per cent of the vote.

Marxism' that Piotr Struve elaborated as a programme for 'progressive' Russian capitalism at the beginning of the twentieth century.[11]

(2) Although the onset of the Cold War in 1947-8 forced a left turn (particularly in relation to American imperialism), the Latin American communists still retained their stagist conceptions. This was most dramatically evident in the case of Guatemala in the early 1950s—the most important left-wing experience of the period. The coalition government of Colonel Arbenz, composed of populists and communists, decided to implement an agrarian reform that included the expropriation of parts of the extensive holdings of the US-owned United Fruit Company. For the communists of the Partido Guatemalteco del Trabajo (PGT) the major aim of this reform was to finish, in alliance with the national bourgeoisie, the tasks of the bourgeois-democratic stage of Guatemalan development. In his report to the Second Congress of the PGT (December 1952), the General Secretary, J. M. Fortuny, announced: 'We communists recognize that because of its particular conditions, the development of Guatemala will still have to take place, for a certain time, along capitalist lines.'[12] In the PGT's conception, therefore, the armed forces were the representatives of a 'progressive and anti-imperialist' national bourgeoisie, and it rejected proposals to arm the workers and peasants as nothing less than the 'manoeuvres of internal reaction, attempting to counterpose a workers' and peasants' front to the Armed Forces'. Fortuny specifically emphasized his confidence in the 'progressively inclined sympathies of the officers and commanders of the Army'.[13] In June 1954, a mercenary army, financed by United Fruit and commanded by Colonel Castillo Armas, invaded Guatemala and overthrew Arbenz. Needless to say, the 'progressive' armed forces rallied to Armas, outlawed the PGT and established the white terrorist dictatorship that has survived until the present day.

In Asia the casualties of stagist illusions were on an even more tragic

---

[11]Revealingly, the Soviet historian Anatol Shulgovsky in his book on Mexico makes precisely a comparison between 'Legal Marxism' and the ideology of Lombardo Toledano, then head of the Mexican trade unions and very close politically to the Mexican communists. See A. Shulgovsky, *Mexico en la encrucijada de su historia*, Mexico 1969, p. 414.

[12]José Manuel Fortuny, *Relatorio sobre la actividad del Comité Central al Segundo Congresso del Partido*, Guatemala 1952.

[13]Manuel Pinto Usaga, *Guatemala, apuntes sobre el movimiento obrero*, 1954, p. 15. In a self-criticism written in 1955, the PGT recognized that it 'did not follow a sufficiently independent line in relation to the democratic bourgeoisie', and that it did 'contribute to breeding illusions about the army'. Yet at the same time, the PGT continued in its advocacy of a bloc with the national bourgeoisie and the struggle for a 'democratic and patriotic revolution'. See Comision Political del PGT, *La intervencion norte-americana en Guatemala ye el derrocamiento del regimen democratico*, 1955, pp. 31-2, 42.

scale; indeed, the destruction of the Indonesian Communist Party (PKI) in 1965 ranks as the greatest defeat suffered by the international labour movement in the post-war epoch. It is necessary to recall that the PKI was the largest communist movement in any capitalist country and the third biggest Communist Party in the world (exceeded only by the Soviet and Chinese Parties). This mass party of three million members organized a periphery of almost ten million people through its various trade unions, peasant organizations, and mass movements of all kinds. Despite its immense resources the PKI provided virtually uncritical and unconditional support to the bourgeois Bonapartist regime of Sukarno. Aidit, the PKI's Chairman, explained the *raison d'etre* of this policy by stressing that 'the Indonesian revolution is at the present stage bourgeois-democratic in character and not socialist and proletarian.'[14] Further, he insisted that to confuse the two stages of the Indonesian revolution was 'demagogic, subjective and reactionary', and that 'the socialist stage cannot be achieved without first completing the national-democratic stage.'[15] Classically, this democratic stage was supposed to be implemented by a 'four class bloc', including the Indonesian national bourgeoisie, conservative Muslim forces, Sukarno's nationalists and the PKI. In a speech before leading Chinese communists in 1963, Aidit painted a glowing account of the successes of this alliance: 'We have now collaborated with the Indonesian bourgeoisie for nearly ten years, and the revolutionary forces have continually grown . . . whereas the reactionary forces have experienced failure after failure.'[16] Although the Soviets repeatedly expressed their support for the PKI's strategy, the Party's closest fraternal links were with the Chinese, and Mao's writings on the 'New Democracy' provided the principal inspiration for its class collaborationist line. There was, however, a central difference between New Democracy as applied in Chinese and Indonesian contexts: *the PKI had no red army*. True, the PKI had begun to organize a red army in 1945, but it was soon dissolved, and in the following years the PKI recanted this 'sectarian and leftist' deviation. As M. H. Lukman, the Second Secretary of the PKI, explained, 'in face of the propaganda of the reactionaries, we feel it necessary to affirm the possibility of a transition to socialism by peaceful means.'[17] As a matter of fact, Sukarno derived most of his power

[14]D. N. Aidit, *The Indonesian Revolution and the Immediate Tasks of the Indonesian Communist Party*, Peking 1965, p. 15.

[15]Aidit, *The Indonesian Revolution, Its Historical Background and Its Future*, Djakarta 1964, p. 77.

[16]Aidit, *The Indonesian Revolution and the Immediate Tasks*, pp. 82-3.

[17]M. H. Lukman, *About the Constitution*, Djakarta 1959, p. 26. See also T. Soedarso, 'Lessons from a Defeat', in *The Catastrophe in Indonesia*, New York 1966.

acting as a Bonapartist broker between the social camps of the PKI and the army. In October 1965, this precarious equilibrium was exploded and the military deposed Sukarno. With the support of fanatic Muslim civilian groups, the Indonesian military launched a campaign of mass murder against the PKI and its supporters that made the defeat of the Shanghai Commune in 1927 look like a minor episode. According to most estimates, at least 500,000 people, including the entire leadership of the PKI, were massacred, while several hundred thousands 'suspects' were imprisoned in concentration camps. Sixteen years later, tens of thousands of Indonesian leftists and democrats still languish in this huge capitalist Gulag Archipelago.

Finally, the most recent example of the depressing chain of disasters associated with stagist strategies is, of course, the Chilean coup of 1973. The Chilean Communist Party, despite the experience of its previous Popular Front fiasco, remained the most indefatigable advocate of a stagist approach. Its General Secretary, Luis Corvalan, had earlier distinguished himself by his sharp polemic against the line of the 1967 OLAS conference in Havana; as he vehemently rejected the possiblity of socialist revolution in Latin America and insisted on the need to traverse an 'anti-oligarchic and anti-imperialist' stage. On the eve of *Unidad Popular*'s electoral victory, the Fourteenth Congress of the Chilean Party (November 1969) solemnly re-affirmed these principles. Corvalan singled out for attack the 'unserious' and 'unscientific' positions of the sections of the left (mainly the MIR, the Trotskyists and the left wing of the Socialist Party) which sought to implement a socialist revolution, rather than concentrating (as the CPC demanded) upon 'anti-oligarchic and anti-imperialist transformations'.[18] This strict adherence to the formalist schema of stages was consistently carried through in the CPC's policies: the search for a rapprochement with the Christian Democratic Party, the return to the national bourgeoisie of enterprises that had been seized by the workers (in response to the employers' lock-out of October 1972), and stout faith in the armed forces' loyalty to the parliamentary system. . . .

The Soviet leadership, of course, has continued to be the principal source of the official formulations of stagism that have been adopted by the communist movement in the peripheral capitalist countries. Without ever abandoning the basic premises of Stalin's doctrinal elaborations of the 1920s, Soviet theoretical production in this field has nonetheless undergone various twists and turns over the last half-century. The latest of these

[18]Luis Corvalán, *Camino de victoria*, Santiago 1971; and Carlos Corda, *El leninismo y la victoria popular*, Santiago 1971, pp. 111-2.

schemas, worked out by eminent Soviet academicians in the late 1960s and early 1970s, is the theory of the 'non-capitalist way', which has become the orthodox line for so-called 'developing countries'. It was probably Professor R. A. Ulyanovsky who first proposed this theory, but its development and elaboration owed most to V. G. Solodovnikov, Director of the Africa Institute of the Soviet Academy of Sciences. According to Solodovnikov, the 'non-capitalist development toward socialism' is the path of 'National Democratic' states like Egypt, Syria, Algeria, Iraq, the Congo, Guinea, Somalia, Burma and others, where there exists a 'democratic dictatorship of the revolutionary people'. This National Democracy 'represents mainly the interests of the national bourgeoisie, the radical intelligentsia, the peasantry and the proletariat' (a barely modified version of the bloc of four classes). The fact that this 'democratic dictatorship' is frequently the authoritarian and most undemocratic dictatorship of the armed forces does not seem contradictory to the Soviet academician: 'the military intelligentsia is the most organized anti-imperialist force. In order to withstand the pressure of the imperialists and the exploiter classes in general, the democratic military intelligentsia takes political power into its own hands. . . .'[19]

Although the term 'non-capitalist' might seem to introduce some ambiguity, this theory is manifestly continuous with classical stagism. According to Solodovnikov, for example, 'at the present stage' the national democratic states 'cannot resolve . . . full liquidation of all the exploiter classes and . . . the building of socialism'. The historical mission of national democracy is to prepare the 'political, economic and social preconditions for a further transition to the building of a socialist society', to create 'the material prerequisites . . . to the future socialist reconstruction of the economy'. Although these 'preconditions' and 'prerequisites' are never concretely explicated, their absence is nonetheless deemed sufficient reason for the contemporary impossibility of socialist transformation in these countries.[20] In this context, what meaning is ascribed to the pivotal term 'non-capitalist'? Solodovnikov himself concedes that the countries in question 'have not fully pulled themselves away from the system of the world capitalist economy'; that they have a 'mixed economy' (including state, national capitalist and foreign capitalist sectors), and that the exploiting classes have not been abolished. The only real argument advanced by Solodovnikov for considering these states to be 'non-capitalist' is the

---

[19] V. G. Solodovnikov, *The Present Stage of the Non-Capitalist Development in Asia and Africa*, Budapest 1973, pp. 13-21.

[20] Ibid., pp. 13, 26.

importance of the state-controlled sector, which constitutes in his view 'the economic basis of the non-capitalist development'. The principal example that he evokes—Egypt—could not demonstrate more ironically the fragility of his thesis. Equally the mass murder of communists in Iraq is a sad commentary on the true nature of the supposedly 'democratic dictatorship of the revolutionary people'. Despite one huge contradiction after another, however, the exigencies of Soviet foreign policy will continue to discover new 'non-capitalist national democracies'—Egypt and Somalia *exeunt*, Ethiopia enters, and so on.

The theory of permanent revolution, in contrast, was largely able to predict, explain and illuminate the red thread that runs through the twentieth century: the social revolutions in the peripheral capitalist countries. In this sense, it is, in our opinion, a crucial key to the understanding of our epoch. What occurred in Russia, Yugoslavia, China, Vietnam and Cuba corresponded closely to Trotsky's central thesis: the possibility of an uninterrupted and combined (democratic/socialist) revolution in a 'backward', dependent or colonial country. The fact that, by and large, the leaders of the post-October revolutionary movements did not acknowledge their 'permanent' character, or did so only *a posteriori* and with a different terminology, does not alter the unmistakenly permanentist character of these revolutions. The concrete unfolding of the global revolutionary process can hardly fit into Plekhanov's or Stalin's rigid stagist models; while the dogma of national democratic revolution as a necessary and anterior stage to anticapitalist transformation is too narrow and rigid to contain the turbulent movements of real history.

This does not mean, of course, that there were no 'phases' or *moments* in the revolutionary process. Trotsky himself wrote in *The Permanent Revolution*: 'No matter what the *first episodic stages* of the revolution may be in the individual countries . . . the *victory* of the democratic revolution is conceivable only through the dictatorship of the proletariat which bases itself upon the alliance with the peasantry and solves *first of all* the tasks of the democratic revolution.'[21] If one examines the dynamics of the various revolutions mentioned above, one can find such 'episodic stages', particularly in Russia (from February to October 1917) and in Cuba (from January 1959 to the summer of 1960); but the 'victory' of the democratic revolution (i.e. the full achievement of its tasks) was attained only through the dictatorship of the proletariat, or, more precisely, through a revolutionary state power which politically represented the proletariat. In Yugoslavia,

[21]*Permanent Revolution*, p. 153.

China and Vietnam the revolution was from its beginning under the leadership of communist parties, and during its first period—lasting from a few months (Yugoslavia) to a few years (China)—it accomplished the agenda of urgent democratic tasks. But this was scarcely a 'democratic stage' in terms of traditional stagist scenarios, since these reforms were inseparably combined ('chemically' not merely mechanically) with socialist measures implemented by proletarian parties holding state power.

As we have seen, however, the question of the possibility of successful bourgeois-democratic revolutions in the twentieth century is both more controversial and ambiguous. The ambiguity resides partially in the question itself: what defines a 'complete' solution of bourgeois-democratic tasks? Since the distinction between a limited and a complete solution is open to various interpretations and assessments, it is very difficult to construct a clear-cut, rigorous and uncontestable answer from the historical data surveyed in Chapter 5. Some authors, for example, would claim that the development of capitalism in agriculture is tantamount to a bourgeois solution of the agrarian question. But this is obviously nonsense: for instance, practically all Mexican Marxist scholars agree today that agriculture in Mexico during the last twenty years of the Diaz dictatorship was largely capitalist.[22] Thus if this had 'solved' the agrarian question, one is left wondering why millions of peasants rose up between 1911 and 1919 in one of the most important social explosions of the century. Certainly the mere substitution of capitalist exploitation for pre-capitalist relations of production only tends to intensify in most Third World settings the rampant contradictions of rural society as it accelerates a polarization between the landless poor and the big capitalist landowners.

If one adopts the criteria (as Trotsky implicitly did) of the long-term achievements of the great historical bourgeois revolutions, it seems not unreasonable to conclude that *none* of the bourgeois revolutions or 'semi-revolutions' in the non-European peripheral capitalist countries have yet been able to achieve both a stable and complete solution to *all* three genera of national democratic tasks.[23] As Ernest Mandel has recently argued, the

[22]See Adolfo Gilly, Arnaldo Cordova, Armando Bartra, Manuel Aguilar Mora, and Enrique Semo, *Interpretaciones de la revolución mexicana*, Mexico 1980.

[23]Even non-Marxist critiques of Trotsky are ready to concede this point: 'That, in fact, the bourgeoisie of these underdeveloped countries, dependent on foreign capital and lacking a strong dedication to national purposes, would fail to realize its own "historical tasks"—this part of Trotsky's theory has been all but entirely vindicated by experience. He, and not the Mensheviks, nor even Lenin, has been proven right on this point. . . . That the bourgeois revolution would now have to be completed without the leadership of, and often in direct opposition to, the bourgeoisie of the underdeveloped nations—this has been shown to be a reality of our time.' (Irving Howe, *Trotsky*, London 1978, p. 35.)

decisive test for this aspect of theory of permanent revolution is whether any dependent country has become through its processes of development actually 'ripe' for a *purely socialist* revolution of the same kind that has become the order of the day in the advanced capitalist societies. 'Is there a dependent capitalist country, or ex-colony, that has undergone sufficient socio-economic transformation that the tasks now facing the proletariat in that country are substantially identical to the tasks now facing the proletariat of countries such as Germany, France, Britain or the United States? Once we pose the question in this manner, the answer becomes evident. There is no such country, and there is no reason to expect that there will be one.'[24] At the same time, however, it must not be forgotten that even the 'classical' French Revolution did not immediately bring about a stable bourgeois democracy: this historical task was only achieved eighty years afterwards with the establishment of the Third Republic in 1870-1. And if we further examine the cases of Italy and Japan, we discover that not only the achievement of democracy, but also the resolution of the agrarian question, were only completed seventy or eighty years (and two world wars) after the inauguration of their semi-revolutions from above. Could it not be the case, then, that some Third World countries are in the middle of their long march towards such a protracted solution of their bourgeois historical tasks? While such a possibility can certainly not be ruled out *a priori*, it does not seem very probable, especially since the process of 'semi-industrialization' in leading Third World countries seems to be increasing rather than reducing their dependence upon imperialism.[25]

However, what the historical evidence examined in Chapter 5 *does* show is that one should not underestimate the capacity of bourgeois or petty-bourgeois-led revolutions or semi-revolutions to accomplish important reforms and to establish relatively stable regimes—even, in some cases, stable parliamentary states—with a considerable degree of political and

[24]*Revolutionary Marxism Today*, London 1979, pp. 88-9.
[25]'Some of the most developed of the underdeveloped countries are experiencing a not insignificant degree of industrialization. . . . But the system as a whole continues to be dominated by imperialism, and there is no sign that this is changing in any important way. There are therefore absolute limits to the industrialization programmes of these countries, and none of them—or at least no country with a significant-sized population—will succeed in making the transition from "semi-industrialized" to fully industrialized, with all the socio-economic consequences this entails. . . . In some ways, stepped-up industrialization has made these countries—the most developed of the underdeveloped countries—more and not less dependent on imperialism than before. They are more dependent on imperialist technology, more closely integrated into and therefore subjected to the imperialist world market. Extensive sectors of the national bourgeoisie are more strongly tied to multinational firms. In fact, their relative economic successes have enhanced their dependence on the international credit system.' (Ibid., pp. 78, 83, 84).

economic autonomy. To invoke an analogy: Lenin repeatedly warned against the revolutionary complacency that the Stolypin reforms were doomed, stressing that they might actually succeed in giving Tsarism a new lease on life. A similar injunction might be made about the contemporary Stolypins of the Third World. The thesis that the bourgeoisie in the peripheral capitalist countries is incapable of democratic reforms, or of achieving a relative socio-political stability through populist demogoguery, are recipes for comfortable passivity and fatalism. Why try to prevent what will never happen anyway? A more sober assessment of the potentialities of bourgeois/petty-bourgeois leadership arms revolutionaries with a more active understanding of their own role in fighting to *prevent* bourgeois stabilization, as well as a dynamic determination, not to rely on events, but to creatively struggle for an *alternative* future.

Trotsky himself, in his 1908 polemic against the Menshevik Cherevanin (see Chapter 2), stressed that the bourgeois or proletarian character of the Russian revolution could not be defined *a priori*. 'The question as to what stage the Russian revolution will reach can, of course, be answered only conditionally.' Such a 'conditional' perspective—intrinsic to the theory of permanent revolution—is the opposite of mechanical fatalism, even where such fatalism is 'optimistic' about the inevitable outcome (as in the outlook of the Second International at the beginning of this century). As a matter of fact, from the perspective of the theory of permanent revolution, the acknowledgment of the possibility of the bourgeois forces establishing a long-term hegemony over the popular masses through national-democratic reforms is the sharpest of all stimuli to a correct understanding of the *urgency* of forestalling such an outcome through the unremitting fight for proletarian hegemony. Such an approach, while recognizing the capacity of bourgeois (or petty-bourgeois or 'Bonapartist') regimes to implement significant reforms, does not call upon the proletariat to support the bourgeois leadership or to help it accomplish its tasks. Instead the strategy of permanent revolution implies that Marxists must learn to seize the advantage from every hesitation or indecision of the bourgeoisie in order to conquer leadership over the popular/peasant masses and to develop the revolutionary process uninterruptedly toward socialist goals. In other words, a combined socialist-democratic revolution under proletarian leadership is an objective possibility in the areas of peripheral capitalism and this possibility does not depend upon the previous completion of bourgeois-democratic revolution (Stalin's classic doctrine of stages). On the contrary, it depends on the partial or total failure of the bourgeoisie to accomplish these tasks, and/or the capacity of the proletarian vanguard to win the leadership of the bloc of popular forces.

As this book is finished, several new revolutionary experiences are occurring that provide new evidence for the contemporary salience of the theory of permanent revolution. The two most successful cases so far are Iran and Nicaragua. Although it is much too soon to attempt a balance-sheet of these complex ongoing historical processes, it may be useful to sketch a provisional and comparative analysis of some of their central features.

In both countries, powerful, well-equipped armies were defeated by vast popular insurrections in which the proletariat and the urban poor played the decisive role. Moreover, in both countries the leadership of the revolutionary movement was overwhelmingly of petty-bourgeois extraction and had developed, through protracted struggle with terroristic dictatorship, an anti-imperialist and anti-autocratic programme. Also in both Iran and Nicaragua (and unlike El Salvador), significant sectors of the local bourgeoisie rallied in the end to the movements against the dictatorships. With these similarities acknowledged, however, enormous differences between the two cases are immediately evident. There is, for example, an abyss between the nature of the leadership and programme represented by the ayatollahs in Iran and the Frente Sandinista de Liberación Nacional (FSLN) in Nicaragua. The Iranian Shi'ite clergy is trying to channel the mass movements into a peculiar form of anti-imperialist bourgeois solution: the 'Islamic state' with an attendant nationalist-capitalist framework that would suppress any independent proletarian politics. The FSLN, in contrast, is a movement with Marxist leanings, very profoundly influenced by the Cuban revolution, and with deep roots amongst the workers, peasants and the slum poor. Its emergent perspective seems unmistakably committed to socialist revolution in Nicaragua and the whole of the Central American isthmus.

The example of the Cuban Revolution and the support that it gave to the FSLN since the early 1960s have certainly contributed to the radicalization of the Sandinistas and the popular movement in Nicaragua. Contrariwise, the Soviet and Chinese bureaucracies' outspoken support for the Shah weakened the influence of the left in the Iranian anti-imperialist movement. If the rabidly anti-communist forces of Khomeini attained hegemony over the popular masses, this was not the inevitable result of some 'innately reactionary' characteristic of Islam *per se*—indeed, significant *left-Muslim* forces (the Mujahadeen, for instance) were active in the anti-Shah struggle—but, to a large extent, the result of the negative image projected by the USSR and China, which helped discredit communism in the eyes of broad sections of the Iranian population.

Further contrasts: The Iranian religious nationalists executed many generals and police officers, organized a new paramilitary 'Revolutionary Guard', but failed to destroy the old imperial army. It is precisely this traditional military apparatus, now 'rehabilitated' by the war with Iraq, which still constitutes the basis for any restoration of the pro-imperialist forces (with or without the support of the Islamic clergy). In Nicaragua, on the other hand, there were practically no executions, but the FSLN completely dissolved Somoza's Guardia Nacional and replaced it with the Ejercito Popular Sandinista, composed of its own guerrilla columns and armed popular militias. Moreover, the Islamic leadership in Iran, despite its vehement anti-imperialist orientation, has failed to establish a real democracy, to emancipate oppressed nationalities or to solve the agrarian question. Indeed it has continued the repression of national minorities (Kurds, Arabs, etc.), attacked the most militant sectors of the labour movement, suppressed the rights of women, and, in general, paved the way for a counter-revolution.[26] The FSLN, in contrast, organizing the masses through an array of unions, militia organizations and the 'Sandinista Defence Committees', has taken increasingly radical measures that have undermined Nicaraguan capitalism: nationalization of Somoza's immense properties (numerous banks, stores, plants and almost half of the country's arable land), a basic agrarian reform, the institutionalization of workers control in factories, and so on. The current sharpening of the economic and political conflicts between the FSLN majority and the bourgeoisie (represented by 'COSEP') suggests that the Sandinista revolution is already organically, and without intermediary stages, growing over into an anti-capitalist revolution.

The particular dynamics of the permanent revolution in Nicaragua can perhaps best be illustrated by comparison with its Cuban predecessor. In the first place, the Sandinista experience reproduces many familiar motifs of the Cuban revolution: (1) the formation of a radical anti-imperialist movement under the banner of a legendary jacobin revolutionary leader of the past (Marti, Sandino); (2) this movement (M-26-7, FSLN) leads the struggle against a brutal dictatorship protected by US imperialism (Batista, Somoza); (3) through a combination of guerrilla warfare and urban insurrection, the old state apparatus and its repressive organs are thoroughly destroyed; (4) a new revolutionary army is organized on a basis of guerrilla units and popular militias, but the government remains a coalition with representatives of the anti-dictatorial bourgeoisie (Urrutia in Cuba, Robelo

---

[26]For an illuminating comparison of Iran and Nicaragua, see Manuel Aguilar Mora, 'Populisme et révolution permanente', *Quatrième Internationale* (July-September 1980).

in Nicaragua); (5) as the masses are mobilized and armed, and as the revolution takes increasingly radical measures (beginning with attacks against the rural oligarchy and foreign capital), the coalition disintegrates and the bourgeois forces go over to the counter-revolutionary camp.

At the same time, however, there are important differences between the two revolutions. The FSLN, for instance, was from its origins in 1961 a movement with a clearer and more left-wing programmatic definition than the M-26-7 at comparable stages of development (between 1954 and 1959). Both the founders of the Frente Sandinista, Carlos Fonseca (killed by Somoza's troops in 1976) and Tomas Borge (present Minister of the Interior), were Marxists who had left the Stalinist Partido Socialista de Nicaragua in protest against its reformist orientation. In a seminal essay on the FSLN's strategy, published in Cuba in 1969, Fonseca wrote: 'Our main goal is the socialist revolution, a revolution which intends to drive out Yankee imperialism and its local agents . . . we must be alert to the danger that the insurrection will be manipulated by the reactionary forces within the anti-Somoza opposition. The aim of the revolutionary movement is dual. On the one hand, the task is to smash the treacherous and criminal clique that has usurped power for so many years, and, on the other hand, to prevent the capitalist component of the opposition, whose submission to imperialism is well known, from profiting from the crisis created by the guerrilla struggle to seize power for themselves.'[27] Another distinctive feature of the Nicaraguan revolution was the relationship between the respective roles of urban insurrection and rural guerrilla warfare: the *decisive* political/military moment in the destruction of Somoza's well-oiled war machine was the massive armed upsurge of workers, urban poor and *youth* in the towns—first in the provincial centres (Masaya, Léon, Esteli), then in the capital (Managua). These two differences suggest that the Sandinista revolution has had, since its beginning, a more consistently 'proletarian' and socialist character than the Cuban struggle in its first years. The relative maturity of the FSLN, however, is easily understandable, since the Nicaraguan revolution has profited from the very beginning from the example of the Cuban permanent revolutionary process.[28]

[27]Carlos Fonseca Amador, 'Nicaragua heure H', *Tricontinentale*, 14 (September-October 1969) pp. 40-7.
[28]Another specificity of the Sandinista revolution has been the important role of the Indian masses. For an analysis of the tradition of Indian revolt in Nicaragua, see the book by the FSLN's current chief of the Institute for Agrarian Reform: Jaime Wheelock, *Raices indigenas de la lucha anti-colonialista en Nicaragua*, Mexico 1974. By contrast, the lack of understanding of the tenets of permanent revolutionary strategy was to have disastrous consequences in Afghanistan. The People's Democratic Party of Afghanistan (PDPA) carried out a defensive coup

Now, if the *politics* of Trotsky's theory of permanent revolution have on the whole passed the tests of history, his *sociology*—that is, his analysis of the roles of the various social classes in the revolutionary process—requires some important clarifications and amendments. Let us re-examine Trotsky's theses on the roles of the five principal social strata—the national bourgeoisie, the petty bourgeoisie, the intelligentsia, the peasantry and the proletariat—in the light of the modern historical experiences of the countries of peripheral capitalism.

The National Bourgeoisie

Although it is true that Trotsky sometimes underestimated the capabilities of the indigenous bourgeoisie in certain countries (expecially India), his general views concerning the historical role of this class have been decisively vindicated on a world-historical scale. As a matter of fact, the most advanced democratic revolutions have been specifically distinguished by the *petty-bourgeois*, rather than bourgeois, character of their leadership.

---

d'etat with the support of its members in the armed forces and overthrew the hated Daud dictatorship in April 1978. Daud had been preparing a massive wave of repression directed against the PDPA. The coup had the support of the masses, but the PDPA's Stalinist training institutionalized a process of manipulation and substitutionism, which rapidly divorced the new regime from the masses, encouraged reaction and ultimately resulted in the Soviet military intervention. Trotsky had stressed in the theses on permanent revolution that democracy was crucial in order to ensure the widest participation of the masses. In his writings on China he further amplified his earlier views in the following way: 'The stage of democracy has a great importance in the evolution of the masses. Under definite conditions, the revolution can allow the proletariat to pass beyond this stage. But it is precisely to facilitate this future development, which is not at all easy and not at all guaranteed to be successful in advance, that it is necessary to utilize to the fullest the inter-revolutionary period to exhaust the democratic resources of the bourgeoisie. This can be done by developing democratic before the broad masses and by compelling the bourgeoisie to place itself in contradiction to them at each step.' (*On China*, New York 1976, p. 400-1). If the PDPA had permitted a flowering of democratic institutions, prepared an electoral register and announced the date for elections to a Constituent Assembly events might have turned out differently. The election campaign would have permitted the PDPA to go to the masses and argue for their programme of reforms. The elections would have also provided the most accurate estimate of the relationship of social forces in the country. This failure to mobilize the masses and encourage mass participation at every level could only lead to an unstable, petty-bourgeois dictatorship. The PDPA's social base was extremely narrow. It was at the time of the coup an organization of 2,000—3,000 members, most of whom were teachers and students. Instead of relying on the masses it sought to use the Army as an instrument of reform. It is indisputable that Hafizullah Amin had more political prisoners executed than all preceding regimes. The consequences of Stalinism have, in this case, meant that the Afghan masses are more alienated from socialism today than they were in the period preceding April 1978.

The national bourgeoisie appears most of the time as a moderate, if not conservative, force, unwilling to initiate social struggles, and obsessed with containing, 'institutionalizing' and halting (if not overtly repressing) popular democratic revolutions.

The Petty Bourgeoisie

In *Permanent Revolution* Trotsky insisted that the petty bourgeoisie, in either the advanced or the backward countries, would not be capable of playing a leading revolutionary role because the logic of capitalist development 'condemns the petty bourgeoisie to nullity'.[29] Yet a few years later he was forced to acknowledge that the petty bourgeoisie was, in fact, the leading force of the nationalist movement in Catalonia;[30] while in the *Transitional Programme* (1938) he even envisioned the possibility that under exceptional circumstances (war, financial, crash, mass revolutionary pressure and so on) the petty-bourgeois parties might 'go further than they wish along the road to a break with the bourgeoisie' and the establishment of a workers and farmers' government.[31] The advents of such 'workers' and peasants' governments' were, of course, quite exceptional; the most notable examples being probably Algeria under Ben Bella (1963-5) and the 1959-60 phase of the Cuban revolution.

But there has been a much more frequent phenomenon, of central importance in the Third World, which Trotsky did not foresee: that petty-bourgeois nationalist forces (particularly the military) would *substitute* themselves for the weak or faltering national bourgeoisie, assume the leadership of the democratic revolution or semi-revolution, and implement important reforms whose radicalism would far exceed the desires or capacities of the bourgeoisie. This, of course, is what happened in Nasser's Egypt, in Boumedienne's Algeria, in Velasco Alvarado's Peru, and, to a certain extent, in both Mexico and Bolivia. Although these substitutionalist petty-bourgeois forces have generally opened the way to the rule of *nouveau riche* bourgeois fractions (Mexico, Bolivia, Egypt and so on), they have sometimes—at least in Algeria—transformed themselves into a *sui generis* 'bourgeois bureaucracy'. In any event, they have played a hegemonic social role for a certain historical period, and have imprinted a *specific*, petty-bourgeois character on the revolutionary process under their leader-

---

[29] *Permanent Revolution*, pp. 126-7.
[30] 'La question catalane' (17 May 1931), in *La révolution espagnole 1930-1940*, Paris 1975, pp. 104-5.
[31] *The Transitional Programme*, London n.d., p. 35.

ship. More recently, one has seen petty-bourgeois jacobin nationalist movements come to power in several African and Asian countries which claim allegiance to scientific socialism, Marxism and sometimes even to Leninism. Furthermore, these states—Angola, Mozambique, Guinea-Bissau, South Yemen, Ethiopia and Afghanistan—have established strong economic, political and military ties with the Soviet Union, Cuba and the Eastern bloc. To what extent this might correspond to the beginning of a permanentist process of social transformation, in a 'Cuba-like' pattern, remains to be seen. Perhaps it can be equally well a transitional stage towards neo-bourgeois stabilization and the renewal of dependence upon imperialism. Whatever may be the actual outcomes, these experiences demonstrate the continued revolutionary vitality of the leftist petty bourgeoisie, the general attraction of Marxism, and, more specifically, the renewed influence of the USSR in the 1970s, following China's complete retreat from the anti-imperialist struggle.

Thus, we must conclude that although Trotsky's thesis of the petty bourgeoisie as a class that must in the last analysis support either the bourgeoisie or the proletariat is ultimately vindicated, the course of modern history has also demonstrated that the nationalist petty bourgeoisie can, for distinct periods of years or even decades, hold power and forge its own distinctive policy. Trotsky verged on recognition of this phenomenon in his notes on Bonapartism in Latin America, but he did not clearly distinguish between a Bonapartism under the hegemony of petty-bourgeois fractions and another variety linked to the national bourgeoisie. This consequential analytical oversight was probably related to the fact that the concrete example most carefully observed and written about by Trotsky— Cardenas's Mexico—was uniquely a border-line case between the two modes of Bonapartist rule.

The Intelligentsia

The intelligentsia is not a social class but a social category, defined by its relationship to the sphere of what Marx called 'spiritual production', and with traditional links to the petty bourgeoisie (although more recently it has been increasingly transformed by the tendency toward the proletarianization of intellectual labour). In his unfinished biography of Lenin (1936), Trotsky developed a remarkable analysis of the role of the intelligentsia in *fin de siècle* Russia, which included the recognition that 'after the abolition of serfdom, the nourishing body for revolutionary ideas was almost exclusively the intelligentsia, or rather its young generation, the poorest elements of the youth in the schools, students, seminarists, high-school pupils, most of whom by their living conditions were not above the proletariat, and frequently even below it.'[32] Unfortunately, however, Trotsky never attempted to extend the implications of this analysis to other 'backward' countries, and the question of the role of the intelligentsia was virtually neglected in the bulk of his writings on the permanent revolution in the colonial and semi-colonial areas (China, India, Mexico, etc.). This is a serious lacuna, since, as we have seen, the intelligentsia (or rather its radicalized sections: intellectual labourers) has played a crucially important role in most of the socialist revolutions in the countries of peripheral capitalism. Moreover, the problem of the intelligentsia cannot be waived away by references to individuals 'breaking with their class'; for, even though only fractions of the intelligentsia have ever participated in revolutionary struggle, they have furnished very considerable proportions of the cadre of the communist and revolutionary socialist movements of the Third World. Thus we are confronted with a massive phenomenon, mostly ignored by 'classical' Marxism, and demanding a rigorous sociological explanation.

Amongst non-Marxist scholars, Alvin Gouldner has provided some of the most provocative hypotheses about the general role of revolutionary intellectuals. In particular, his essay 'Prologue to a Theory of Revolutionary Intellectuals' is full of fertile insights, but his central thesis on the dynamic of the revolutionary intelligentsia in the Third World is far from convincing. In his view the struggle of the intelligentsia against the national bourgeoisie is 'an internecine struggle *within* the 'elite', a struggle

[32]Trotsky, *La jeunesse de Lénine* (1936), Paris 1970, pp. 35-6. This analysis was prefigured to a certain extent by Trotsky's earlier writings on students, particularly his 1910 essay, *The Intelligentsia and Socialism* (London 1966): 'The student, in contrast both to the young worker and to his own father, fulfils no social function, does not feel direct dependence on capital or the state, is not bound by any responsibilities and—at least objectively, if not subjectively—is free in his judgement of right and wrong. At this period everything within him is fermenting, his class prejudices are as formless as his ideological interests, questions of conscience matter very strongly. . . . If collectivism is at all capable of mastering his mind, now is the moment, and it will indeed do it through the nobly scientific character of its basis and the comprehensive cultural content of its aims, not as a prosaic "knife and fork" question.' (p. 12) However, Trotsky developed in this essay a rather pessimistic view of the possibility of winning significant numbers of students and intellectuals to the Western European socialist movement before the victory of the proletarian revolution. We know from his later writings that he was aware of the revolutionary role of students in countries such as Spain, but he never attempted to elaborate the larger implications of the phenomenon. Finally it is important to note that while the students and young intellectuals had been a key source of revolutionary cadres in the peripheral capitalist countries from the beginning of the century, in the advanced countries, by contrast, they remained rather conservative, if not reactionary, in their majority until the 1960s.

within the ruling group itself.[33] The vague term 'elite' is not able to establish any real social link between the bourgeoisie and the intellectuals, while the characterization of the latter as being members of the 'ruling class' is highly debatable. Moreover, as Eric Wolf has shown in a comparative study of revolutions in Mexico, Russia, China, Vietnam, Algeria and Cuba, the intellectuals who played the leading roles in these movements were by and large 'rootless', 'marginal' and divorced from the traditional sources of power.[34] In order to defend his analysis, therefore, Gouldner is compelled to define the intelligentsia—including professionals, technicians, clerks, journalists, lawyers, and so on—as a *'cultural* bourgeoisie whose capital is *knowledge* and language acquired during their education'[35]—a definition that completely empties the concepts of 'bourgeoisie' and 'capital' of any determinate socio-economic meaning and reduces them to simple metaphors.

In our opinion, the opposition of the intellectuals o the bourgeoisie, far from being an internecine struggle within the 'ruling group' or a conflict between two fractions of the bourgeoisie, is above all related to their links with a different social class: *the petty bourgeoisie.* The spontaneous ideology of the so-called 'democratic petty bourgeoisie', of which intellectuals comprise the most vocal and active segment, is not bourgeois liberalism but rather *jacobinism*: the specific combination of plebeian democracy and romantic moralism of which Rousseau and Robespiere were the first historical representatives. In the countries of 'belated' capitalist development (e.g. Germany in the nineteenth or Russia in the early-twentieth centuries), where the bourgeoisie was non-revolutionary and allied by fear of the masses with landowners and/or imperialism, this petty-bourgeois jacobinism tended to become more radicalized. In some cases, such a radicalization eventually led sections of the petty bourgeoisie, particularly the intellectuals, to a complete break with the bourgeoisie and to the adoption of a socialist stance. The two classic examples were, first, the case of Marx himself and the 'Hegelian left' in Germany before 1848, and, second, the Russian intelligentsia at the end of the nineteenth century.[36] Gouldner has discussed this process in one of the most perceptive passages of his essay: 'Marxism arises in part as an outcome of the propertied middle-class thermidorian halt to its own revolution. After that, revolutionary intellectuals

---

[33]Alvin Gouldner, 'Prologue to a Theory of Revolutionary Intellectuals', *Telos,* 26 (Winter 1975-6), p. 5.
[34]Eric Wolf, *Peasant Wars of the Twentieth Century,* New York 1973, p. 289.
[35]Gouldner, p. 6.
[36]On the role of Marx's conflict with the liberal Rhenish bourgeoisie as part of his evolution toward communism, see our book, *La théorie de la révolution chez le jeune Marx,* Paris 1970.

could *no longer ally themselves with the propertied middle class* and had to move in search of another "historical agent", an identity they later assigned to the proletariat.'[37] During the twentieth century, moreover, this process of the radicalization of the intelligentsia in the countries of peripheral capitalism has become increasingly massive. This is the combined result of the growing penetration of imperialism (and its destructive impact on native culture, bitterly resented by nationalist intellectuals), the conciliatory or even openly pro-imperialist positions of the local bourgeoisie and the *cumulative impact of the victorious socialist revolutions*. The convergence of these three developments has produced an explosive fusion of anti-imperialist, anti-bourgeois and socialist sympathies in broad sections of the intelligentsia.

The Peasantry

The crucial role of the peasantry in all the victorious socialist revolutions after 1917 reveals some important common traits: First, the peasants constituted the main social base for the revolutionary process, at least until the seizure of power. They furnished the vast majority of members of both the revolutionary party and the popular army. Second, unlike the experience of Russia in 1917, where peasant unrest was stimulated by the working-class upsurge in the towns, the mobilization of the peasantry in these other cases was *not* a result of the mass activity of the urban proletariat. Third, the peasants massively supported and were recruited to parties that proclaimed allegiance to communism and did not hide their socialist revolutionary aims (with the exception of Cuba until 1960). Fourth, the progressive collectivization of agriculture after the seizure of power (with the exception of Yugoslavia where a small peasantry has remained entrenched) was supported by vast sections of the rural poor and did not encounter the massive opposition of the peasantry as had been the case in the Soviet Union.

These facts, while being perfectly compatible with the fundamental postulates of the theory of permanent revolution, do, however, contradict several of Trotsky's specific assertions about the peasantry, especially with regard to China. (Although, as we have seen, he was ready to revise in 1939 the classical Marxist conception of the peasantry as a 'non-socialist class'.) Moreover, Trotsky's views on the peasantry reflected traditional Russian Marxist views, and these attitudes, because of their profound purchase on modern revolutionary theory, require a thorough re-assessment. The revolutionary role of the peasantry is simply a huge historical fact that occupies

---

[37]Gouldner, p. 4.

a central place in the unfolding dynamic of revolution in the twentieth century. It cannot be pushed aside as an 'historical accident' or as an episodic 'deviation from the norm'. It must be squarely confronted and scientifically explained.

In our view it is precisely the theory of permanent revolution itself that offers the most consistent and comprehensive explanation of the two most important underlying determinants of the peasantry's revolutionary inclinations: (1) the unequal and combined development of capitalism in agriculture has produced a deep crisis in the rural life of the colonial and semi-colonial countries. As Eric Wolf has stressed, 'the spread of the market has torn men up by the roots and shaken them loose from the social relationships into which they were born'. A situation of acute instability has been created where 'new wealth does not yet have legitimacy, and old power no longer commands respect. Traditional groups have been weakened, but not yet defeated, and new groups are not yet strong enough to wield decisive power.'[38] A similar view has been expressed in a recent essay by James Petras, who rightly insists on the social consequences of imperialist penetration: 'The immediate effect of imperial domination has been to accentuate the uprootedness of the rural labour force: the decomposition of the village through force, commercial relations and/or corporate expansion has been a central feature of pre-revolutionary societies. . . . It is the dispossessed former peasant, uprooted by the combined politico-military-economic efforts of imperial powers, who has set in motion the movement of peasants toward political action. . . . Indeed this transformation of the peasantry is clearly the reason that rural labour has been so prominent in all successful socialist revolutions to date;'[39] (2) the failure of the national bourgeoisie to provide radical democratic solutions to the agrarian and national questions has, thus, led the rebellious peasantry to support and/or join communist movements.

The 'peasantry' is, of course, a very broad concept that conflates heterogeneous social strata which have engaged in quite different ways with the revolutionary process. Rich peasants, obviously, have in general been hostile or at least neutral to communist-led revolutionary movements. Paradoxically, the first section of the peasantry who usually have been mobilized have not been the poorest strata, but rather the *middle peasantry*, peasant smallholders. In his well-known essay on peasants and revolution, Hamza Alavi exposes as mythical the famous assertion of Mao's that the

---

[38]Wolf, pp. 282-3, 295.
[39]James Petras, 'Socialist Revolutions and Their Class Components', *New Left Review* 111 (September-October 1978), pp. 44-5.

struggle in Hunan was waged and led by primarily poor peasants; in fact, it was the middle peasants who were from the first the most militant of the rural masses.[40] Similar trends, as we have seen, characterized the Cuban revolution; indeed, as Eric Wolf has observed, the central role of the middle peasantry has been common in all the great 'peasant wars' of the century (Mexico, Russia, China, Vietnam, Cuba and Algeria). 'Possession of some land grants the property-owning peasant a measure of independence not possessed by the peasant who depends for his livelihood primarily on his immediate overlord. The property-owning peasant thus has some independent leverage which he can translate into protest more easily than a man who options are severely restricted by a situation of total dependence.'[41]

The poor and landless rural population (sharecroppers, tenants, wage-labourers and so on), potentially more radical than the middle peasants and more objectively inclined to the collectivist aims of the communist movement, generally join the 'peasant war' only at a second stage when the power of the landlords and local authorities has already been shaken. Comparing the various experiences of peasant insurgency in the Third World, Wolf concludes that 'the poor peasant or landless labourer who depends on a landlord for the largest part of his liveliehood, or the totality of it, has no tactical power: he is completely within the power domain of his employer, without sufficient resources of his own to serve him as resources in the power struggle. Poor peasants and landless labourers, therefore, are unlikely to pursue the course of rebellion, *unless* they are able to rely on some external power to challenge the power which controls them.' As examples of such 'external' forces, he cites the peasant soldiers who returned to the villages, weapons in hand, after the collapse of the Russian army in 1917, and the role of the red army in China's rural areas.[42] Analysing the Chinese 'peasant war', Alavi criticizes the distorted portrait of the struggle in Mao's writings: 'The poor peasant is depicted to be spontaneously and unconditionally playing a revolutionary role; a picture which obscures the crucial role of the Communist Party, a party with a proletarian revolutionary perspective, and the Red Army which broke the existing structure of power in the village, which prevented the Chinese revolution from degenerating

[40]Hamza Alavi, 'Peasants and Revolution', *Socialist Register 1965*, pp. 258-61.

[41]Wolf, p. 202. According to Wolf, another section of the rural classes with a propensity to rebellion are the 'marginal', 'free' or 'tactically mobile' peasants not directly under the control of the landowners. (pp. 290-3) Our analysis of the role of the peasantry of the Sierra Maestra in the Cuban revolution would tend to confirm this hypothesis.

[42]Ibid., p. 290.

into an ineffective peasant uprising.'[43] In this respect Trotsky was correct in insisting that the peasantry could only play a consistent revolutionary role under proletarian and communist leadership. The rebel peasants required an urban intellectual and working-class revolutionary vanguard in order to attain socialist consciousness and to become organized on a national scale. In the absence of such leadership, the peasant movement either remained local and ineffective, or followed bourgeois or petty-bourgeois leadership, as in Mexico and Algeria. The peasant movement by itself could not seize power or undertake the transformation of society.[44] Even Wolf, a particularly sympathetic historian of peasant insurgency, recognizes this fact: 'Marxists have long argued that peasants without outside leadership cannot make a revolution; and our case material would bear them out. Where the peasantry has successfully rebelled against the established order—under its own banner and with its own leaders—it was sometimes able to reshape the social structure of the countryside closer to its heart's desires; but it did not lay hold of the state, of the cities which house the centers of control. . . .'[45]

It may be predicted, however, that because of the accelerated urbanization and industrialization of many peripheral capitalist countries, especially in Latin America, the revolutionary class struggles of the next decade may increasingly shift to the cities, and the working class will play a more central role. The end of the twentieth century may see a return to the 'classical' October pattern of proletarian revolution.

The Proletariat

In October 1917 the working class was *directly* the principal social actor and architect of the revolution through its organization into soviets. Simultaneously, the Bolshevik Party was proletarian, not only by its ideology and programme, but also in social composition. Contrary to Trotsky's

---

[43] Alavi, p. 260.

[44] This does not mean, however, that Marxists should consider the peasantry merely as an *instrument*; as Alavi justifiably insists, 'for socialists, the question is not merely that of mobilizing peasant support as a *means* for achieving success in their struggle. The question is not just that of *utilizing* the forces of the peasantry. The free and active participation of the peasantry in transforming their mode of existence and giving shape to the new society, in itself, must be an essential part of the socialist goal.' (ibid., p. 242).

[45] Wolf, p. 294. Considering the Chinese case, the French scholar Lucien Bianco has shown how the communists 'revolutionized' the peasants, filling them with a global vision that went beyond their inarticulate discontent and anger. (Bianco, 'Les paysans dans la revolution', in *Regards froids sur la chine*, Paris 1976, pp. 291-4. See also Roland Yew, 'Révolution en Asie et marxisme', *Critique Communiste* 24, September 1978.)

expectations, however, this configuration of a hegemonic proletarian party and massive working-class self-organization was not repeated in the Chinese or other post-1917 revolutions. Although the proletariat did play a seminal role in the early stages of the struggle in China, Vietnam and Yugoslavia (as well as in Cuba in the 1930s), it was largely absent during the actual revolutionary seizure of power. The situation in Cuba was somewhat different because of the role of the general strike of January 1959, but it was still the peasantry that provided the main social support for the revolutionary war. We cannot enter here into a detailed discussion of the reasons for the subordinated role of the urban working classes in the final phases of these revolutions, except to note the fateful consequences of repression. In all societies in question, the proletariat was the victim of terrible, systematic white terror: China after 1927, Vietnam after 1939, Yugoslavia during the Nazi occupation and Cuba after 1957. This wide-scale repression not only destroyed or disorganized the workers' vanguard, but also precipitated a mass displacement of revolutionary cadre to the relatively more secure areas. It must also be recognized, however, that internal political factors also contributed to a weakening of the urban labour movements. In China, for example, there was the CCP's policy of seeking an alliance with the national bourgeoisie, while in Cuba an important factor was the non-revolutionary character of the political leadership of the organized workers' movement (the old Stalinist PSP). All the post-1917 revolutions, therefore, can be designated as 'proletarian' only *indirectly*, by the nature of the political leadership of the revolutionary process. Indeed, not only was the proletariat not directly the social agent of revolution, but *the revolutionary party was not the direct, organic expression of the proletariat.* How can we, then, meaningfully describe the Chinese, Vietnamese, Yugoslav or Cuban communist parties as 'proletarian movements'? In our view, these parties acted as 'representatives' of the proletariat in the four following ways:

(1) With the exception of M-26-7, all parties had their *historical roots* in the labour movement and the struggles of the urban proletariat.

(2) The working class was socially present in the party structure, especially among its middle cadre. This was most of all true of the Yugoslav Party, but also in differing degrees true of the Chinese, Vietnamese and Cuban movements.

(3) The parties were the *political* and *programmatic* expression of the proletariat by virtue of their adherence to the historical interests of the working class (abolition of capitalism, etc.).

(4) The parties' *ideologies* were proletarian and the membership and periphery were systematically educated to accept the values and world-view of the international working-class movement.

These last two aspects are the decisive ones, and the only ones indisputably present in all four post-1917 cases. This implies that these parties were not directly proletarian in the sense of the Bolshevik Party, but only through certain political and ideological *mediations*. They are proletarian in an indirect sense not merely because of the predominance of non-proletarian layers (peasants, intellectuals, etc.), but especially because of the presence of a *bureaucracy* which, whatever its specific social origins, constitutes a 'separate body' with characteristics and interests distinct from the proletariat. Some authors have tended to confuse such bureaucracies with intellectual strata, and present the revolutionary party as an instrument for the seizure of power by intellectuals. But the two social categories are not identical; indeed, in certain European communist parties a large proportion of the *apparatchiks* are of working-class background. The crucial element in the bureaucratization of the communist movement, including those parties that actually led revolutions, was not the hegemony of intellectuals, but the dominance of the political and ideological model of the Soviet Union.

If the political forces that led the uninterrupted revolutions in Russia, China, Vietnam, Yugoslavia and Cuba were, directly or indirectly, proletarian, can the same be said of the *states* which they established? Trotsky, as we know, developed the concept of a 'bureaucratically degenerated worker's state' to characterize the USSR after Stalin's 'Thermidor' of the 1920s. In the post-war era the Fourth International extended Trotsky's theory to the new Yugoslav, Chinese and Vietnamese regimes, which they designated as 'bureaucratically deformed states'; the terminology indicating that since the bureaucratic dimension had been inherent from the beginning, there was no need for a bureaucratic counter-revolution to destroy the old proletarian party, as in the USSR.

The problem is that the character of bureaucratization in a *state* is qualitatively distinct from that of a *party*, for the simple reason that the state bureaucracy holds real power and can assure itself access to broad social and economic privileges. A thorough discussion of this problem of the nature of the so-called socialist states is beyond the scope of this book and would demand another volume, at least. Nonetheless it seems to us that it would be more accurate to characterize these regimes—with the possible exception of Cuba—as *bureaucratic states of proletarian origin*: meaning that while

they are the products of socialist revolutions under the leadership of proletarian-socialist parties, the real power in these states is monopolized by a
bureaucratic layer with specific social and economic interests. In these
post-capitalist societies, the transition to socialism which began with the
revolution has been arrested by the bureaucratic character of the regime and
the absence of socialist democracy. But the proletarian-socialist origin of
the bureaucratic state generates a series of contradictory structural traits:

(1) Its economic system still incorporates certain revolutionary features: the
abolition of private ownership, state planning and so on. This also means
that certain limits are imposed on social inequality and unemployment.
But the economic plan expresses the interests of the bureaucracy first and
above all, and not the needs and aspirations of the population.

(2) The power of the bureaucracy is also constrained, within certain limits,
in its appropriation of the means of production (which it cannot dispose of
as private property) and, particularly in Yugoslavia, in its control of the
labour process.

(3) A significant percentage of the bureaucracy is from a proletarian background; moreover, the bureaucracy tends to reproduce itself through a
system of selective, working-class 'upward mobility'.

(4) Marxism is the official doctrine of the regime, although it has been
transformed into an official dogma which empties it of its critical dimension and transforms it into a device for the ideological legitimation of the
bureaucratic system.

(5) The state remains integrated in the world communist movement and
continues to give support to other socialist revolutions, but the principal
objective of its foreign policy becomes the promotion of national interests
as interpreted by the bureaucracy.

Thus the working class *per se* is excluded from the direct exercise of
power, which becomes concentrated in the bureaucratic apparatus. The
dictatorship of the bureaucratic layer can assume more totalitarian or more
enlightened, more terrorist or more liberal, more personal or more institutional forms: in any case, its foundation is the absence of democratic rights
for the mass of working people. The bureaucratic stratum enjoys a broad
spectrum of material, social and political privileges, ranging from special
shops to differential access to education.

The most complex problem is accurately defining the precise nature of
this bureaucratic layer: is it a 'new class', a 'caste', a 'new bourgeoisie', or

just a 'fraction of the proletariat'? Although the bureaucracy—particularly in the USSR—has its historical roots in the working class and the labour movement, it cannot be considered merely a special 'fraction of the pro- letariat'. As the Soviet Left-Oppositionist Christian Rakovsky showed in his remarkable essay, 'The Professional Dangers of Power' (1928), the *functional* differentiation between those who exercise power and those who do not, tends to become a determinate *social* difference as well: the life conditions and the socio-economic privileges of the bureaucracy increasing- ly separate them from the working class. With time, Rakovsky empha- sized, 'the function modifies the organ', and individuals exercising the tasks of political and economic leadership, objectively and subjectively, materially and morally, become a distinct and consolidated layer.[46]

If we take the classical Marxist definition of a social class—a group of individuals who occupy the same position in the social process of produc- tion and share the same relationship to property in the means of produc- tion—it is difficult to consider the post-capitalist bureaucracy as a social class in a rigorous sense. The high-ranking officer in the KGB, the professor of 'Marxism-Leninism' and the manager of a hydro-electric trust, scarcely hold the same places in the production process and certainly are not owners of the means of production. What they do have in common are the follow- ing *political* and *ideological* characteristics: first, their membership of the ruling political institution, the party; second, its monopoly of social pow- er; and third, as a consequence of these first two conditions, their access to a system of socio-economic privileges.

Trotsky refused to characterize the Stalinist bureaucracy as a social class, designating it, instead, as a 'caste'. But he was the first, however, to recognize that 'this definition does not of course possess a strictly scientific character' and that 'the makeshift character of the term is clear to every- body, since it would enter nobody's mind to identify this Moscow oligar- chy with the Hindu caste of the Brahmins'.[47] Indeed, the term is not at all accurate, since the caste system as it exists in India is a totally *closed* and

---

[46]Rakovsky, 'Les dangers professionels du pouvoir', in *Les bolchéviks contre Staline 1923-28*, Paris 1958, pp. 157-61. A year after the publication of this essay, Rakovsky, in collaboration with other exiled Trotskyists, wrote a document that has only recently been discovered in the sealed section of the Trotsky Archives at Harvard. The document contains a characterization of the USSR which, in our opinion, is extremely perceptive: *'From a proletarian state with bureaucra- tic deformations*—as Lenin defined the political form of our state—*we are becoming a bureaucratic state with proletarian-communist remnants.* (K. Rakovsky, V. V. Kossior, N. I. Mouralov, V. S. Kasparova, 'Déclaration en vue du XVI Congrès du PCUS' (12 April 1930), *Cahiers Leon Trotsky*, 6, 1980, p. 97.)

[47]Trotsky, *In Defence of Marxism*, London 1966, pp. 6-7.

hereditary system of social stratificaction without social mobility: characteristics that obviously are not applicable to the Soviet bureaucracy. The
rationale for Trotsky's employment of the term, however, becomes clearer
when some of his other writings are considered. In an analysis of Tsarist
society, for instance, he refers to the several social estates as 'castes'. It is
likely, therefore, that Trotsky used 'caste' as synonymous with 'estate'.[48]
Now, we would argue that this concept of 'estate', defined by political and
ideological criteria, actually is the most adequate for grasping the specificity of a system of social stratification based on a bureaucracy. According to
Max Weber's well-known definition, a social estate (*Stand*) is a plurality of
individuals which has been able to impose special rights and (*Ständische*)
monopolies; these monopolies can take different forms, one of the most
important being the monopolistic appropriation of political power.[49]

Estates are not social classes, but a separate and subordinate system of
stratification. In the feudal mode of production, for example, a structure of
estates (nobility, clergy, third estate) existed side-by-side and partially
combined with the class structure: the nobility, largely, but not completely, coincided with the landowners as a social class. The third estate, in
contrast was primarily an *inter-class* layer, composed of the bourgeoisie,
petty bourgeoisie, peasants, urban plebs, and so on. The clergy was an even
more complex case: on one side, it was also an inter-class bloc, divided
between an aristocratic high clergy and a plebeian low clergy; on the other
side, however, its unity as an estate was quite real and assured to the
totality of its membership certain juridical and socio-economic privileges.
Thus the pre-capitalist clergy, constituted as an estate, possessed several
salient characteristics that are analogous with the post-capitalist bureaucracy: first, its institutional definition; second, institutional forms of property
(absence of private accumulation or the hereditary transmission of wealth);
third, an elaborate hierarchical structure with a concentration of power and
privilege at the top; fourth, the central role of ideology in the cohesion of
the estate and operation of its social power (as a corollary, ideological
monolithicity had to be defended at any price: thus witch hunts, inquisi-
tions, confession and abjuration of sinners, dogmatism, scholasticism and
so on).

The Stalinist party has frequently been compared to the medieval
church. It is obvious, however, that the two phenomena are radically

---

[48]See *La Jeunesse de Lénine*, p. 55.
[49]Max Weber, *Wirtschaft und Gesellschaft*, I, Tübingen 1921, p. 180. Marx and Engels also
distinguished estates from classes; see Marx, *The German Ideology*.

distinct and it would be superficial and ahistorical to see them as similar or equivalent. The feudal mode of production has nothing in common with post-capitalist society, and the Communist Party of the USSR is not a new incarnation of the Roman *Ecclesia*. Nevertheless, we would suggest that it is a fruitful hypothesis to consider the post-capitalist bureaucracy as a new form of *estate*, defined by political/ideological criteria, with an articulated institutional unity and a *de facto* monopoly of power in society. Further, we would argue that very nature of the post-capitalist social formation, especially its economic structure, founded on state property and centralized planning, *determines in the last instance* the possibility (although certainly not the inevitability) of the bureaucracy constituting itself as the dominant and privileged estate. Without being a class, the post-capitalist bureaucracy nonetheless fulfills some of the traditional functions of a ruling class: appropriation of the surplus, exercise of power and so on. The same, of course, can be said of a pre-capitalist estate such as the clergy. But while the mode of exploitation of the producing classes operated by the clergy was similar or overlapping with that of the feudal lords, the economic parasitism of the bureaucracy is *sui generis* and different from any social class. Thus, we can say that while the high energy of pre-capitalist society was partially assimilated to a ruling class (the feudal landowners); the high bureaucracy of the post-capitalist states *takes the place of a non-existent ruling class*.

In 1905 Trotsky expressed the hope that the permanent revolution would lead to the establishment of a workers' democracy. Although this was indeed briefly realized in Russia during the first year of the revolution, none of the post-1917 revolutions have achieved real proletarian deomcracy or even temporary phases of 'soviet' or councilist mass democracy. It is an essential question for the future of the socialist movement whether this absence of democracy has been inscribed as an inevitability in the nature of the objective conditions prevailing in backward and underdeveloped countries.

Some famous Marxist thinkers, following the example of Karl Kautsky, have interpreted the evolution of the USSR and other post-capitalist states in precisely such a fatalistic framework. Such a 'neo-Menshevik' perspective differs from traditional Menshevism in that it does concede the possiblity of anti-capitalist revolution in peripheral countries, but at the same time it insists that such a revolution is doomed to degenerate into totalitarian despotism. Because Kautsky was the first to coherently formulate such a position and because he contributed to an important reconstruction of the stagist problematic, it is useful to briefly chart the evolution of his analysis of the Russian revolution.

Initially Kautsky clung to traditional Menshevik orthodoxy, arguing as late as 1918 that the Russian revolution could not escape its fundamentally bourgeois-democratic destiny. In his first anti-Bolshevik pamphlet (*The Dictatorship of the Proletariat*—1918), for example, he argued that according to Marxism, 'the coming revolution . . . owing to the economic backwardness of Russia, could only be a middle-class one'; the Bolsheviks were repudiating Marx when they 'attempt to clear by bold leaps or remove by legal enactments the obstacles offered by the successive phases of *normal* development' (our emphasis). He emphatically denied that the Soviet regime could accomplish durable socialist tasks: 'That it has radically destroyed capitalism can be accepted by no one . . . capitalism will again rise, and must rise. Probably it will reappear very quickly. . . .'[50] But a year later, in *Terrorism and Communism*, there was a certain change in Kautsky's emphasis; the main argument revolved around the inevitable collapse of Bolshevism in the near future.[51] It was only in the 1920s, when the post-capitalist character and stability of the USSR had become irrefutable, that Katusky began to create a new theoretical formulation. He acknowledged that the Soviets had been capable of smashing capitalism, but he claimed that the new regime—which he sometimes designated as 'state capitalism'—was, if anything, *worse than capitalism* and even compared it unfavourably to Mussolini's Italy. By 1930 he arrived at a position that seemed like almost an exact mirror image of the 'social fascist' conception of Third Period Stalinism: Bolshevism and Fascism are basically identical ('Mussolini is only the ape of Lenin'), while the main enemy of the working class became no longer the 'primitive' or 'white-guard' counter-revolution so much as the 'Fascist-Bolshevik' (*faschistisch-bolchevistisch*) threat.[52]

Of course, these polemical excesses should not be taken too seriously, particularly because they were vehemently rejected by Kautsky's own Menshevik and Austro-Marxist friends. Rather more important and interesting, are Kautsky's contributions to the fatalist doctrine of the inevitable degeneracy of 'premature revolution'. In all of his post-1917 writings, for instance, he repeatedly argued that the Bolsheviks' unbridled subjectivism and voluntarism led them to violate the limitations of historical conditions and to attempt a socialist project on an immature socio-economic base that

[50]Kautsky, *The Dictatorship of the Proletariat*, 1964, pp. 98, 124-6, 136.

[51]*Terrorismus und Kommunismus* (1919) quoted by M. Salvadori, *Karl Kautsky and the Socialist Revolution 1880-1938*, London 1979, p. 301.

[52]Kautsky, *Der Bolschewismus in der Sackgasse*, Berlin 1930, pp. 102-3.

inevitably generated a brutal bureaucratic dictatorship.[53] Interestingly, he did not attribute the responsibility for this historical catastrophe solely to the Bolshevik Party, but also blamed the *'debasement' of the Russian proletariat itself*—the same proletariat which he had so extolled in his pre-1917 writings. 'The World War led to the moral and intellectual debasement of the toiling classes, not only because it brutalized nearly all strata of the population and elevated the least developed section of the proletariat to the vanguard of the social movement, but above all because it aggravated the proletariat's misery enormously, and thus replaced calm deliberation with the most bitter exasperation.[54] He went as far as to criticize the Bolsheviks for opportunistically yielding to the radicalism of these backward masses: 'The Bolsheviks owe their accession to power to the fact that they said Yes and Amen to all that the masses wanted, whether it was reasonable or not'.[55] The Bonapartist dictatorship in the USSR was, therefore, the punishment sent by the laws of history for the foolish, 'unreasonable' and 'exasperated' radicalism of the Russian working class.

In Kautsky's view, the only alternative to this bureaucratic dictatorship was the re-establishment of the 'successive phases of normal development': the restoration of *democratic capitalism* (the proper successor to feudal absolutism). In 1930 he advanced a 'democratic programme' for Russia which actually called for the abolition of the state monopoly of foreign trade in order 'to make room for free exchange' and for the establishment of capitalist, rather than state enterprises, 'when it is advantageous for consumers and workers'.[56] The rationale for this retrogressive programme had already been formulated back in 1919: 'The more a State is capitalistic on the one side and democratic on the other, the nearer it is to socialism.'[57] Only through capitalist democracy would the proletariat grow in numerical strength and acquire the necessary socio-cultural *maturity* that would allow it to implement a socialist transformation. Indeed, for Kautsky capitalism and democracy are virtual synonyms, and he had averred in the 1920s that fascism would necessarily be confined to backward agrarian countries such as Italy, since modern industrial capitalism was not compatible with such forms of reaction or authoritarianism.[58] Thus, no one was more tragically surprised or taken unawares by the events of January 1933 than Kautsky

---

[53]See Salvadori, p. 266.
[54]Quoted in ibid., p. 265.
[55]Kautsky, *Der Bolschewismus*, p. 46. See also Salvadori, p. 271.
[56]*Der Bolschewismus*, p. 137.
[57]*The Dictatorship of the Proletariat*, p. 96.
[58]Salvadori, p. 333.

himself. But it is important to recognize that his arguments were only restatements and reformulations of the premises of classical and inflexible stagist doctrine: the only road to socialism is through the evolution of advanced, democratic capitalism.

Kautsky and his followers, however, consistently turned their heads away from one of the most fundamental contradictions in their theory: if the 'backward' Russian masses had wanted socialist revolution, and if the original sin of the Bolsheviks had been to say 'Yes and Amen to all the workers demanded', then how could the October Revolution have been avoided without a bloody repression of the 'unreasonable' proletariat? In other worlds, was not the rule of Denikin's white terror the only real historical alternative to the relentless defence of proletarian revolution? And, after the formation of the USSR, would not the attempt to restore capitalism inevitably lead, as Max Adler argued against Kautsky in 1932, not to a 'normal', 'democratic' capitalism', but rather to counter-revolutionary dictatorship hardly conducive to further democratic or socialist evolution?[59] Furthermore, has not the historical record of the overwhelming majority of unrevolutionized dependent capitalist countries shown that democracy is a rare, episodic exception, and that the most common form of state rule has been some form of autocratic or military dictatorship?

The central motif in Kautsky's stagist conception of history is precisely this fetishism of 'maturity'. It is part of a general theoretical pattern in which socio-historical development is conceived, in neo-Darwinist terms, as 'the evolution of an organism' obeying laws of 'historical necessity'.[60] Furthermore, Kautsky directly linked the political 'immaturity' of the Russian proletariat to that country's economic immaturity, and attempted to explain that the virtual economic collapse of the Soviet Union at the end of the Civil War 'does not mean that socialism is impossible in itself. . . . But it means that the proletariat of a certain country and at a certain time is not yet mature for socialism, for industrial self-administration. That the productivity of its labour decreases as soon as the worker is no longer under the lash of the capitalist whip; that he lacks the necessary economic know-ledge and the necessary feeling of duty, which are as much a presupposition of socialism as a certain level of the concentration of capital'.[61] Only

[59]See ibid., pp. 310-1.
[60]'Marxism teaches us that socialism will arrive inevitably, according to natural necessity, at a certain level of capitalist development. But with this is indissolubly linked the other knowledge, that *socialism is impossible at an earlier stage of development*.' (Kautsky, *Die proletarische Revolution und ihr Programm*, Berlin 1922, p. 89.)
[61]Ibid., p. 159.

by going through 'the school of capitalist production' could the proletariat, in Kautsky's opinion, achieve the level of maturity requisite for
socialism and self-management.[62]

It is interesting to note the paradoxical affinity between Kautsky's
schema and certain emphases of the early Lenin on the crucial educative role
of the factory in acculturating the proletariat to discipline and organization.[63] Rosa Luxemburg, on the other hand, had already anticipated and
criticized this theory of the 'maturation' of the proletariat in the 'capitalist
school', in the course of her polemic with Lenin in 1904: 'What is there in
common between the regulated docility of an oppressed class and the
self-discipline and organization of a class struggling for its emancipation? . . . The working class will acquire the sense of a new discipline, the
freely assumed self-discipline of Social Democracy, not as a result of the
discipline imposed on it by the capitalist state, but by extirpating, to the
last root, its old habits of obedience and servility.'[64]

Although the direct descent of Kautsky's theses was limited, more diffuse
versions of his ideas can be encountered, in diverse contests, amongst many
Marxist writers from the 1920s to the present day. For instance, the
argument that capitalism and bourgeois democracy are the indispensable
'bridge to socialism', requisite for the political and moral 'ripening of the
proletariat', is central to Bill Warren's recent (posthumous) book, *Imperialism, Pioneer of Capitalism* (1980). According to Warren, 'bourgeois political
democracy would provide the working class the best conditions to acquire
the cultural depth required to becoming a ruling class.' This is a typically
Kautskian theme, as Warren himself recognizes in an adjoined footnote
('Cf. K. Kautsky: "Democracy is indispensable as a means of ripening the
proletariat for social revolution. . . ." ').[65]

There are some undeniably strong points in Warren's work, which could
be considered as healthy antidotes to the Khomeini-type irrational rejec-
tions of Western heritage, to other similar nationalist-religious mytholo-
gies in the Third World and even to certain anti-industrial, romanticist
tendencies in the First World. Warren, for instance, is unquestionably
correct to stress that imperialism *has* developed the productive forces in the
peripheral countries and that this development has, in turn, brought some

---

[62]Ibid., p. 335.

[63]See, for example, *One Step Forward, Two Steps Back.*

[64]Luxemburg, 'Organizational Questions of Russian Social Democracy' (1904), in *Selected
Political Writings,* London 1972, pp. 100-1.

[65]Bill Warren, *Imperialism: Pioneer of Capitalism,* London 1980, pp. 26-7.

important social improvements in terms of health, life expectancy, education, and so on. Moreover, his criticism of the famous 1928 Comintern resolution, which proclaimed that imperialism necessarily retarded the development of the productive forces and industrialism, is also cogent and useful, expecially since such vulgar and propagandistic conceptions are still flourishing in the revolutionary and/or nationalist movements of the Third World.

Warren's opus, however, is compromised by a very astonishing (for a Marxist) bias in favour of the 'progressive historical roles' of capitalism and imperialism, which, in turn, supports a stagist conception of socialist transformation. Warren's prejudices on these matters are so extreme that it reminds one less of classical Menshevism, and more of Piotr Struve and the 'Legal Marxist' apologia for Russian capitalism. Warren refers frequently to Marx's admiring remarks about the progressive role of world capitalism while forgetting the proper context of Marx's statements: the fact that Marx consistently emphasized the *contradictory* character of capitalism and its peculiar combination of progressive *and* regressive features *vis á vis* the development of social productive forces. Warren systematically opposes Marx to anti-capitalist romanticism, but seems to forget the interest and sympathy that Marx demonstrated towards some of the most famous romantic critics of industrial capitalism (Sismondi, Carlyle, Balzac and so on) precisely because they were able to grasp—albeit in a one-sided and utopian way—the *dark side* of capitalist civilization. He quotes extensively from an article by Marx on India, where the 'progressive' role of British imperialism is praised (railroad building, integration into the world market and so on), but omits mentioning its conclusion: after the triumph of socialism ('when a great social revolution shall have mastered the results of the bourgeois epoch'), 'then only will human progress cease to resemble that hideous pagan idol, who would not drink the nectar but from the skulls of the slain'.[66] Nor does Warren draw any of the proper conclusions from Marx's hope that Russia, through the alternative socialist path of the mir, might spare itself the 'fatal vicissitudes of the capitalist regime'.[67]

In his eagerness to prove the beneficial and civilizing destiny of imperialism—and, therefore, by implication to demonstrate that socialist revolutions in 'less developed' countries are a costly and useless detour—Warren systematically minimizes the horrors of the imperialist era, becoming a kind of modern Doctor Pangloss who tries to convince the wretched of the

---

[66]See Marx, 'The Future Results of the British Rule in India' (1853), in Marx and Engels, *On Colonialism*, p. 90.
[67]See Warren, p. 34.

earth that they actually live in the best of all possible worlds. He goes so far
as to claim that the 'colonial record, considering the immense numbers of
people involved, was remarkably free of widespread brutality'.[68] The least
that can be said of such an intepretation is that it obviously owes more to
Cecil Rhodes than to Karl Marx (whose chapter in *Capital* on 'The Genesis
of the Industrial Capitalist' is one of the fiercest indictments of colonial
brutality every written). But Warren does not stop here. Indeed, he goes
on to deny that imperialism is intrinsically responsible for malnutrition or
starvation in the Third World. In his rather astonishing view, famines are
only 'the result of mistaken policy, lack of suitable incentives and alloca-
tion of insufficient resources to agriculture'. Moreover, there is no need to
worry about the future, since 'these policy errors are now being rectified',
and 'sooner or later major advances will result, as agrarian capitalism
becomes sufficiently developed to use more productive methods and
inputs'.[69] When confronted with the fact that social inequality tends to rise
as backward countries industrialize, Warren cavalierly observes that this
'cannot be regarded automatically as negative, since there are strong,
though not yet conclusive, reasons to believe that this rising inequality is as
much a cause as a consequence of growth'. Furthermore, 'the pursuit of
economic equality for its own sake is both unjust and undemocratic'.
'Unjust' because 'it would tend to equally reward different groups and
individuals with different value judgements about consumption, leisure,
intensity of work' and so on. And 'undemocratic', because the majority of
the inhabitants of the Third World have a deep 'aspiration to keep up with
the Joneses' which does not imply 'a desire for an egalitarian economic
policy'.[70] Translated into present Third World reality, Warren's arguments, if they are to be taken in their literal sense, would mean that to
abolish the rising inequality between, say, Birla, the big Indian tycoon,
and the pauper masses of Calcutta would be 'unjust' since they have 'different value judgement about leisure and consumption' (indeed!); and 'undemocratic', since the hungry urban poor are obsessed with the 'aspiration
to keep up with the Joneses'. . . .

Although Warren does not make an assessment of the socialist revolutions in the peripheral capitalist countries explicitly, the scattered remarks
in his book tend to suggest that imperialism offers a preferable, less costly
and more efficient path to the modernization and industrialization of the
'less developed countries' (his stock phrase). While recognizing that the

[68]Ibid., p. 128.
[69]Ibid., pp. 238, 253.
[70]Ibid., pp. 208-11, 251.

Soviet Union did industrialize in a fantastically short period, he says this was 'due to specific factors that are not necessarily or easily repeatable'; and China is only mentioned to stress that 'several decades of civil war were necessary for the establishment of an egalitarian regime in China, with all that implied in terms of economic loss.'[71] For Warren, as for Kautsky, socialism can only be the direct outcome of advanced industrial capitalism, and he insists on the necessary economic and cultural *continuity* between them.[72] The idea that socialism should inaugurate an entirely new civilization, radically breaking with present modes of production/consumption and eliminating the irrationalities inherent in capitalist development (waste, planned obsolescence, consumerism, ecological destruction, and so on), seems totally alien to him.

But the principal pillar of Warren's neo-stagist conception, as well as his most obvious point of intersection with the Kautskian tradition, is the idea that a whole era of bourgeois democracy is an indispensable precondition for 'schooling' the working class for socialism. As was Kautsky, Warren is deeply convinced that 'capitalism and democracy are linked virtually as Siamese twins'[73]; but, as he explains in a footnote, he limits his discussion of this assertion to Western Europe. This is most unfortunate, since the fundamental problem is precisely whether this putative equation between capitalism and democracy can be discerned as tendentially true of the less developed countries as well. As we have already had several occasions to emphasize, the political norm in the most rapidly industrializing peripheral countries (and with a few *partial* exceptions such as India or Venezuela) is authoritarian or military rule, not parliamentary democracy. Thus, what kinds of skills 'for running a socialist society' are likely to be acquired under such despotisms? And, even in the advanced capitalist democracies, what level of socialist culture is developed by working classes whose main political activity is to vote every four, five or seven years, while technocrats and politicians of the bourgeoisie run both economy and state in the meantime? Finally, if bourgeois democracy is the decisive 'training ground' for socialism—or as Kautsky puts it, 'the indispensable means of ripening the proletariat'—why is it that the US proletariat, after more than a century of representative democracy, is still politically one of the most backward and 'unripe'—from a socialist standpoint—in the world?

It seems to us that Warren, like Kautsky before him, has simply ignored the basic difference between bourgeois and socialist democracy:

[71]Ibid., pp. 116, 210.
[72]Ibid., p. 24.
[73]Ibid., p. 28.

while the first is grounded on the passivity of the workers, the second can only exist through their *self-activity* on both political and economic planes. The proletariat can learn the skills required to become a new ruling class only through its own experiences, its own revolutionary *praxis* and its own exercise of power, from the level of the factory floor to the overall administration of the state. It is only by riding that one learns to ride and not by watching other people ride or helping them—every few years or so—climb on the horse's back. There is a fundamental and unbridgable contradiction between the naturalistic ideology of evolutionary 'maturation', so typical of the Kautskian school, and the decisive conception of historical materialism, first formulated by Marx in his 'Third Thesis on Fuerbach': 'the coincidence of the changing of circumstances and of human activity or self-changing can be conceived and rationally understood only as *revolutionary practice*'.

Other echoes of the Kautskian neo-stagist problematic, albeit in a very different inflection from Warren, have appeared in the recent work of Rudolf Bahro. At first glance, Bahro does not seem to have much in common with the Kautskian tradition. For example, he considers the Soviet Union and other post-capitalist countries as 'proto-socialist' societies, representing real historical progress from backwardness: 'Revolutions such as the Russian and the Chinese are the precondition for victory over hunger.'[74] At the same time, however, Bahro shows in his remarkable book (without doubt one of the most important *Marxist* contributions to a theory of post-revolutionary society) that none of those states has yet achieved real socialism and that their political nature is bureaucratic and despotic. Where Bahro does overlap with the fatalist historiography of Kautsky and company is his assertion that his 'industrial despotism'—the bureaucratic dictatorship—is an *inevitable* stage along the 'non-capitalist road' of the underdeveloped, post-revolutionary societies. In the case of the USSR, for example, Bahro is convinced that Stalinism corresponded to an objective necessity. Although he readily concedes that most extreme forms of terror and absolutism (the 'Caesarist folly') might have been avoided by a leader with different subjective qualities than Stalin; he nonetheless insists that the divergence between material progress and socio-political emancipation was inevitable since 'only a great leap in the technical and cultural level of the masses could create the preconditions for socialist relations of production'.[75]

[74]Rudolf Bahro, *The Alternative in Eastern Europe*, London 1978, p. 58.
[75]Ibid., p. 117.

The double functions of the Soviet state in the Stalin era—to discipline labour and to resist the egalitarian tendencies of the masses—were a necessary condition for the country's economic development, given the backwardness and uneven development inherited from the ancien regiem. Furthermore, Bahro criticizes Trotsky for considering only the subjective determinants of Stalinism, dismissing *The Revolution Betrayed* as only an early version of the thesis of the 'cult of the personality'. In Bahro's view, Trotsky did not appreciate that if Stalin had seized power and brutally centralized it around himself, this was due to the fact that 'he possessed the historically necessary passion to create the apparatus of power for the terroristic transformation from above that Russia then needed'.[76]

In a similar vein, Bahro polemicizes against Mandel and argues that a socialist democracy in the USSR of the 1920s and the 1930s would have been impossibly inefficient and economically disastrous.[77] Yet at the same time he makes no attempt to show why 'bureaucratic despotism', with its attendant waste, corruption and general irrationality, is a more 'efficient' management of the economy than socialist democracy, and, therefore, the only alternative that guaranteed the development and survival of the USSR.

But Bahro's historical analysis goes well beyond the Soviet case, and he argues that not only in the USSR, but also in China and all the countries of the Third World, the state is 'the taskmaster of society in its technical and social modernization'.[78] In all the not yet fully industrialized countries 'the discipline of obedience to instructions, which can only be made effective with a despotism of some kind or other, is the surest guarantee that the progressive interests will carry the day'.[79] He honestly and frankly recognizes that such a perspective easily incurs the danger of appearing as *apologetic*, but he insists that 'critical realism' shows that the various forms of despotic domination that arise in the course of non-capitalist industrialization are 'practically unavoidable consequences of a definite historical progress'.[80]

Only after the creation of the industrial and cultural infrastructure for socialism can proletarian democracy become a concrete historical possibility: such is now the stage attained in the USSR and the industrial states of Eastern Europe.

Thus, in contrast to Kautsky, Bahro clearly opts for the *non-capitalist*

[76]Ibid., pp. 19-20.
[77]Ibid., pp. 104-5.
[78]Ibid., p. 129.
[79]Ibid., p. 130.
[80]Ibid., p. 163.

road for the industrialization and modernization of the underdeveloped countries, but, at the same time, he shares the Kautskian belief that in the absence of the crucial preconditions of proletarian democracy—industrialization, modernization, and the 'technical-cultural qualification of the masses'—bureaucratic despotism is inevitable. Furthermore, Bahro implies that only after the (non-capitalist) industrialization of these post-revolutionary societies will the proletariat be competent to rule directly as a class. Once again, Rosa Luxemburg had anticipated precisely such an argument, and in her 1918 polemic with the Bolsheviks she asserted: 'Socialist democracy is not something which begins only in the promised land after the foundations of socialist economy are created; it does not come as some sort of Christmas present for the worthy people who, in the interim, have loyally supported a handful of socialist dictators. Socialist democracy begins simultaneously with the beginning of the destruction of class rule and of the construction of socialism . . . it must arise out of the growing political training of the masses of the people'.[81] In other words, the decisive precondition for socialist democracy—far more important than the degree of industrialization or level of technical skills—is the accumulated *revolutionary praxis* of the proletariat as a class, both before and after the seizure of power.

What Bahro shares, then, with the Kautskian tradition, is a *passive* conception of 'maturation' (mechanically linked to modernization, economic development, and so on), which does not grasp the centrality of mass *self-activity and self-organization* in the 'education' of the proletariat to become masters of the new society. Behind Bahro's historiography lurks the old materialist philosophy of the eighteenth century, which believed that 'circumstances make men' and that, therefore, backward conditions make 'backward' classes. This doctrine (which Marx criticized devastatingly in the *Theses on Feuerbach* and other writings) leads logically to an impasse whose classical resolution was the idea of an 'enlightened despot' who would alter circumstances and open the way for a pedagogical transformation of the people. In this respect, Bahro is a socialist Diderot explaining the historical role of Stalin as the simulacrum of Catherine the Great. . . .

In conclusion, however, we must recongize a certain 'rational kernel' in the views of Kautsky, Warren and Bahro: it is undoubtedly true that social, economic and political underdevelopment are major obstacles to the establishment of socialist democracy and constitute a very favourable environ-

---

[81] Rosa Luxemburg, *The Russian Revolution* (1918), in *Selected Political Writings*, p. 249.

ment for the growth of bureaucratic parasitism, economic authoritarianism and ideological monolithism. Trotsky himself was keenly aware of this and, in his *The Revolution Betrayed*, emphasized the powerful role of objective conditions—particularly scarcity—in facilitating the triumph of Stalinism. He was also convinced that in an advanced country such as the United States, with a high level of industrialization and a long tradition of democracy, the danger of bureaucratic degeneration in the wake of proletarian revolution would be much smaller. But at the same time he believed in the realistic possiblity of combating, even in the poorest and most underdeveloped countries, the tendencies toward bureaucratization and the usurpation of proletarian democracy. In contrast with Kautsky and his ilk, Trotsky never accepted the thesis that bureaucratic despotism is somehow the unavoidable punishment inflicted upon those mass movements who dare to smash capitalism and imperialism before their full 'maturation'.

Historical evidence does not yet allow us to weigh definitively the balance between the antagonistic positions of Kautsky and Trotsky, but it does seem to support the politics of the latter more strongly than those of the former. For at the very least, it shows that there is no direct relationship between the degree of the industrialization of a post-capitalist society (or its parliamentary traditions) and its level of bureaucratic ossification. Indeed, the most important variable seems to be whether or not—and to what degree—the post-capitalist state was the product of an authentic popular revolution. Certainly this is what distinguishes Cuba and Yugoslavia on the one side (where the post-revolutionary state enjoys a genuine popularity and where certain forms of local popular power—in the factories or neighborhoods—exist) from the GDR or Czechoslavkia on the other (notwithstanding their industrialization or the democratic traditions of the latter). The USSR is not, as it might seem at first glance, an exception to this rule: the Bolshevik Revolution produced a revolutionary state with more elements of pluralism (until 1920-21 other socialist groups were legal and participated in the soviets) and socialist democracy than any other post-capitalist regime. Unquestionably these elements of democracy were deeply corroded by the Civil War and the forced retreat of the NEP, but it took a massive and systematic extermination of the old revolutionary party to definitively establish the bureaucratic dictatorship in the 1930s.

It seems reasonable to assume, therefore, that the intervention of the so-called 'subjective factors'—the participatory character of the revolutionary process, the democratic/pluralistic outlook of the socialist vanguard, the degree of proletarian self-activity and popular self-organization, and so on—can, if not abolish, then at least limit and *counterbalance* the tendencies toward bureaucratization inherent in the transition toward socialism in a poor and underdeveloped country. Considering the bureaucratic degeneration of the USSR, for example, we must count amongst the negative 'subjective' determinants, the lack of socialist-democratic awareness on the part of the revolutionary leadership. The mistakes of the Bolsheviks in 1917-23 paved the way for the emergence and, later, the triumph of the Stalinist bureaucratic estate. The revolutionaries of October created, by default of maintaining the vigour of proletarian democracy, a Golem—a bureaucratic apparatus—that soon escaped their control, ran amock and finally destroyed them. Once again, the prescience of Rosa Luxemburg commands admiration. In opposition to Kautsky and the Mensheviks, she expressed her full solidarity with the audacious project of the Bolshevik Revolution, but at the same time, she warned Lenin and Trotsky that the curtailment of socialist democracy would, sooner or later, lead to a bureaucratic Thermidor.[82]

It is, therefore, far from clear that bureaucratic despotism is inevitably in-built into the process of permanent revolution in peripheral capitalist countries. In particular, it remains to be seen whether the existence of massive forms of popular self-organization combined with a profound commitment to socialist democracy by the hegemonic revolutionary political organizations cannot check the 'natural' tendencies towards bureaucratism that arise out of scarcity and backwardness. Historical research and sociological analysis cannot provide unequivocal replies to this question; the answer belongs to the realm of future *praxis*, in the classical Marxist sense of the word.

---

[82]Ibid., pp. 247-8.

5
Permanent Revolution in the Twenty-First Century
Interview with Michael Löwy by Phil Gasper, 2010

What led you to write your book?

I had been interested in the issue for many years, since my time as a socialist activist in Brazil. At that time—the late 1950s—the main force of the left was the Brazilian Communist Party, whose aim was a 'national-democratic revolution" in alliance with the "progressive national bourgeoisie'. I soon discovered, by reading *The Permanent Revolution*—in an old French stenciled edition—the best arguments against this Stalinist conception. Although my main theoretical reference was Rosa Luxemburg rather than Leon Trotsky, I was persuaded that the idea of permanent revolution was not only useful, but indispensable to elaborate a radical political strategy in Latin America. The astonishing development of the Cuban revolution during the years 1959–61 seemed to bring a striking confirmation of Lev Davidovitch's insights.

As a student in Paris I had planned, after my 'first PhD' (Doctorat de troisième cycle) on Young Marx (1964), to write a 'Second PhD' (Doctorat d'Etat) on 'Marx's Conception of Permanent Revolution'. I even registered the subject and found a thesis advisor, the well-known historian of the French revolution, Ernest Labrousse. I started to work on the issue, and produced an article discussing Marx's little-known writings on the Spanish revolution of 1854–56, as an example of his "permanentist" approach. But for various reasons, this project was never completed, and in the 1970s I decided to take up a new PhD subject, the political evolution of Georg Lukacs (presented in 1974).

In answer to a request from my Latin American comrades, I wrote in 1972 a small booklet—62 pages—*Permanent Revolution in Latin America*, published in Paris by François Maspero, and in a Spanish version in Buenos Aires in 1973. I suppose this was one of the reasons why, a few years later, I was invited by my friends from New Left Books to write an essay that would both examine the origins of the theories of uneven and combined development, and of permanent revolution, from Marx to Trotsky, and discuss its relevance to understanding events in the twentieth century. The idea came from Perry Anderson, who thought there was a need to systematically reassess some of the key theoretical tools of Marxism. My first draft was given to a rather hostile reader whose comments were very unfriendly, but forced me to strengthen some of my arguments, and take into account some objections.

The book came out in 1979 and was later translated into German and Korean. It was divided in two sections: Part One discussed the genesis of the theoretical argument, and Part Two tried to analyze historical events in the light of the theory: on one side, the social revolutions in "backward" capitalism: Russia, China, Vietnam, Yugoslavia, Cuba; on the other, the failure of the unfinished bourgeois revolutions in Mexico, Algeria, India, Egypt, Turkey.

Thirty years later, I feel that much of it has become outdated. Among other reasons, because most of the societies that I characterized as "post-capitalist" have simply restored capitalism, without much resistance from the exploited classes. I think however that the first chapter, with the history of the theory, and the conclusion, which tries to assess its relevance, are still of some interest—I hope!

Trotsky first wrote about 'combined and uneven development' in the global capitalist system at the time of the 1905 Russian Revolution. Over a century later has the nature of the capitalist world system changed qualitatively in any way that means we have to reevaluate Trotsky's conclusions?

Of course, there have been very substantial changes in the capitalist world system since 1905! Colonial empires have practically disappeared, new capitalist powers have emerged—China!—and the process of globalisation, under the hegemony of financial capital, has dominated the world economy to an unprecedented scale. But the system is still characterized by the unevenness between center and periphery, between the highly industrialized countries of the Atlantic North and the 'underdeveloped' world of the global South: Africa, Latin America, and most of Asia. UN statistics, showing that 1 per cent of the world population—the richest minority in the North—possess as much as the poorest 50 per cent, living in the South, is a striking illustration of this 'unevenness'. On the other hand, the center and periphery of the system have never been so powerfully 'combined', i.e., unified, under the aegis of multinational enterprises and banks, financial markets, and international capitalist institutions (International Monetary Fund, World Bank, World Trade Organisation, etc.).

Trotsky was mainly interested in the way that capitalist development in peripheric countries—Russia in 1905, China in 1930—combined a remarkably advanced and modern industry with "backward" economic and social conditions in the rural areas. Does this still apply? It is difficult to give a general answer. For instance, in many countries in Latin America one has seen a strong development of agribusiness, producing export crops with modern methods—

fertilizers, GMOs, pesticides, machinery—all of which, by the way, are highly destructive of the environment. On the other side, in many big towns in the South, industrial development has been limited, and the majority of the urban population, living in the slums, survives on the margins of the productive system, in the so-called 'informal economy'. One could, however, consider this as a new form of 'uneven and combined' development: in the megacities of Brazil, India, or Egypt, a small island of modern industrial, financial, and commercial enterprises—often multinational—is surrounded by a sea of urban poor, composed of street vendors, prostitutes, unemployed workers, rubbish collectors and small-time drug dealers. Similarly, in the rural areas, modern agricultural capitalist ventures combine with traditional latifundia, and brutally exploit small sharecroppers, subsistence farmers and a mass of poor landless peasants. These contradictions may not be similar to those of Tzarist Russia in 1905, but are still forms of "uneven and combined" peripheric capitalism, which generate explosive social tensions and, sometimes, semi-insurrectionary uprisings.

You've written: 'In the struggle of the countries of the South against neo-liberal globalisation, against the world financial institutions, against the inhumanity of the foreign debt system, against the imposition by the IMF of "adjustment" policies with dramatic social consequences, the national question regains a burning relevance.' Could you describe struggles today you think are important examples of this?

As Trotsky argued, in the 'colonial and semi-colonial' countries, the social confrontation is not only one between labour and capital, but also between the popular classes and the colonial powers. Well, today there are a few colonial situations—Puerto Rico, Martinique, but also the occupied territories in Palestine are some examples—and a few situations of direct imperial military intervention—Iraq and Afghanistan!—but imperialist hegemony over the so-called Third World is still the rule.

The national question in the capitalist-dependent countries—quite different in nature from the national question in, say, Spain or the United Kingdom— concerns the resistance against any form of foreign/imperial domination, be it economic, political or otherwise. The issue of 'national liberation' is still relevant in those countries, and any movement for social emancipation has to integrate it in its program and strategy. For instance, in Sub-Saharan Africa, how can one imagine a social/revolutionary movement that is not also, at the same time, directed against French neocolonial domination? And the same applies, in Latin America, to US imperial power. The struggles I mentioned against neoliberal globalisation, the foreign debt system, the IMF and the WTO, are still very much relevant today, everywhere in the global South.

Let me give some examples from Latin America, with whose developments I'm more familiar. In 1994, when the Zapatista uprising took place in Chiapas, the immediate reason for the rebellion was the imposition of NAFTA, the North American Free Trade Agreement, which submitted the Mexican economy to the interests of US capital. Not by accident, the organization that led the uprising, and is still active in southern Mexico, called itself the 'Zapatista Army of National Liberation'. The struggle against US 'free trade' schemes was one of the key issues in social mobilizations south of the Rio Grande during the 1990s and the beginning of the new century until finally the US-sponsored 'Free Trade Association of the Americas' (ALCA in Spanish) was defeated.

More recently, the new leftist governments in Venezuela—Hugo Chávez— and Bolivia—Evo Morales—have put anti-imperialism, i.e., the confrontation with economic and political interests of the US, very high on their agenda. Whatever their shortcomings, this anti-imperialist stance is certainly one of the reasons for the popular support they enjoy (for the moment, at least).

While nationalism can be, even in Latin America, quite narrow and often reactionary, anti-imperialism has a more radical potential, leading to the cooperation between various countries, aiming at a common emancipation from the economic and political grip of the United States. This is the case with ALBA, the Bolivarian initiative, including Cuba, Venezuela, Bolivia, Ecuador, Nicaragua and other countries.

Since the Zapatista uprising, a new form of 'national question' has become decisive in Latin America: the struggle of indigenous communities and 'nations'. The aim here is not separation, independence or setting up a new state, but local autonomy and the dismantling of the colonial (racist) structure of the existing states. Mexico, Guatemala, Ecuador, Peru and Bolivia are the main countries where such indigenous movements have developed. The most important success for indigenism has been achieved in Bolivia, with the election of a peasant of indigenous origin, Evo Morales, and the establishment, by popular vote, of a new Constitution, transforming Bolivia into a multinational state. Of course, such developments have not been predicted by Trotsky, but they illustrate the relevance of the 'national question' for any revolutionary process in Latin America—or, as the great Peruvian Marxist José Carlos Mariategui used to say, *Indoamerica*.

You have noted that Trotsky emphasized 'the necessarily international character of the revolutionary process'. Do you see the germs of such internationalism today? Have changes in the means of communication complicated or enhanced how internationalism is expressed today?

The most promising development in terms of internationalism during the last decade has been the rise of the global justice movement. In the Spanish, *el movimiento altermundialista.* This is not yet a 'revolutionary process' but has contributed to the rise of anti-imperialist and anti-neoliberal mobilisations around the planet. Its diversity reflects the 'uneven and combined' nature of capitalist globalisation.

This vast galaxy, a sort of 'movement of movements', whose most visible manifestations are the social forums—local, continental or international—and the great demonstrations of protest—against the World Trade Organisation (WTO), the G-8 (annual meeting of the eight great powers), or the imperial war in Iraq, do not correspond to the usual forms of social or political action. Being a large decentralized network, it is multiple, diverse and heterogenous, associating workers unions and peasant movements, NGOs and indigenous associations, women's movements and ecological initiatives, senior intellectuals and young activists (or vice versa). Far from being a weakness, this plurality is one of the sources of the movements' growing and expansive power.

The international solidarities that grow inside this vast network are of a new sort, somewhat different from those of the internationalist mobilisations of the 60s and 70s. In those years, solidarity networks would *support* liberation movements, either in the global South—the Algerian, Cuban or Vietnamese revolutions—or in Eastern Europe: the Polish dissidents, the Prague Spring. A few years later, in the 1980s, important solidarity movements developed in support of the Sandinistas in Nicaragua, or of Solidarnosc in Poland.

This fraternal and generous tradition of solidarity with the oppressed has not disappeared from the new movement for global justice that started during the 90s—far from it. An obvious example is the sympathy and the support, on an international scale, for the Zapatistas, after the indigenous uprising of January 1994 in Chiapas, Mexico. But one sees here already something new emerging, a change of perspective. In 1996, the Zapatista Army of National Liberation called an Intercontinental—ironically described by Subcommander Marcos as 'Intergalactic'—Encounter against Neoliberalism and for Humanity. The thousands of participants, originating from forty countries, who came to this encounter—which could be considered the first event of what would later be called *movimiento altermundialista*—where motivated, without doubt, *also* by feelings of solidarity with the Zapatistas. But the aim of the meeting, defined by its organizers, was much larger: the search for convergencies in the *common struggle* against a *common ennemy*, neoliberalism, and the discussion of possible alternatives for humanity.

Here is therefore the new characteristic of the solidarities that are woven inside or around the movement of global resistance to capitalist globalisation: the fight for immediate aims common to all—for instance, the defeat of the WTO—and the common search for new paradigms of civilisation. In other words; instead of a solidarity *with* it is a solidarity *between* the various organizations, social movements or political forces from different countries or continents, which help each other and cooperate in the *same battle*, against the same planetary enemies.

The dynamics of the global justice movement includes three distinct but complementary moments: *the negativity of resistance, the concrete proposals, and the utopia of another world.*

The first moment, the starting point of the movement, is the *great refusal,* the protest, the imperative need to *resist* against the existing order of things. This is why the global justice movement constitutes, in fact, the International of Resistance that Jacques Derrida hoped for in his book *Specters of Marx* (1993). The initial motivation for the multitudes that mobilised against the WTO in Seattle (1999) was the wish to oppose, actively, not "globalisation" as such, but its capitalist and liberal form, i.e., *corporate globalisation* with its sequel of injustices and catastrophes: growing inequality between North and South, unemployement, social exclusion, destruction of the environment, imperial wars, crimes against humanity. Not by accident the *altermundialista* movement was born with a cry, issued by the Zapatistas in 1994: *Ya basta!* Enough of that! The strength of the movement comes first of all from this *radical negativity*, inspired by a deep and irreducible *indignation.* Celebrating the dignity of indignation and of the unconditionnal rejection of injustice, Daniel Bensaïd wrote: 'The burning current of indignation cannot be dissolved into the lukewarm waters of consensual resignation ... Indignation is a beginning. A way to stand up and to start on the road. People are indignated, they rise up, and then see what happens.'[1] The radicality of the movement results, to a large extent, from this capacity of rebellion and insubmission, of this uncompromising disposition to say *no!*

The hostile critics of the movement and the conformist media insist heavily on its excessively 'negative' character, its nature of 'pure protest', the absence of 'realist' alternative propositions. One must resolutely reject this blackmail: even if the movement did not have one single proposition to make, its rebellion would be *entirely justified.* The street protests against the WTO, the G-8 or the imperial war are the visible, concentrated and vocal expression of this defiance against the powers that be, and their rules of the game. The movement is proud of its active negativity, its rebellious complexion. Without this radical feeling of refusal, the global justice movement would simply not exist.

Against which enemy is this rejection directed? The international financial institutions (WTO, World Bank, International Monetary Fund)? Or the neoliberal policies? Or still the great multinational monopolies? All these forces, responsible for the commodification of the world, are among the favourite tar-

---

[1] D. Bensaïd, *Les irréductibles. Théorèmes de la résistance à l'air du temps,* Paris, Textuel, 2001, p. 106.

gets. But the movement is more radical. This word means, as we know, to go after the roots of the problems. Now, what is at the root of the banks and monopolies' total domination, of the financial market's dictatorship, of the imperialist wars, if not *the capitalist system* itself ? For sure, not all components of the global justice movement are ready to draw this conclusion: some still dream of a return to neo-Keynesianism, of the 'thirty glorious' years of growth, or of a regulated capitalism, with a human face. These 'moderates' have all their place in the movement, but usually the radical tendency predominates. Most of the documents issued by the movement challenge not only the neo-liberal and bellicist policies, but the power of capital itself. Let us take, for instance, the World Social Forum(WSF)'s 'Charter of Principles', issued by the Brazilian Organising Committee—composed not only of delegates from the unions and peasant movements, but also of the NGOs and of the Peace and Justice Commission of the Catholic Church—and approved, with small changes, by the International Council of the WSF. This document, one of the most representative and 'consensual' of the *altermundialista* movement states:

'The World Social Forum is an open space of encounter whose aim is to deepen reflection, debate democratic ideas, formulate propositions, freely exchange experiences, and articulate in view of efficient actions, organizations and movements of civil society that are opposed to neoliberalism and to the domination of the world by capital and all form of imperialism, and which wish to build a planetary society grounded on the human being ... The alternatives proposed by the WSF are opposed to a process of capitalist globalisation commanded by the great multinational enterprises ...'[2] The main parole of the movement, 'the world is not a commodity', is not so far from the ideas of a certain Karl Marx, who denounced in his *Manuscripts of 1844* a system—capitalism—where 'the worker becomes a commodity, whose worthlesness increases with the quantity of commodities it produces. The depreciation of the human world increases in direct relation with the rise in value of the world of things'.[3] The radicality of the movements' *great refusal* concerns the capitalist nature of domination.

However, in contrast to the assertions of the establishment scribes, the global justice movement does not lack concrete, urgent, practical and immediately feasible *alternative propositions*. For sure, none of its bodies has approved a 'common program', and no political force has imposed its project. But there appear, during the forums and mobilisations, several demands that are, if not unanimous, at least largely shared and carried by the movement: for instance, suppression of the Third World's debt, taxation of financial trans-

[2] En annexe dans Bernard Cassen, *Tout a commencé à Porto Alegre...*, Paris, Mille et une nuits, 2003, p. 166.
[3] K. Marx, *Manuscrits de 1844*, Paris, Ed. Sociales, 1962, p. 57.

actions, suppression of fiscal paradises, a moratorium on GMOs, the right of peoples to nourish themselves, effective equality between men and women, defense and extension of public services, priority for health, education and culture, protection of the environment. These demands were elaborated by the movements' international networks—Womens World March, Attac, Focus on the Global South, Via Campesina, Committee for the Abolition of the Third World's Debt—and by various other social movements, and discussed in the Forums. One of the great qualities of those is to provide the space for the gathering and mutual exchange of knowledge of feminists and trade unionists, ecologists and Marxists, believers and non-believers, activists from the North and the South. In this process of confrontation and mutual enrichment, the disagreements do not disappear, but little by little there emerges a body of common propositions.

We touch here the third moment, as important as the previous ones: the *utopian dimension* of the 'movement of movements'. It also is radical: 'another world is possible'. The aim is not simply to correct the excesses of the capitalist/industrial world, and its monstruous neoliberal policies, but to dream, and to struggle, for *another civilisation,* another economic and social paradigm, another way of living together on the planet Earth. Beyond all the multiple concrete and specific propositions, the movement harbors a more ambitious, more 'globa', more universal transformative perspective. Here too, one would search in vain for a common project, a consensual reformist or revolutionary program. The *altermundialista* utopia shows itself only in the sharing of certain *common values.* It is they that sketch the outlines of this other 'possible world'.

The first of these values is the *human being itself.* The utopia of the movement is resolutely humanist, it requires that the needs, the aspirations of human beings become the vital center of a reorganisation of economy and society. Its rebellion against the commodification of human relations, against the transformation of love, culture, life, health, into commodities, supposes another form of social life, beyond reification and fetishism. Not by accident the movement addresses itself to all humans, even if it privileges the oppressed and the exploited as social change actors. The defense of the environment also stems from humanist inspiration: to save the ecological equilibrium, to protect nature against the predatory attacks of capitalist productivism is the condition to assure the continuity of human life on this planet.[2] Another essential value of the *altermundialista* utopia is *democracy.* The idea of participatory democracy, as a superior form of citizenship, beyond the limits of the traditional representative systems—because it permits the population to exercise directly its power of decision and control—takes a central place in the discussions of the movement. It has an 'utopic' value, in so far as it questions the existing forms of power, but at the same time it is already being put into practice, under limited and experimental forms, in several towns, beginning, of course, with Porto Alegre, the first meeting place of the WSF. The great challenge, from the view point of an alternative society project, is to extend democracy to the economical and social sphere. Why permit in these areas the exclusive power of an elite that one rejects in the political sphere?

Capital has replaced the three great revolutionary values of the past—*liberty, equality, fraternity*—with more "modern" concepts: liberalism, equity, charity. The utopia of the global justice movement takes up the values of 1789, but gives them a new scope: for instance, liberty is not only the freedom of expression, organisation, thought, criticism—won at a high price by fierce struggles, which took centuries, against absolutism and dictatorship. It is also, today more than ever, the freedom from another form of absolutism: the dictatorship of the financial markets and the oligarchy of bankers and heads of multinational enterprises, which impose their interests on the whole planet. As for equality, it concerns not only the 'social fracture' between the richest elite and the dispossessed masses, but also the inequality between nations, continents—the North and the South—as well as between men and women. Finally, fraternity—which seems to limit itself to the brothers (*frates* in latin)—wins by being replaced by *solidarity*, i.e., by relations of cooperation, sharing and mutual help. The expression *civilisation of solidarity* is perhaps the best summary of the movements' alternative project. This requires not only a radically different economic and political structure, but also an alternative society that cherishes the ideas of common good, general interest, universal rights, gratuity.

Another important value of the global justice culture is *diversity*. The new world of which the movement dreams is anything but a homogeneous one, where all are supposed to imitate a unique model. We want, said the Zapatistas, 'a world where different worlds can find their place'. The plurality of languages, cultures, music, food and life forms is an immense wealth that one must learn to cultivate.

All these values do not define a model of society for the future. They provide paths, openings, windows toward the possible. The road to utopia is not yet traced: it is the marchers themselves who are going to trace it.

For many of the participants in the forums and the demonstrations, *socialism* is the name of this utopia. It is a hope shared by Marxists and anarchists, radical Christians and left ecologists, as well as by a significant number of activists of the labour, peasant, feminist or indigenous movements. A socialist democracy would mean that the great socioeconomic and ecological choices, the priorities in terms of investment, the basic orientations of production and distribution, would be democratically discussed and *decided* by the population itself, and not by a handful of exploiters, in the name of the so-called 'laws of the market' (nor, in a variant that has already failed, by an all-powerful politiburo). It wouldn't make sense to impose socialism as the program of the global justice movement, but the debate on socialism—very much at the center of political life in several countries in Latin America, under the form of a debate on 'socialism in the twenty-first century'—is a legitimate part of the confrontation of alternative projects and ideas.

In any case, the global justice movement is not waiting for this utopian future to arrive, but is acting and struggling, here and now. Each social forum, each local experience of participatory democracy, each collective land occupation by peasants, each internationally coordinated action against war is a prefiguration of the *altermundialista* utopia, and is inspired by its values, which are those of a civilisation of solidarity.

What do you think is the importance of Trotsky's theory of permanent revolution for political activists in the twenty-first century?

I think that Trotsky's theory, on the condition that one doesn't take it as closed system that has answers to everything, is a very precious tool to understand the 'uneven and combined' nature of the system, and the 'combined' nature of the possible revolutionary processes in the capitalist periphery. It has all sorts of shortcomings, to which I refer in my conclusion, but it still has the great advantage of pointing to the connection between anti-imperialist, agrarian, democratic and anticapitalist struggles: not one of them can triumph if not 'combined' with the others ... One should not take the theory as being predictions about the future, it only can propose conditional perspectives: if movements for national liberation, or agrarian reform, or radical democratisation do not develop, in an 'uninterrupted' process, into a socialist revolution, they will sooner or later be defeated. This applies also to the more promising developments in Latin America today, such as those in Venezuela, Colombia or Ecuador.

New problems have emerged in the twenty-first century, not predicted by Trotsky, but which can be approached by using his method. For instance, the ecological issue, about which Lev Davidovitch hardly had an inkling. However, the key ecological issues—such as the catastrophic process of global warming—are intimately linked with the logic of the capitalist system. The expansion of capital, and the destruction of the environment are 'combined' and inseparable. Therefore, a struggle to save the climate has to become an anticapitalist combat, otherwise is it doomed to failure. This is not 'permanent revolution' as Trotsky formulated it, but there is a sort of analogous argument.

Index

Address of the Central Committee to the Communist League (Marx & Engels), 14, 16, 17, 47

Adler, Max, 134

Afghanistan, 116n, 117n, 119

Age of Permanent Revolution (Deutscher ed.), 44

Aidit, P. N., 107

Alavi, Hamza, 123–5

Algeria, 109, 118, 121, 124, 125

Allende, Salvador, 105

The Alternative in Eastern Europe (Bahro), 139, 140

Althusser, Louis, 84

Alvarado, Velasco, 118

Amador, Carlos Fonseca, 116

Amin, Hafizullah, 117n

Anarchists, 33, 102

Anderson, Perry, 32n

Angola, 119

Anti-Duhring (Engels), 74

April Theses (Lenin), 33, 59–61, 63, 68, 84

Arabs (in Iran), 115

Arbenz, Jacobo, 106

Armas, Colonel Castillo, 106

Aux origines de la revolution permanente, la pensée politique du jeune Trotsky (Brossat), 27n, 42n, 44n, 53n

Austria, 29

Australia, 42

Axelrod, Pavel Borisovitch, 25, 44, 45

Babeuf, François Nöel, 19

Bahro, Rudolf, 139–41

Balzac, Honored dé, 136

Batista, 105, 115

'Before the 9th January' (Trotsky), 41, 44

Ben Bells, 118

Bernstein, Eduard, 16, 17, 26

Bianco, Lucien, 125n

Birla, 137

Bismarck, Otto von, 5, 28, 29

Blackburn, Robin, 16n

Blanqui, Louis-Auguste, 8n, 16, 20

Bolivia, 118

Bolsheviks, 2, 20, 33–6, 43, 44n, 46, 48, 57–64, 68, 70, 73, 75–9, 84, 97, 101, 125, 127, 132, 133, 141, 143

The Bolshevik Revolution (Carr), 61

Der Bolchewismus in der Sackgasse (Kautsky), 132, 133

Bonch-Bruevich, Vladimir, 60

Borge, Tomas, 116

Boumedienne, Houari, 118

Britain, 6, 12, 14, 18–21, 74, 212

Brossat, Alain, 27n, 42n, 44n, 53n

Bukharin, Nikolai Ivanovitch, 56, 74–76, 80, 84

Burma, 109

Camino de victoria (Corvolán), 108

Capital (Marx), 2n, 3, 23, 24, 137

Cardenas, Lazaro, 92, 119

Carlyle, Thomas, 136

Carr, Edward Hallett, 61, 81n

Catalonia, 118

The Catastrophe in Indonesia (Soedarso), 107n

The Challenge of the Left Opposition (Trotsky), 68
Chang Tso-lin, 78
Le chemin du pouvoir (Kautsky), 2
Chen Tu-hsui, 78, 80
Chernov, Victor, 64
Chiang Kai-shek, 75, 78–80, 82, 91
Chile, 104, 106, 108
Chilean Communist Party, 104, 108
Chilean Trotskyists, 108
China, 12, 64, 65, 67, 69, 70, 75–87, 89, 98, 103, 105, 110, 111, 114, 117n, 119, 127, 138, 140
Chinese Communist Party, 12, 77–82, 85, 94–6, 107, 124, 126
Christian Democratic Party (Chile), 108
The Civil War in France (Marx), 5, 6, 18–20
Claudin, Fernando, 12, 74, 102
CNT (Spain), 102
Codovilla, 102
Comintern, 64–9, 75–85, 90, 91, 95, 97, 98, 101, 103, 105, 136
Communist League, 7, 16
Communist Manifesto (Marx & Engels), 4, 5, 11, 12, 14, 26, 47
La concepción materialista de la historia (Labriola), 46
The Conflicts & Dilemmas of the Marxist Path of G V Plekhanov (Feldman-Belfer), 33n, 34
Congo (Brazzaville), 109
La correspondance internationale, 67n
Corvalan, Luis, 108
COSEP (Nicaragua), 115
Critique of the Gotha Progamme (Marx), 74
Cuando fui communista (Claraval) 103n
Cuba, 85, 103, 105, 110, 114, 115, 118, 119, 121, 122, 124, 126, 127, 142
Cuban Communist Party (see also PSP), 103

Czechoslovakia, 142

Dan, Fedor, 75, 77
Daud, Mohammed, 117n
'Declaration en vue de XVI congres du PCUS' (Rakovsky et al), 129
Democratic Association of Cologne, 12, 13
'Democracy & Narodism in China' (Lenin) 65
Denikin, Anton, 134
Deutsch, Leo, 34
Deutscher, Isaac, 70, 81n
Diaz, Porfirio, 111
The Dictatorship of the Proletariat (Kautsky), 132, 133
'A Discussion with Trotsky on Latin American Questions' (International Press), 92
Draft Programme of the Comintern (Stalin & Bukharin), 83–5, 91
'The Driving Forces $ the Perspectives of the Russian Revolution' (Kautsky), 36, 43n

Economique et politique dans la pensée de Trotsky (Avenas) 45, 49
Edinstvo, 33
Egypt, 109, 110, 118
The Eighteenth Brumaire of Louis Bonaparte (Marx), 20, 96
El Salvador, 103, 104, 114
El Salvador Communist Party, 103, 104
Engels, Frederick, 1–31, 46, 47, 74, 101, 130
Espartero, General, 21
Ethiopia, 110, 119
Eurocommunistm & Socialism (Claudin), 74

Feuerbach, Ludwig, 31, 139, 141
The First Five Years of the Comintern (Trotsky), 69

'Foundations of Leninism' (Stalin), 70
Fortuny, J. M., 106
Fourth International, 101, 127
France, 4, 7, 11, 12, 18–21, 28, 54, 86, 96, 112
Frankfurt Assembly, 13
'From the Great Logic of Hegel to the Finland Station of Petrograd' (Löwy), 36n, 60n
'The Future Results of British Rule in India' (Marx), 136

Gandhi, Mahatma, 91
German Democratic Republic, 142
The German Ideology (Marx & Engels), 130
German Marxism & Russian Communism (Plamenatz), 16
German Social Democratic Party, 59
Germany, 4, 9, 10–12, 23, 27–9, 52, 59, 75, 79, 86, 112, 121
Geroe, Erno, 102
Die Geschichte der Russichen Sozial-Demokratie (Martov), 40
Geschichte Frankkreichs im Revolutionsalter (Wachsmuth) 9n
Gouldner, Alvin, 120, 121
GPU, 56
Gramsci, Antonia, 2, 3, 4n, 29, 46
Guatemala, 106
Guatemala, apuntes sobre el movimiento obrero (Usaga), 106n
Guatemalan Communist Party, (see PGT)
La guerre et l'Internationale (Trotsky), 58
Guinea, 109

Hegel, Georg Wilhelm Frederich, 17, 60
Helvétius, Claude-Adrien, 31
Hilferding, Rudolf, 64
Hillquit, Morris, 64
Histoire dy marxisme contemporain (Walecki), 31n
History & Class Consciousness (Lukács), 48
History of the Russian Revolution (Trotsky), 51, 87, 88
Hoare, Quintin, 2n
Ho Chi Minh, 76
The Holy Family (Marx & Engels), 8
Howe, Irving, 111n
Hungary, 18, 29, 75

Imperialism, the Highest Stage of Capitalism (Lenin), 60
Imperialism, Pioneer of Capitalism (Warren), 135–8
In Defence of Marxism (Trotsky), 129
'In Defence of the Party' (Trotsky), 57
India, 69, 84, 86, 91n, 117, 120, 136–8
Indonesia, 107, 108
Indonesian Communist Party, 107, 108
The Indonesian Revolution, Its Historical Background and Its Future (Aidit), 107
The Indonesian Revolution & the Immediate Tasks of the Indonesian Communist Party (Aidit), 107
Inprekorr, 78
'The Intelligentsia & Socialism' (Trotsky), 120
Intercontinental Press, 92n
L'International communiste, 67n
Internationalismus und Klassenkampf (Luxemburg), 38
Interpretaciones de la revolución Mexicana (Gilly et al), 111
La Intervencion norte-americana en Guatemala y el derrocamiento del regimen democratico (PGT), 106
Introduction to the Critique of Hegel's Theory of Right (Marx), 9, 11
Iran, 114, 115
Iraq, 109, 110, 115

Iskra, 41
Italy, 28, 29, 112, 132, 133

Japan 28, 112
Jaurés, Jean, 54
La jeunesse de Lénine (Trotsky), 119, 120, 130
The Jewish Question (Marx), 8
July 26th Movement (Cuba), 115, 116, 126

Kadets, 33, 48
Kamenev, Lev, 46, 61, 62, 68
Karl Marx (Nicolaievski & Maenchen-Helfen), 13n, 16
Kautsky, Karl, 1, 2, 26, 36, 37, 39, 40, 43, 59, 61, 64, 131–5, 138–43
Karl Kautsky & the Socialist Revolution (Salvadori), 2n, 36n, 39n, 132n, 133n, 134n
Khomeini, Ayatollah, 114, 135
Kossuth, Leo, 18
Krasso, Nicolas, 9, 49, 50
Kuomintang, 12, 67n, 75–82, 84, 91, 97
Kurds, 115

Labarca, Carlos Contrera, 104
Labriola, Antonio,, 46
Lamettrie, 31
Lassale, Ferdinand, 44, 48
Latin American Perspectives, 88
Left Opposition, 56, 71, 77, 83, 103, 129
The Legacy of Rosa Luxemburg (Geras), 26n, 29n, 54n
Lenin, Vladimir Ilich, 12, 18, 33–8, 40, 41, 43, 44n, 45, 48, 49n, 53, 54, 57, 59–67, 70, 72, 73, 75, 76, 83, 85, 93n, 97, 101, 111, 112, 119, 129n, 132, 135, 143
Lenin, *Collected Works*, 36, 54, 63, 64, 71

Leninism (Stalin), 39
Lenin of the National & Colonial Question, 65, 66
El Leninism y la Victoria popular (Corda), 108n
Letters from Afar (Lenin), 60
Letters on Tactics (Lenin), 62
Longuet, Jean, 64
Lukács, Georg, 48
Lukman, M. H., 107
Luxemburg, Rosa, 12, 37–41, 43, 54, 58, 135, 141, 143
Luxemburg, 'Gesammelte Werke', 12n, 38

Macdonald, Ramsey, 64
Machado, Gerardo, 103
Maenchen-Helfen, O., 13n
Mandel, Ernest, 49, 111, 112, 140
'Manifesto of the Fourth International on the Imperialist War & Proletarian Revolution' (Trotsky), 94, 95n
Mannheim, Karl, 45
Man's Estate (Malraux), 78
Mao Tse-tung, 76, 83, 88, 95, 96, 107, 123
Mao Tse-tung (Schram), 96n
Marat, Jean-Paul, 18, 19
Mariategui, José Carlos, 103
Marti, José, 115
Martov, Julius, 40, 46, 64
Martynov, General E. G., 75, 77, 80, 81, 98
Marx, Karl, 1–31, 37, 46, 47, 53, 74, 79, 96, 101, 121, 130, 136, 137, 139, 141
Marx, 'Early Writings', 8, 10, 11
Marx & Engels, 'Ausgewählte Briefe', 7, 22, 24, 26
Marx & Engels, 'Ausgewählte Schiften', 18, 28
Marx & Engels, *Collected Works*, 4n,

6n, 7, 13, 13n, 14, 20
Marx & Engels, *Selected Works*, 4n, 5, 18, 74
Marx & Engels, *Werke*, 13, 28n
Marx & Engels, *Werke*, 19, 24
Marx et la revolution française (Bruhat), 9
Marx, Engels, y la revolución de 1848 (Claudin), 12
Marx und das Russiche Problem (Nicolaievski), 25
Marxism (Lichtheim), 16
'Marxism: Theory of Permanent Revoltion' (Blackburn), 16
Le marxisme er l'Asie (d'Encaussee & Schram), 65n, 95
Le marxisme et la question nationale et coloniale (Stalin), 76n
Matanza, El Salvador's Communist Revolt of 1932 (Anderson), 104
Materialism & Empiro-Criticism (Lenin), 34, 60
Mehring, Franz, 39, 40, 47
Mella, Julio Antonio, 103
Mensheviks, 27, 32–6, 40, 43, 44, 46–8, 50–7, 61–4, 77–9, 81, 84, 90, 105, 111, 113, 131, 132, 136, 143
Merchant of Revolution: The Life of A. I. Helphand (Parvus) (Zeman & Scharlau), 41, 42
Mexican Communist Party, 105, 106
Mexico, 86, 89, 92, 105, 106, 111, 118–21, 124, 125
Mexico en la encrucijada de su historia (Shulgovsky), 106
Meyers, S., 6n
Miguel Marmol: El Salvador 1930–32 (Dalton), 104
Miliukov, Paul, 33, 41, 51
MIR (Chile), 108
Mora, Manuel Aguilar, 115n
Mozambique, 119
Mujahadeen, 114

Mussolini, Benito, 132
My Life (Trotsky), 38, 40, 45, 46

Nachalo, 33, 40
Napoleon I, 8
Napoleon II (Louis Bonaparte), 5, 22, 28
Narodniks, 24–6, 32, 45, 47, 51, 65, 96
Nashe Slovo, 58
Nasser, Colonel, 118
Neue Rhinische Zeitung, 3, 12, 13n, 14, 18
Neue Zeit, 37, 39, 42, 57
The New Course (Trotsky), 39, 68
New Left Review, 9, 16n, 32n, 102, 123
New York Daily Tribune, 21
Nicaragua, 114–6
Nicaragua heure H (Amador), 116
Nicaraguan Communist Party, see PSN
Nicolaievsky, Boris, 13n, 16, 25n
1905 (Trotsky), 9, 39, 47, 48n, 51, 52, 57, 58, 68

O'Donell, General, 21
OLAS, 108
On Britain (Marx & Engels), 6n
On China (Trotsky), 67, 78, 80–3, 89–91, 92n, 94, 95, 97, 98, 117
'On Cooperation' (Lenin), 73
'On the Opposition' (Stalin), 70, 71, 76n, 79, 80
'On Tactics' (Lenin), 62
One Step Forward, Two Steps Back (Lenin), 135
'Organizational Questions of Russian Social Democracy' (Luxemburg), 135
Open Society & Its Enemies (Popper), 1
L'ottobre cubano (Tutino), 105
'Our Controversies' (Plekhanov), 32
'Our Differences' (Trotsky), 43

'Our Revolution' (Lenin), 61, 64

Paris Commune, 24, 36, 45, 61
Les paysans dans la revolution
(Bianco), 125n
PDPA (Afghanistan), 116n, 117n
The Peasant War in Germany
(Engels), 29
'Peasants & Revolution' (Alavi), 123–5
Peasant Wars of the Twentieth Century
(Wolf), 121, 123–5
Pensamiento Criticio, 104
'The People of Chile Unite to Save
Democracyy' (Labarca), 104
The Permanent Revolution (Trotsky),
17n, 38n, 57, 58n, 59n, 63n, 68,
70, 72n, 73, 84–6, 89, 91, 93–5,
97, 98, 110, 118
Peru, 118
Peruvian Communist Party, 103
Petras, James, 104, 123
PGT (Guatemala), 106
Philosophical Notebooks (Lenin) 59, 60
Pilsudski, Marshal J., 81
Plekhanov, 'Liternaturnie Nasledie', 32
Plekhanov, *Oeuvres philosophique*, 31
Plekhanov, *Sochinennya*, 32n
Poland, 5, 81
'Politics & Social Forces in Chilean
Development' (Petras), 104
'The Political Ideas of Marx & Engels'
(Hunt), 16n
'Political Parties in Russia & Tasks of
the Proletariat' (Lenin), 62
Political Power & Social Classes
(Poulantzas), 4n
Poulantzas, 4n
POUM (Spain), 102
Pravda, 61, 64, 77
'Preface to "Before the 9th October"'
(Parvus), 41, 44n
*Preface to a Contribution to the
Critique of Political Economy*
(Marx), 6, 31
Preobrazhensky, Evgeni, 83, 97
Les presupposés du socialisme
(Bernstein), 16, 17
*The Present Stage of the Non-Capitalist
Development in Asia & Africa*
(Solodovnikov), 109
Prison Notebooks (Gramsci), 46
Problems of Leninism (Stalin), 93
'The Professional Dangers of Power'
(Rakovsky), 129
'El proletariado y su organizacion'
(Mariategui), 103
'The Proletariat & the Russian
Revolution' (Trotsky), 48, 50
*Die proletarische Revolution und ihr
Programm* (Kautsky), 134, 135
*Prologue to a Theory of Revolutionary
Intellectuals* (Gouldner), 121, 122
The Prophet Armed (Deutscher),
40, 51
PSN (Nicaragua), 116
PSP (Cuba), 105, 126
Prussia, 9, 21, 29

Quatrieme Internationale, 37, 115
'Que es el APRA?' (Mella), 103
*La question chioise dans l'Internationale
Communiste* (Broué), 76
*Les questions fondementales du
marxisme* (Plekhanov), 31

'Raices indigenas de la lucha anti-
colonialists en Nicaragua'
(Wheelock), 116n
Rakovsky, Christian, 129
Ramagnolo, David J., 88n
Results & Prospects (Trotsky), 27, 20,
47–58, 67, 87, 101
*La revolución Mexicana y el desarrallo
capitalista de Mexico*
(Cardenas), 105
Revolution Betrayed (Trotsky), 70, 72,

98, 140, 142
La revolution chinoise (Serge), 83
La revolution democratique bourgeois en Allemagne (Engels), 28, 29
Révolution en Asie et marxisme (Yew), 125
Le revolutions espagnole (Trotsky), 118
Revolutionary Marxism Today (Mandel), 112
La revolution d'octobre (Golikov), 60
'Die Revolution in Permanenz' (Mehring), 39, 47
'Revolution in Spain' (Marx & Engels), 21, 22
The Revolutions of 1848 (Marx & Engels), 4, 7, 12, 13, 15, 16, 18
La revolution russe de 1917 (Sukhanov), 61
Rheinische Zeitung, 9, 14
Rhodes, Cecil, 137
Riazanov, David, 25, 32n
Robespierre, Maximilien, 121
Roa, Blas, 105
'Le role du CP Chinois' (Martynov), 77
Rousseau, Jean-Jacques, 121
Roy, M. N., 65
RSDLP (Russia) 4, 30, 33, 38, 40, 45, 47, 54, 57, 77, 135
Ruge, Arnold, 10, 11
Russia, 1–3, 7, 15, 20, 23–7, 30–79, 82, 84–7, 90, 91, 94, 96, 102, 106, 107, 110, 114, 119, 121, 122, 124, 127, 129–34, 136, 138–40, 142, 143
'The Russian Menace to Europe' (Marx & Engels), 23, 25, 26
The Russian Revolution (Liebman), 63n
The Russian Revolution (Luxemburg), 141, 143

Sandino, Augusto César, 115
Sandinistas, 114–6
Schram, Stuart, 96n

Science of Logic (Hegel), 59
Second International, 1, 3, 4, 7, 30, 33, 35, 39, 42, 43, 46, 58, 59, 64, 101, 113
Serge, Victor, 83
Shachtman, Max, 67n
Shulgovsky, Anatol, 106n
Siete ensayo de interpretacion de la realidad peruana (Mariategui), 103
Siéyes, Abbé Emmanuel, 10
Sismondi, Jean Charles Simonde de, 136
'Sobre la liberacion nacional' (Trotksy), 89
Social Revolutionaries, 62
'Socialism & Political Struggle' (Plekhanov), 32
Le socialisme dans un seul pays (Bukharin), 74n
Socialism: Scientific & Utopian (Engels), 4n
Socialist Party of Chile, 104, 108
'Socialist Revolutions & their Class Components' (Petras), 123
Solodovnikov, V. G., 109, 110
Somalia, 109, 110
Somoza, Anastasio, 115, 116
South Yemen, 119
Sozialdemokratie und Leninismus (Mandelbaum), 26n
Spain, 14, 21–3, 86, 102, 120
'Spain—The Untimely Revolution' (Claudin), 102
Spanish Communist Party, 102
Spanish Socialist Party, 102
Spanish Trotskyists, 102
Spinoza, Baruch, 48
Stalin, Joseph, 21, 38–40, 56, 62, 68–84 88, 93, 98, 101, 103, 105, 108, 110, 113, 117, 139–41
Stalinism & Bolshevism (Trotsky), 72
Stolypin, Píotr, 113
Struve, Piotr, 42, 106, 136

Sukarno, President, 107, 108
Sukhanov, N. N., 61, 64, 83
Sul moviemento operaio internazionale (Togliatti), 102
Sun Yat-sen, 64
Surveys from Exile (Marx & Engels), 19–21
Syria, 109

Tcherny Peredel, 25n
Terrorism & Communism (Kautsky), 132
Le theorie de la revolution chez le jeune Marx (Löwy), 10n, 121n
The Theory of Permanent Revolution (Michail), 48n, 62n
Theses on the Eastern Question (Comintern), 66
Theses on Feuerbach (Marx) 31, 139, 141
These, Resolutions & Manifestos of the First Four Congresses of the Third International, 65, 66
'Theses on the Situations in China' (Comintern), 76
Third International After Lenin (Trotsky), 72, 73n, 74n, 75, 86
'The Three Conceptions of the Russian Revolution' (Trotsky), 42n, 96
Togliatti, Palmiro, 102
Toledano, Lombardo, 106
The Tragedy of the Chinese Revolution (Isaacs), 78, 80, 98
The Transitional Programme (Trotsky), 72, 118
Trotsky, Leon, 1, 3, 9, 15, 17n, 18, 21, 27, 28, 30, 33, 35, 38–59, 62–4, 66–99, 101, 103, 110, 113, 117, 122, 125, 127, 129–31, 140, 142, 143
Trotsky (Howe), 111
'Trotsky y le opposicion comunista' (Mariategui), 103n
'Trotsky' (Johnstone), 62

Trotsky, *Writings*, 89, 92, 96, 97
'Trotsky's Kampf um die Nachfolge Lenins … ' (Brahm), 70n
'Trotsky's Marxism' (Krasso), 9
Turati, Augusto, 46, 64
Turkey, 91
The Two Revolutions (Martynov), 77
Two Tactics (Lenin), 34 35, 61, 62

Ulyanovsky, R. A., 109
United States, 53, 86, 112, 138, 142
Urrutia, Manuel, 115
Usaga, Manuel Pinto, 106n

Venezuela, 138
Vietnam, 86, 110, 111, 121, 124, 126, 127
Vietnamese Communist Party, 85, 126
Volna, 62
Vogt, Karl, 6n
La Voz de Mexico, 105

Wage Labour & Capital (Marx), 13, 14
Wang Chin-wei, 79, 80, 82
War and Revolution (Parvus), 41
Warren, Bill, 135–41
Weber, Max, 130
Weydemeyer, Joseph, 7
What Is to Be Done? (Lenin), 43, 77
Wolf, Eric, 121, 123–5
Workers Association of Cologne, 13

Yugoslavia, 110, 111, 122, 126–8, 142
Yugoslav Communist Party, 85, 126

Zasulich, Vera, 23–6, 45
Zinoviev, Grigori, 68
Zur Deutschen Geschichte (Marx et al), 12n, 18n

Also from Haymarket Books

From Rebellion to Reform in Bolivia: Class Struggle,
Indigenous Liberation, and the Politics of Evo Morales
Jeffery R. Webber • Evo Morales rode to power on a wave of popular mobilizations against the neoliberal policies enforced by his predecessors. Yet many of his economic policies bear a striking resemblance to the status quo he was meant to displace. Based in part on dozens of interviews with leading Bolivian activists, Jeffery R. Webber examines the contradictions of Morales's first term in office. ISBN 9781608461066

History of the Russian Revolution
Leon Trotsky • Regarded by many as among the most powerful works of history ever written, Trotsky's account of the events of 1917 reveals the October revolution's profoundly democratic, emancipatory character. Collected in a single, portable volume, with a thorough new index. ISBN 9781931859455

How Revolutionary Were the Bourgeois Revolutions?
Neil Davidson • In this panoramic historical analysis, Neil Davidson defends a renovated concept of bourgeois revolution. Davidson shows how our globalized societies of the present are the result of a contested, turbulent history marked by often forceful revolutions directed against old social orders, from the Dutch Revolt to the English and American Civil Wars and beyond. ISBN 9781608460670

Revolution and Counterrevolution:
Class Struggle in a Moscow Metal Factory
Kevin Murphy • Based on research in four factory-specific archives, *Revolution and Counterrevolution* is the most thorough investigation to date on working-class struggle during Russia's revolutionary era. ISBN 9781931859509

Witnesses to Permanent Revolution: The Documentary Record
Edited and translated by Richard B. Day and Daniel F. Gaido • Providing a window into the debate that raged between the leading figures of late nineteenth-century Marxism, these newly translated documents by Karl Kautsky, Rosa Luxemburg, Leon Trotsky, and others reveal critical insights and unearth new evidence for interpreting the formative years of Marxism in Russia. ISBN 9781608460892

About Haymarket Books

Haymarket Books is a nonprofit, progressive book distributor and publisher, a project of the Center for Economic Research and Social Change. We believe that activists need to take ideas, history, and politics into the many struggles for social justice today. Learning the lessons of past victories, as well as defeats, can arm a new generation of fighters for a better world. As Karl Marx said, "The philosophers have merely interpreted the world; the point, however, is to change it."

We take inspiration and courage from our namesakes, the Haymarket Martyrs, who gave their lives fighting for a better world. Their 1886 struggle for the eight-hour day, which gave us May Day, the international workers' holiday, reminds workers around the world that ordinary people can organize and struggle for their own liberation. These struggles continue today across the globe—struggles against oppression, exploitation, hunger, and poverty.

It was August Spies, one of the Martyrs targeted for being an immigrant and an anarchist, who predicted the battles being fought to this day. "If you think that by hanging us you can stamp out the labor movement," Spies told the judge, "then hang us. Here you will tread upon a spark, but here, and there, and behind you, and in front of you, and everywhere, the flames will blaze up. It is a subterranean fire. You cannot put it out. The ground is on fire upon which you stand."

We could not succeed in our publishing efforts without the generous financial support of our readers. Many people contribute to our project through the Haymarket Sustainers program, where donors receive free books in return for their monetary support. If you would like to be a part of this program, please contact us at info@haymarketbooks.org.

Order these titles and more online at www.haymarketbooks.org or call 773-583-7884.

Printed in the USA
CPSIA information can be obtained
at www.ICGtesting.com
JSHW012033140824
68134JS00033B/3035